APPROACHING CIVIL WAR
AND
SOUTHERN HISTORY

APPROACHING CIVIL WAR AND SOUTHERN HISTORY

WILLIAM J. COOPER

LOUISIANA STATE UNIVERSITY PRESS
BATON ROUGE

Published with the assistance of the V. Ray Cardozier Fund

Published by Louisiana State University Press

Manufactured in the United States of America
First printing

Designer: Michelle A. Neustrom
Typeface: Sentinel, text
Printer and binder: Sheridan Books, Inc.

Library of Congress Cataloging-in-Publication Data

Names: Cooper, William J., Jr. (William James), 1940– author.
Title: Approaching Civil War and Southern history / William J. Cooper.
Description: Baton Rouge : Louisiana State University Press, [2019] | Collection of essays initially published between 1970 and 2012. | Includes bibliographical references and index.
Identifiers: LCCN 2018035313 | ISBN 978-0-8071-7058-8 (cloth : alk. paper) | ISBN 978-0-8071-7096-0 (pdf) | ISBN 978-0-8071-7097-7 (epub)
Subjects: LCSH: Southern States—History—1775–1865. | Confederate States of America—History. | United States—History—Civil War, 1861–1865.
Classification: LCC F214 .C77 2019 | DDC 975/.03—dc23
LC record available at https://lccn.loc.gov/2018035313

The paper in this book meets the guidelines for permanence and durability of the Committee on Production Guidelines for Book Longevity of the Council on Library Resources. ♾

FOR

My Colleagues and Students

IN THE

LSU History Department

Who Over a Half Century

Created an Ideal Environment

FOR

This Historian to Do His Work

CONTENTS

PREFACE

The essays in *Approaching Civil War and Southern History* span almost my entire scholarly career. Until now only one of them, "A Reassessment of Jefferson Davis as War Leader" (chapter 1), has been reprinted.[1] Initially published between 1970 and 2012, these works also range widely across a broad spectrum of Civil War and southern history. They are placed here in the chronological order in which they initially appeared in print. In the introduction to each essay, I note its genesis and purpose. Thus, I will not describe each one here.

Throughout the bulk of my years as an historian, my chief interest has been southern political history in the nineteenth century. That has been the main highway I have traveled. Yet the variety of topics investigated in this volume illustrates the many lesser roads this historian has taken over time. Invitations from individuals and institutions led to some; my own inquisitiveness turned me into others. All I found both worthwhile and interesting.

Reprinting a body of work done over almost half a century is cause for both satisfaction and trepidation—satisfaction because knowledgeable and respected people believe my scholarship has continuing merit, trepidation because bringing forward essays from decades ago can reveal what some might see as the naiveté or the plain wrongheadedness of a younger historian.

Yes, I am indeed pleased that the Louisiana State University Press saw value in bringing out this volume. My association with the Press has been long and, for me certainly, rewarding. I served two different terms on the Press Committee between 1972 and 1981. Additionally, between 1979 and 1993, I was editor of the Press's Southern Biography Series.

Furthermore, counting this one, the Press has published three of my own books as well as three others that I edited or coedited. Finally, the Press is part of the university where I spent a most gratifying career. For an historian with my interests, few places could have matched LSU, either for scholarly environment or the research support given me.

Rereading these essays brought back many fond memories of people and events involved in one way or another in their preparation. Moreover, I did not find myself wondering how I could ever have put forward the interpretations central in them individually. In fact, I found the cases I made still mostly sound. Without question, if writing any of them today, I would modify particulars in some, but in none would I fundamentally change my argument.

Concluding, I want to make clear that each essay is reprinted as it originally appeared in either journal or book, adjusted only for consistency of presentation within this collection. The notes, however, where necessary, have been reformatted for uniformity.

APPROACHING CIVIL WAR AND SOUTHERN HISTORY

1

A Reassessment of Jefferson Davis as War Leader

THE CASE FROM ATLANTA TO NASHVILLE

This essay had its genesis in my senior thesis at Princeton University, written under the direction of David Herbert Donald, who later would become my major professor in graduate school. It deals with Confederate strategy and the command structure in the western theater from the Atlanta Campaign to the effective collapse of the major Confederate army in the West at the Battle of Bentonville, North Carolina, in March 1865. For this "reassessment," I focused on President Jefferson Davis, his thoughts and actions, from Atlanta to the ill-fated Confederate invasion of Tennessee in late 1864. When I did the research for my thesis and on to the preparation of this essay, the historiography presented Davis in an overwhelmingly negative light, basically depicting him as an unfit and even incompetent chief executive, who did not understand the demands of his role as presidential commander in chief and lacked the ability to fulfill these demands even if he had comprehended them. The evidence led me to a different conclusion, however. I discovered a chief executive who exhibited a keen sense of his and his country's situation as well as what his duties, as both political leader and military commander in chief, entailed. Of course, at that time I had no premonition that within two decades I would begin a lengthy journey with that same Jefferson Davis. Yet even with the additional scholarship on the man and the Confederacy as well as my own vastly more extensive research, I find the interpretation advanced in this early essay largely substantiated.[1]

The failure of the southern Confederacy has often been correlated with the failure of Jefferson Davis as war leader. Davis's shortcomings as commander in chief of the armed forces, as political head of a new nation, and as chief spokesman to and for the public often lead the list of reasons for southern defeat. For example, Davis pales beside Abraham Lincoln in any comparison of the two presidents as war leaders. Recently Eric L. McKitrick, summing up the views of many, wrote: "It seems apparent that the leadership of Abraham Lincoln was superior to that of Jefferson Davis."[2] Lincoln was flexible; Davis was rigid. Lincoln wanted to win; Davis wanted to be right. Lincoln had a broad strategic vision of Union goals; Davis could never enlarge his narrow view. Lincoln searched for the right general, then let him fight the war; Davis continuously played favorites and interfered unduly with his generals, even with Robert E. Lee. Lincoln led his nation; Davis failed to rally the South.[3] Simply, Lincoln contributed mightily to the Union victory; Davis contributed mightily to the Confederate defeat.

The attack on Jefferson Davis began during the war. Davis, according to the acerbic Richmond editor Edward Alfred Pollard, ran an administration from which neither the Confederate States of America nor its citizens could expect "anything wise, or magnanimous, or unselfish." Editor Pollard scorned "the pitiful personal feelings, of a single man [President Davis]" who wrecked the war effort and the careers of generals "with cold and insolent neglect."[4] Writing in 1863, Pollard viciously indicted Davis for "his intermeddling" which "removed a decisive victory [Antietam] from the grasp of our army, and turned back the war for years."[5]

Final southern defeat failed to temper Pollard's written assaults on the former Confederate president. "Mr. Davis," wrote Pollard in the preface to a biography of Davis he published in 1869, "[was] the prime cause of the failure of the South in the late war."[6] Three years earlier Pollard had attributed to Davis "a peculiar obstinacy, which, stimulated by an intellectual conceit, spurned the counsels of equal minds, and rejected the advice of the intelligent."[7]

Modern historians, while not always adopting the bitterness of Pollard's assessments, have echoed his basic interpretation that Jefferson Davis's failure as a war leader was a crucial factor in the ultimate defeat of the Confederacy. Clifford Dowdey, who found Davis after the fall of

Atlanta a man dominated by "a wishful thinking that produced no more than fantasies, daydreams," has published two general studies of the Confederacy which have made major contributions to the preservation of Pollard's estimate of Davis.[8] In a book lauding Lincoln as "a great war President," T. Harry Williams dismissed Davis as a "mediocre one."[9] Perhaps the most damning indictment of Davis's ability by a serious scholar has come from David M. Potter—Davis, in Potter's judgment, was a man "who cared more about proving he was right than about gaining success."[10]

Davis, of course, has had his defenders. The most recent attempt—and the most voluminous—came in Hudson Strode's massive three-volume biography.[11] Strode devotes half of his study to Davis's experiences as president of the Confederate States of America. From Strode's pages Davis emerges as an omniscient hero who failed because of the bitterness, incompetency, and jealousy of "little" subordinates. Although certain of Davis's lieutenants undoubtedly did not give unselfish service to their president, Strode's eulogistic effort to depict Davis as a great man and a great war leader is unsuccessful because his biography is written in a historiographical vacuum and fails to evaluate men and events critically.[12]

Other works viewing Davis more favorably have greater validity. Archer Jones, in a study of early Confederate strategy, concludes that Davis's strategic "method was sound; his application competent."[13] Writing about Davis and his cabinet, Rembert W. Patrick asserted that "Davis's claim to conspicuous ability as a leader is incontestable."[14]

A thoughtful article by Frank E. Vandiver, "Jefferson Davis and Confederate Strategy," stands as probably the most convincing and persuasive attempt to rehabilitate the reputation of Davis. Basic to Davis's strategic planning, according to Vandiver, was the concept of the offensive-defensive, which meant "the Confederates would stand on the defensive because they had fewer men and feebler resources than the Yankees, but they would exploit every chance to counterattack, to take the initiative, to carry the war to the enemy." Vandiver finds "Confederate strategy to have been logical, consistent, and realistic," mainly because it "enable[d] the Confederates to outlast their resources."[15] Unlike Potter, Vandiver found Davis's strategy consistent with reality, and he pictured Davis as striving to institute a comprehensive, overall strategy for the Confederacy.

None of Davis's defenders, however, has caused any significant reassessment of the view initiated by Pollard in the 1860s. To test Davis's performance, this paper examines his actions as war leader during an extremely critical period of Confederate history. Davis functioned energetically as such a leader during the crucial months beginning with the campaign for Atlanta in the spring and summer of 1864 and the subsequent destruction of the Army of Tennessee in the Battles of Franklin and Nashville, which sealed the fate of the Confederate West.

Jefferson Davis lived in Richmond, the Confederate capital. Here, at the northeastern edge of the Confederacy, he found himself in the midst of one of the major theaters of the war. For four years Union and Confederate armies fought over and through the one hundred miles separating Richmond from Washington, the Union capital. The geographical location of the Confederate seat of government could have focused President Davis's mind on Virginia.

Davis, however, did not forget the Confederate West. A Mississippian, he maintained a strong interest in western affairs and in the career of the single most important Confederate force in that vast area, the Army of Tennessee.[16] As its first commander, Davis appointed his friend Albert Sidney Johnston, the man Davis believed to be the best southern general. During his short tenure Johnston showed few signs of military genius. His death at Shiloh in April 1862 required a new commander for the Army of Tennessee, and Davis advanced Pierre G. T. Beauregard, who had been Johnston's deputy at Shiloh. After only two months Davis replaced Beauregard with Braxton Bragg. Initially, it seemed that Davis had acted wisely, for Bragg made a rapid dash into Kentucky—a campaign that marked the northernmost advance made by the Army of Tennessee. But once in Kentucky, Bragg became indecisive and hesitant, and after installing a Confederate governor and fighting an inconclusive battle, he returned to Tennessee.

Although Davis never lost faith in Bragg's abilities as a general, Bragg's subordinates did. Aware of the anti-Bragg feeling in the Army of Tennessee, Davis realized that he had to make some changes. Rather than remove Bragg, he created the Department of the West and placed Joseph E. Johnston in command of Confederate troops from Georgia to the Mississippi. This arrangement failed to work and lapsed after the fall of Vicksburg, but its failure cannot be blamed on lack of support from Davis.

By the autumn of 1863 President Davis faced another crisis in the Army of Tennessee. Bragg won a victory at Chickamauga in September, but he frittered away his opportunity and finally was driven away from Chattanooga two months later. This time Davis knew Bragg would have to go. Certain of Davis's closest advisers, including Secretary of War James A. Seddon, recommended the assignment of Joseph Johnston.[17] Neither Davis nor Seddon had been pleased with Johnston's performance as commanding general of the Department of the West,[18] but as commanding general of the Army of Tennessee he would have only a single field army under his charge. And Johnston, after all, ranked third among Confederate full generals. The president therefore ordered him to Georgia.

In contrast to his situation in Virginia, President Davis found himself constantly searching for the right general in the West. In Virginia Robert E. Lee, who enjoyed Davis's confidence, had military successes unmatched by any other Confederate commander. He and Davis discussed strategy and other matters, and Davis never lost confidence in him as a general or as a loyal subordinate. In the West Davis never found both qualities in one man. Sidney Johnston, probably, and Braxton Bragg, certainly, were loyal, but neither showed consistent ability as military commanders. For Davis, Beauregard and Joseph Johnston proved even less satisfactory. Showing little, if any, more competence than Sidney Johnston or Bragg, neither Beauregard nor Joseph Johnston exhibited much loyalty to Davis as their president and commander in chief. When the 1864 campaigns opened, Abraham Lincoln had found his general; Jefferson Davis was not at all sure that he had.

Joseph Johnston had had a particularly unsatisfying career as a Confederate general. Piqued initially at being placed fourth on the list of full generals, Johnston seemed to carry this resentment until 1865—and even afterward. Convinced of this own great ability, Johnston resented directions from his civilian superiors and also their requests for information about his intentions. He commanded at First Manassas, but Beauregard directed the battle. A wound cut short his defense of Richmond in the spring of 1862. Excellent strategical and tactical ideas but no action marked his tenure as commanding general of the Department of the West. The spring of 1864 found Joseph Johnston still an unproven general.[19]

Beset with massive Union offensives in both Virginia and the West, Davis relied on Lee and Johnston to turn back the attacks of Ulysses S. Grant and William Tecumseh Sherman. To the new commander of the Army of Tennessee Davis gave only general instructions. Secretary of War Seddon expressed the hope that Johnston could carry the attack to the enemy, but in the same letter Seddon emphasized that "your own experience and judgment are relied on to form and act on your own plans of military operations."[20]

Johnston's "experience and judgment" counseled against taking the fight to his opponent. Sherman began his move southward from Chattanooga toward Johnston's army and Atlanta on May 4, 1864. Retreating for some two months before Sherman's advance, Johnston abandoned defensive position after defensive position.[21] Unlike Lee in Virginia, who constantly struck out at Grant and who viewed the relentless Federal surge with foreboding, Johnston never hurled his divisions at Sherman.[22] By early July Johnston had his troops in the fortifications protecting Atlanta.

Jefferson Davis had watched Johnston's retreat with increasing concern. As early as June 7 General Bragg, military adviser to Davis, told Johnston that he had informed the president that "[t]he condition of affairs in Georgia is daily becoming more serious."[23] By mid-July an official in the Confederate War Department recorded in his diary: "A very gloomy view of Affairs in Georgia prevails in the cabinet."[24] The paucity of communications from Johnston about his plans particularly distressed Davis.[25] No one in Richmond knew his intentions; and after Johnston's continuous retreat of some two months, Davis grew anxious to know what they were. Did he plan to fight for Atlanta, the psychological goal of the campaign, the gateway to central Georgia, and an important rail and supply center? Did he intend to withstand a siege in Atlanta? Did he envision continued retreat to Mobile or Savannah (depending upon Sherman's direction)? What chance would Johnston have against Sherman in the plains of central Georgia, if he had not been able to defend against him successfully in the hilly, even sub-mountainous, terrain of north Georgia. Johnston gave Davis reason to expect the third alternative, when on July 11 he "strongly recommended" the immediate removal of prisoners of war from Andersonville some one hundred miles south of Atlanta.[26]

To ascertain Johnston's intentions, Davis on July 9 ordered Bragg to Atlanta to confer with Johnston about his military plans. Davis instructed Bragg to investigate "dispositions and preparations of the Army of Tennessee."[27] In Atlanta Bragg found "but little encouraging"; elaborating, he told Davis that "[m]uch disappointment and dissatisfaction" existed in the army. General Johnston, observed Bragg, had "ever been opposed to seeking battle." Bragg implied that only a new commanding general could ensure that the Army of Tennessee would fight Sherman.[28]

Davis never planned to rely solely on Bragg's recommendation in a matter so crucial. Even before he sent Bragg to Georgia, he had Secretary of War Seddon request from Senator Benjamin H. Hill of Georgia an account of the talk he had with Johnston. After meeting with Johnston on July 1, Hill reported that the general hoped Sherman would attack his trenches, but Hill concluded, as did Bragg, that Johnston had little desire to fight.[29]

Davis next turned to the hard-pressed Lee. "*Gen. Johnston,*" wrote Davis, "has *failed* and there are strong indications that he will *abandon Atlanta.*" Believing "the case [to be] hopeless in present hands," Davis broached the possibility of Johnston's removal and asked Lee, "Who should *succeed* him?"[30] Lee cautioned the president not to act hastily. He thought it "a grievous thing to change [the] commander of an army situated as is that of the Tennessee," but added, "Still if necessary it ought to be done."[31]

Davis's chief cabinet advisers thought a change essential. Secretary of War Seddon, who had been enthusiastic in 1863 about giving Johnston the Army of Tennessee, now advised the president to replace him.[32] From one of his closest confidants Davis heard the same refrain; for some time Secretary of State Judah P. Benjamin had argued that Johnston's strategy could result only in disaster.[33]

Bragg's report, Senator Hill's views, the advice of his most trusted cabinet advisors, Lee's concurrence (although reluctant), and political pressure from Georgia governor Joseph E. Brown taken together built an impressive case against Johnston.[34] Davis turned to Johnston himself. On July 16 he requested from Johnston information about the "present situation and your plan of operations." Replying the same day, Johnston pointed out that Sherman outnumbered him and that his "plan of operations must therefore, depend upon that of the enemy."[35] That exchange convinced Davis that his advisers were right. The following day Davis relieved Johnston, not only for failing to stop Sherman but mainly for "express[ing] no confidence that you can defeat or repel him."[36]

To repel Sherman, Davis and the Confederacy turned to John Bell Hood. Hood, thirty-three, had been a corps commander in the Army of Tennessee since April 1864. Best known for his battle leadership as a division commander under Lee, he had had no experience as an army commander. Lee, for one, feared for Hood's success in the larger job and told Davis so.[37] Removal of Johnston left Davis no alternative to Hood. The other full generals and prominent senior lieutenant generals—Lee, Edmund Kirby Smith, Beauregard, Bragg, James Longstreet, William J. Hardee—were for various reasons unavailable. The ability of the new commander to assume control quickly dominated all other considerations because it was believed that the fight for Atlanta could not be delayed. That need in effect limited the choice to someone serving with the Army of Tennessee. Nine months earlier, in a situation not nearly so pressing, Hardee had declined the position; no one remained save Hood.[38] And no one doubted that Hood would fight. Jefferson Davis gave him his chance.

Hood fulfilled Davis's expectations; he fought for Atlanta. And he lost. Hood's critics are legion; they accuse him of destroying the fine army he inherited from Johnston by a series of rashly fought, sanguinary clashes in and around Atlanta that bled the Army of Tennessee almost to death.[39] Voicing a contrary view, the distinguished English military historian Alfred H. Burne pointed out that Hood had lost by an extremely narrow margin. Burne asserted, "It would be difficult to find, in the history of any campaign, a more dazzling series of blows" than Hood delivered in Atlanta. His measured judgment found Hood's fight for Atlanta "sound—even brilliant."[40]

While Hood's fight for Atlanta did not surprise Davis, the fall of the city six weeks after Hood assumed command dealt "a stunning blow" to the president and his advisors.[41] He had gambled with Hood; he had gambled that a strong blow could force Sherman to retreat northward and preserve both Atlanta and central Georgia and Alabama. He accepted the risk of battle because he could see no alternative. When that program received a setback, Davis hurried to begin anew. Aware of rumbling dissatisfaction with Hood and hoping to renew fervor and patriotism in the citizens of Alabama, Georgia, and South Carolina—the states most immediately threatened by the fall of Atlanta—Davis determined to visit the Army of Tennessee and that section of his country.[42]

Only three weeks after the loss of Atlanta, on September 25, 1864, Davis arrived at Palmetto, Georgia, Hood's headquarters, where he and Hood discussed strategy and command.[43] Hood proposed to move his army into north Georgia, believing that this maneuver would draw Sherman away from Atlanta.[44] If Sherman refused to oblige the Confederates and marched south from Atlanta, then Hood would be close on his heels. A receptive Davis authorized Hood to proceed with these plans. Davis knew he could not approve a retreat by Hood after he had removed Johnston for following such a policy. He also knew that retreat toward the Atlantic Ocean or the Gulf of Mexico could have but one result. Aggressiveness he felt essential, so he supported Hood rather than those who urged a more cautious and static autumn for the Army of Tennessee.[45]

Davis thought talking to the citizens in this invaded and threatened portion of his country was just as important as military discussions with General Hood. On this western trip he made four major speeches—at Macon, Montgomery, Augusta, and Columbia.[46] In each city he exhorted his listeners to rededicate themselves to the success of the Confederate cause. Supreme sacrifices by each individual would result in "final success" for southern arms. Sherman's invasion of Georgia, in Davis's rhetoric, became the counterpart of Napoleon's march into Russia, with the same fate awaiting the new trespasser. Davis was convinced that the innate sense of duty, which he believed dwelled in every southern heart, would ensure southern independence. This faith dominated the four speeches. This personal effort by the president did rekindle flames of confidence; even a hypercritical Edward Pollard admitted that "[c]onfidence was in a measure revived."[47]

In addition to military strategy and public opinion, Davis was thinking about command structure. He knew that elements within and without the Army of Tennessee would have welcomed the dismissal of Hood.[48] To remove Hood meant, of course, to find a replacement, not an easy task in the Confederacy of late 1864. Most generals who had sufficient rank had by that time proved themselves indispensable in their jobs or unavailable, either for military or political reasons. Besides, Hood, even if he had failed to dislodge Sherman, had indeed fought the army; he had done exactly what Davis put him in command to do. Still, Davis had to consider the political climate of the post-Atlanta weeks.

Even before leaving Richmond for Georgia, Davis corresponded with General Lee on the availability and willingness of General Beauregard to accept a western assignment. Because neither Lee nor Beauregard was satisfied with the latter's difficult position in Virginia as Lee's deputy, both generals eagerly welcomed Davis's suggestion.[49] In Augusta, on his return from Hood's army, Davis conferred with Beauregard on the West. After outlining the strategy he and Hood had decided upon and which Beauregard supported, the president appointed him commanding general of the Military Division of the West.[50] This command arrangement, which put Beauregard over everything between Georgia and the Mississippi, harked back to the Department of the West, when Joseph Johnston had held a similar position.

Davis, in giving Beauregard this command, has been accused of "lay[ing] on the shelf a general who was out of favor."[51] Political considerations undoubtedly influenced Davis's decision. Sending the hero of 1861 to the West to support Hood and to lead the citizenry Davis had rallied was a popular move, although an official in the Confederate War Department probably exaggerated public sentiment when he rejoiced at Davis's "response to the universal call to the people."[52] Without doubt, however, Beauregard's appointment met with public approval.

Davis had not placed Beauregard on a shelf. He knew that he could not direct all military activities from Richmond, and he was making another attempt to create a "unified command of the sort so popular in World War II," to give one man the authority, discretion, and mobility to control and coordinate activities over a large area.[53] His first effort with Joseph Johnston had failed, in large part because Johnston would not use the power he had been given.[54] To Beauregard, Davis gave the same general powers "to secure the fullest co-operation of the troops" under his charge.[55] Davis intended Beauregard to exercise command authority in the Military Division of the West; he did not envision Beauregard's becoming tied down in any one place with any particular segment of his command. To enable Beauregard to act as a theater or group commander, his assignment orders authorized him to operate "wherever in your judgment the interest of your command render it expedient."[56]

Davis gave Beauregard sufficient authority to command, but Beauregard, like Johnston before him and like many other Civil War generals, could not conceive of commanding without actually leading troops in the field.[57] General responsibility over a geographical area or theater rather than a specific army made Beauregard uncomfortable. That "he would be without troops directly under him" and "that he was not superseding General Hood" left Beauregard unsure about the new command structure, but Davis's promise of support persuaded him to accept the position.[58]

The device of the Military Division of the West and the selection of Beauregard as its commanding general constituted, in certain ways, a master stroke. It provided advice and restraint for a young field commander, it muted public criticism after Atlanta, and it resurrected an old hero to repel the invader from the southern heartland.

Davis, back in Richmond, watched the strategy he had approved for his western army go into operation. And that strategy functioned as designed. Even before Beauregard's arrival, Hood started for northwestern Georgia. Receiving word that the Confederates had advanced north of the Chattahoochee River, Sherman moved his divisions out of Atlanta in pursuit of Hood.[59]

For the better part of a month the two armies played a cat-and-mouse game in northwestern Georgia and northeastern Alabama. Neither commander enjoyed this charade. Although Hood had accomplished his purpose of drawing Sherman out of Atlanta, he wanted a fight, and Sherman made that difficult. Sherman had promised to "make [Hood] suffer" if his "army attempt our rear," but the futility of the chase chafed him.[60] "To pursue Hood is folly," Sherman grumbled, "for he can twist and turn like a fox and wear out an army in pursuit." To Sherman, his army some sixty miles behind Hood, the possibilities in a march to the sea contrasted vividly with the fruitless pursuit of Hood.[61]

While Sherman thought of Savannah, Hood had visions of Confederate divisions in Middle Tennessee. The strategy decided on by Hood and Davis at Palmetto and agreed to by Beauregard at Augusta permitted a northern campaign only so long as Sherman dutifully followed. Should Sherman turn back south to Atlanta and central Georgia, then Hood was to become the hunter. Hood's new idea dropped that contingency. The Army of Tennessee would simply forget about Sherman and invade Tennessee.[62]

Hood made this proposal to Beauregard at Gadsden, Alabama, on October 20. Beauregard, who had returned to Hood's army after visiting Richard Taylor, exhibited little enthusiasm for the plan. After two days of discussion, however, Beauregard, though still dubious, authorized Hood to make preparations for the advance and urged on his subordinate the absolute necessity for speed. Hood had to get into Middle Tennessee before the Federals were ready for him.[63]

His decision made, Beauregard informed the War Department on October 22 and 24 of the change in operations.[64] A week later he sent President Davis a letter outlining the new strategy.[65] Nothing came from the president or the War Department countermanding Hood's invasion.

On October 31 Hood arrived at Tuscumbia, Alabama, the place he and Beauregard had decided to use as a jumping-off point for the invasion. Once in Tuscumbia, Hood failed to heed Beauregard's admonishment to make haste and get into Tennessee as quickly as possible. For three weeks, in spite of repeated pleas from Beauregard to "[p]ush on active offensive immediately," Hood waited in Tuscumbia.[66] The dashing, energetic, even impetuous Hood sat down. Not until November 21, for reasons not yet convincingly explained, did he advance into Tennessee.[67]

This three-week delay greatly decreased the chances for Confederate success in Tennessee. While Hood marched between Gadsden and Tuscumbia, Sherman turned back toward Atlanta and began the march to the sea. He placed Major General George H. Thomas in charge of defending Tennessee against attack by Hood, but Thomas did not begin to get his troops positioned until November 4. Disarray pervaded Federal concentration efforts to such an extent that Hood, when he finally did begin his advance, came close to cutting off and isolating from Thomas a sizable portion of his force. Once in Tennessee, ill fortune and poor execution plagued Hood every bit as much as Federal opposition.[68]

Hood's Tennessee campaign was crucial for Davis and the Confederacy. On its accomplishments depended the western war. When the Battles of Franklin and Nashville crushed Hood and the Army of Tennessee, the Confederacy had no military force of consequence left in the West. Sherman, opposed only by militia units and paltry remnants of the Army of Tennessee, gutted Georgia and the Carolinas.

Jefferson Davis backed Hood all the way in the autumn of 1864. He did not countermand Beauregard's authorization of the invasion. Before Hood left Tuscumbia, Davis wrote him a long, vague letter expressing the hope that Hood might beat the Federals in detail and "advance to the Ohio River."[69] To Beauregard he spoke of Hood's "reach[ing] the country proper of the enemy" from whence he could "change the plans for Sherman's or Grant's campaigns."[70]

After the war Davis tried to exempt himself from complicity in Hood's project. Claiming in his memoirs that the invasion was "ill-advised," he asserted that he had no knowledge until after the fact that Hood had decided not to follow Sherman.[71] In the bitter battles the Confederate chieftains fought long after Appomattox, Davis denied that Hood conceived the idea of the Tennessee invasion and insisted that Beauregard forced it on Hood.[72] Neither of these claims has any basis in the contemporary documents. Davis knew from the beginning what Hood was about. He hoped, as did Beauregard and Hood, that Hood would succeed in Tennessee. He hoped that Sherman would be forced out of Georgia. He hoped that the invasion of Tennessee would rejuvenate the Confederate military effort in the West.

Supporting Hood's invasion meant taking a great risk for Davis; not to support it meant certain disaster. The evidence from the Atlanta Campaign and from the battles for Atlanta itself gave no indication that the Army of Tennessee could do more than delay, for brief moments, the inexorable southward advance of Sherman. But resounding victory in Tennessee might make a substantial difference. Davis gambled—with higher stakes than those before Atlanta because the times were more desperate—and according to Beauregard and Federal commanders, it might have paid off had Hood acted quickly.[73] He did not.

This essay suggests a somewhat different Jefferson Davis from the one portrayed over a century ago by Pollard and brought down to the present. In the late period of the western war, Davis did not exhibit a rigidity that refused advice. He showed more than a little political sense and made a strong effort to gain the support of a threatened public. He did not play favorites nor needlessly interfere with his generals in the field. Davis's every act in those months was calculated for victory.

2

Economics or Race

AN ANALYSIS OF THE GUBERNATORIAL ELECTION OF 1890 IN SOUTH CAROLINA

My book The Conservative Regime: South Carolina, 1877–1890 *(1968) concluded with the insurgency led by Benjamin Tillman capturing the state Democratic party and thus overwhelming the Conservatives, who had dominated the state since the end of Reconstruction. Rather than the generally accepted explanation that throughout the South an economically distressed agrarian class revolted against and defeated more probusiness interests, I argued that a generational divide best explained what happened in South Carolina. My study ended when Tillman and his associates took over the Democratic party apparatus and in August 1890 awarded the party's gubernatorial nomination to Tillman. At that point almost every leading Conservative, Democrats all, rallied behind their old foe as the legitimate party leader and nominee. Yet in the general election in November, a group of diehard anti-Tlllmanite Conservatives offered an alternate candidate. It appeared to me that this contest presented a superb opportunity to test whether Tillman brought out heretofore politically dormant farmers. After all, in 1890 South Carolina opposition to the Democratic party was akin to treason to white political domination. Facing such an ominous threat to their cause and their hero, it seemed logical that distressed farmers would rush to back their own chieftain, who upheld the Democratic banner. The failure of such a surge would reinforce my contention that occupational or class antagonisms mattered little in Tillman's triumph over the Conservative regime. To test my hypothesis, I employed two statistical techniques widely used when I wrote the essay.*[1]

Historians usually view the political fight between Bourbon Democrats and agrarian insurgents in the South during the 1880s and 1890s as class warfare.[2] Recently I registered a dissent and argued that in at least one state, South Carolina, the contest between the Conservative Democrats and Benjamin R. Tillman precipitated a battle of generations, not of classes.[3] Tillman, his followers, and their antagonists shared much, including an abiding reverence for the Democratic party. Tillman never stepped outside its bounds; instead, in the summer of 1890, he captured the party by controlling the state convention and winning the Democratic nomination for governor. Afterward an overwhelming majority of the Conservative leadership—United States senator Wade Hampton, patriarch of the Conservative regime, United States senator Matthew C. Butler, the congressmen, most of the county leaders, the *Charleston News and Courier,* the leading Conservative newspaper—acknowledged Tillman as head of the party and renewed their pledge of allegiance to the party.[4] "I would not wish it [Tillman's triumph]," wrote one state senator, expressing the attitude of many Conservatives, "but I accept it."[5]

While most men put the sanctity of the Democratic party above enmity for Tillman, a small group of ultra-Conservatives placed hatred of Tillman above party loyalty.[6] Led by Alexander C. Haskell, a Columbia attorney and close friend of Hampton's who had been chairman of the state Democratic Executive Committee in 1876 and an associate justice of the South Carolina Supreme Court, they declared: "Let us swear that B. R. Tillman shall never be Governor of South Carolina."[7] These ultras met in convention in Columbia on October 9, 1890; this gathering, "notable in numbers and character," from 20 of the state's 35 counties seemed willing to bolt the party.[8] In an address justifying their independent action, the ultras claimed that Tillman "has done more harm and brought greater sorrow on the State than the sword or fire or the hand of man in any other share has ever before effected."

Confident they could win, the ultras asserted that they represented all the people, black as well as white. They made an open appeal to Negroes; Haskell said that "we should ask the support and maintain the rights of colored voters as we did in 1876." While ardently courting the Negro vote, Haskell and his associates did not appeal to blacks as equals.

Haskell told the Negroes that he would maintain white supremacy but he also promised to "maintain the rights of colored voters," treatment they could not expect from his opponent.[9]

The question of the Negro and his status had seldom arisen during the five-year political debate between Tillman and the Conservatives.[10] By 1885, the year of Tillman's rise to statewide prominence, the Negro had been successfully removed from the political scene, except in the special preserve the Conservative Democrats had created for him. The Seventh Congressional District, popularly called the Black District, had been gerrymandered by the Democrats when they drew up new congressional districts in 1882. The gerrymander created one district overwhelmingly Negro (more than 4 to 1 in potential voters) and six with relatively equal racial alignments.[11] Throughout the 1880s, Negroes in the Black District had enjoyed a political life; they elected black legislators and black congressmen—Republicans all. Negroes outside the Black District had had, with few exceptions, no political life.[12] The political fate of the Negro appeared so settled in South Carolina in 1890 that the statewide canvass preceding the Democratic gubernatorial nominating convention generated great excitement and bitter speeches by Tillman and his two Conservative opponents but included hardly a passing reference to Negroes.[13]

I

Between 1876 and 1888, voting in South Carolina elections declined precipitously.[14] Some 183,388 votes were officially counted in the corrupt election of 1876 that put Wade Hampton in the governor's chair and the Democratic party in power. Since that year, South Carolinians had become increasingly lethargic in their use of the franchise. Disturbed at this trend, the *News and Courier* observed, in 1886, "there is in fact, throughout South Carolina an indisposition to take the trouble to vote at elections, which is both significant and shocking."[15] Two reasons can be advanced for the sharp drop: (1) after 1876 the Democratic nominee had no serious challenger in the general election, so many Democrats neglected to vote, and (2) efforts by whites to decrease substantially the Negro vote, combined with the failure of the Republican party to present

Table 2.1. Voting in South Carolina Gubernatorial Elections

Election	*Democratic Vote*	*Other*
1876	92,261	91,127 (Republican)
1878	119,550	213
1880	117,432	4,369 (mostly Greenback)
1882	67,719	17,719 (Greenback)
1884	67,921	None
1886	33,114	None
1888	58,730	16
1890	59,159	14,828 (Haskell)

Note: These figures were taken from the *Tribune Almanac* for 1877, 1879, 1881, 1883, 1885, 1887, 1889, and 1891. The vote for any one year is found in the almanac for the following year.

candidates for statewide office after 1876, significantly reduced Negro voting except in the Black District.

The Tillman-Haskell race in 1890 seemingly had all the ingredients necessary to reverse the trend.[16] In this election, held in November 1890, Tillman stood before the public for the first time (he had won the Democratic nomination in convention). With their champion heading the Democratic ticket and running against a bitter enemy who had dared ask for assistance from Negroes, any class appeal Tillman held should have come forth in a torrent of new Democratic voters. The contest also affords the opportunity for an assessment of Haskell's electoral strength.

II

To find out whether Tillman did bring new voters to the polls, I analyzed the returns in the Tillman-Haskell gubernatorial election. The major centers of Tillman's strength—and of new voters—would be those counties in which the number of Democratic votes increased between 1888 and 1890. I used certain indices to determine whether or not the rise of poor, debt-ridden farmers could account for the increased Democratic vote. If Tillmanism meant class conflict and division, the Tillman counties would be those burdened with mortgages and imprisoned by poor land that provided little agricultural wealth for the county or for the

Table 2.2. Counties in Which Democratic Vote Increased between 1888 and 1890

County	*1888 Democratic Vote*	*1890 Democratic Vote*	*Percentage Increase*
Orangeburg	1,183	2,923	141
Pickens	505	812	59
Laurens	1,300	2,062	59
Greenville	2,248	3,399	51
Kershaw	1,005	1,388	37
Lexington	1,636	2,187	34
York	2,004	2,624	31
Anderson	1,632	2,043	25
Horry	1,099	1,370	25
Edgefield	3,034	3,657	21
Lancaster	1,600	1,920	20
Newberry	1,556	1,694	9
Union	1,729	1,830	6
Clarendon	1,095	1,145	5
Hampton	1,520	1,548	2

Note: The figures for 1888 are in *Reports and Resolutions of the General Assembly for the State of South Carolina at the Regular Session Commencing November 27, 1888* (Columbia, 1889), 1:569; those for 1890 are in the *Tribune Almanac* for 1891.

The percentages given here will not appear separately in successive tables; refer back to this table for them.

individual farmer.[17] Tillman's appeals and Haskell's challenges to Democratic solidarity increased Democratic votes in only 15 of South Carolina's 35 counties.[18] Thus, fewer than half of the state's counties gave Tillman more votes than they had given the unopposed Conservative John P. Richardson in 1888. These Tillman counties ranged from Hampton in the low country to mountainous Pickens.

Neither in the fifteen Tillman counties nor in the state as a whole did a poor agricultural class turn out in greater numbers than before. There is no evidence that the increased Tillman vote came from the poorer counties, whether defined as counties with low per-capita agricultural wealth or low per-capita land values.[19] If the Tillman counties were not the poorer ones, neither were those giving Alexander Haskell a substantial portion of their vote the richer ones.[20] The wealthier of the state did not tend to desert the Democratic party because of Tillman.

Although most important, wealth does not stand alone as a measure of agricultural depression. In his campaign for gubernatorial nomination Tillman often condemned the crop lien system, the post-Civil War farm credit system in the South.[21] Under this arrangement many Southern farmers carried heavy mortgages. Yet neither value of land mortgaged nor the number of mortgages caused men who had previously shown little interest in politics to become politically active for Tillman.[22]

Tillman's new support did not stem significantly from the dissatisfaction among agricultural renters or sharecroppers.[23] The marginal farmers in the small-farm counties depended primarily on cotton for their welfare and cotton prices had been falling in the 1880s, but no ev-

Table 2.3. Agricultural Statistics in Tillman Counties, 1890

County	*Average Size of Farms (in acres)*	*Cotton Production (in bales)*	*Value of Mortgages (in dollars)*	*Number of Mortgages*	*Percentage of Farms Rented or Share-cropped*
Orangeburg	112	47,157	260,326	431	57
Pickens	118	9,587	79,128	191	53
Laurens	129	34,112	189,621	328	59
Greenville	96	28,485	362,840	906	54
Kershaw	158	11,993	280,991	256	57
Lexington	170	12,760	94,767	237	27
York	105	32,256	220,076	256	59
Anderson	83	41,530	448,996	665	65
Horry	210	2,808	26,416	256	13
Edgefield	115	42,743	248,342	494	66
Lancaster	135	11,178	126,359	269	53
Newberry	129	27,416	128,115	226	62
Union	112	23,703	138,507	195	70
Clarendon	82	15,274	108,464	174	67
Hampton	141	10,303	94,726	196	55

Note: Farm sizes are given in the *Eleventh Census: 1890, Statistics of Agriculture,* 178; for cotton production, see ibid., 396; for farm tenure, see ibid., 178–79. Mortgage figures can be found in *Eleventh Census: 1890, Real Estate Mortgages,* 620–25.

Table 2.4. Statistics of Wealth in Tillman Counties, 1890

County	*Per Capita Agriculture Wealth*	*Per Capita Industrial Wealth*	*Total Per Capita Wealth*	*Per Capita Value of Land*
Orangeburg	$58	$7	$65	$99
Pickens	47	7	54	121
Laurens	61	5	76	94
Greenville	43	58	101	121
Kershaw	32	5	37	70
Lexington	45	10	56	128
York	52	20	72	97
Anderson	60	40	100	111
Horry	28	18	46	48
Edgefield	52	5	58	107
Lancaster	35	3	38	85
Newberry	57	18	75	114
Union	56	3	60	83
Clarendon	46	10	56	71
Hampton	44	12	56	79

Note: Population figures are in *Compendium of the Eleventh Census: 1890, Part 1, Population,* 505. For agricultural wealth and land values, see *Eleventh Census: 1890, Statistics of Agriculture,* 226. Industrial wealth is given in *Eleventh Census: 1890, Report on Manufacturing Industries in the United States,* 586–87.

idence exists to demonstrate that a greater number of wool-hat boys or rednecks turned out in 1890 to ensure Tillman's victory.[24]

Some might argue that Tillman, even though he made no specific appeal to textile workers or other industrial laborers, would draw support from the few manufacturing centers in the state because the workers would vote for a champion of the lower classes. Yet the presence or absence of industry did not affect the Democratic vote.[25]

Most new Democratic voters did, however, live above the fall line in South Carolina. Ten of the fifteen counties showing more Democratic ballots in 1890 than in 1888 lie in the up country, with three in the midlands and two in the low country. But agricultural and wealth statistics do not reveal economic reasons for this sectional alignment.[26]

Table 2.5. Haskell Counties

County	*Percentage for Haskell*	*Per Capita Agricultural Wealth*	*Total Per Capita Wealth*	*Per Capita Value of Land*	*Percentage Negro**
Beaufort	70	$28	$47	$44	90
Berkeley	61	29	56	54	85
Sumter	47	55	62	148	68
Richland	46	29	76	59	64
Fairfield	44	49	53	82	70
Horry	39	28	46	48	25
Georgetown	33	25	59	33	78
Williamsburg	32	28	41	51	59
Charleston	31	7	190	12	57
Florence	29	39	58	80	52
Marion	29	56	63	111	47
Union	28	56	60	83	49
Colleton	27	21	33	53	84

* Of total number of potential voters.

Note: Number of males twenty-one and over are presented by race in *Compendium of the Eleventh Census: 1890, Part 1, Population,* 798–99; for total population by race, see ibid., 505. Figures for agricultural wealth and land value can be found in *Eleventh Census: 1890, Statistics of Agriculture,* 226.

Tillman did not draw to the polls a new class, or even larger numbers, of depressed agriculturalists. That the wealthy counties did not desert the Democratic party because of Tillman reinforces this conclusion. An analysis of Tillman's electoral strength does not support a class-conflict interpretation of Tillmanism.

III

Still, certain counties increased their Democratic vote and certain others gave a substantial share of their vote to Alexander Haskell. Race points to a probable answer. The Tillman counties were mainly white;[27] the 13 Haskell counties had large numbers of Negroes; and eight of the nine counties wholly or partially in the Black District were Haskell

Table 2. 6. Sectional Comparison (Averages)

Section	*Average Size of Farm*	*Total Per Capita Wealth*	*Per Capita Value of Land*	*Per Capita Value of Mortgages*	*Agriculture Wealth*
Low Country	117 acres	$65	$55	$197,000	$34
Middle Country	129	66	106	248,000	49
Up Country	103	67	99	216,000	50

Note: In dividing the state I followed the method of the most thorough student of South Carolina sectionalism: W. A. Schaper, "Sectionalism and Representation in South Carolina," *Annual Report of the American Historical Association for the Year 1900* (Washington, 1901), 1:253–54.

Table 2.7. Tillman Counties and Percentage of White Voters

County	*Percent White Voters (of total number potential voters)*
Orangeburg	35
Pickens	80
Laurens	47
Greenville	65
Kershaw	43
Lexington	64
York	51
Anderson	60
Horry	75
Edgefield	40
Lancaster	53
Newberry	38
Union	49
Clarendon	35
Hampton	38

Note: Figures on males twenty-one and over are given by race in *Compendium of the Eleventh Census: 1890, Part 1, Population*, 798–99.

counties.[28] Winning the congressional election in this district in 1882, 1884, 1888, and 1890, the Republicans sent to Washington three different men, two Negro and one white. Haskell made a plea for Negro votes, and the state Republican party, almost totally Negro, backed him.[29] The evidence also indicates that those who voted for Benjamin Harrison for president in 1888 cast their ballots for Alexander Haskell for governor in 1890.[30] That Haskell solicited Negro votes, that the state Republican party supported his candidacy, that he ran best in Republican areas, and that most South Carolina Republicans were Negroes strongly suggests that the bulk of Haskell votes came from Negro citizens.

When Haskell announced his candidacy in late September 1890, most prominent South Carolina Democrats cried for a closing of the ranks against this threat to the party and to white supremacy. The *Charleston News and Courier* urged: "Stand by the ticket, not for the ticket's sake, but for the party and the State."[31] The chief up-country newspaper, the *Greenville News,* asserted that safety and party principles demanded a

Table 2.8. Republican Presidential Vote in 1888 and Haskell Vote in 1890

County	*Percentage for Haskell in 1890*	*Percentage for Benjamin Harrison in 1888*
Beaufort	70	74
Berkeley	61	45
Sumter	47	32
Richland	46	19
Fairfield	44	omitted (less than 0.5)
Horry	39	23
Georgetown	33	47
Williamsburg	32	32
Charleston	31	14
Florence	29	not yet created
Marion	29	23
Union	28	omitted (less than 0.5)
Colleton	27	20

Note: The presidential votes in South Carolina in 1888 are in the *Tribune Almanac* for 1889. Haskell received only about 1,000 more popular votes than did Harrison. Ibid. See also table 2.1.

Tillman victory. Going further the *News* admonished the voters: "Let the people rise up in November as they have never risen before."[32] The white people did; the increased Democratic vote came from white counties whose men heeded the cries of the *News* and the *News and Courier.* White control had been secured only since 1877; the white men of the state had no intention of allowing the Negro to regain any political influence.

3

The Cotton Crisis in the Antebellum South

ANOTHER LOOK

An intriguing aspect of the antebellum territorial issue focused on whether, by 1860, farmers and planters in the existing slave states had exhausted productive cotton land. Historians had addressed this matter in various ways—some have responded yes, others no. In the early 1970s it seemed to me that none of them had taken a systematic approach to the problem. In 1973 I presented the question to a graduate seminar at LSU. In developing an answer, the seminar adopted a two-dimensional approach. First, instead of following politicians' speeches and professional expansionists' assertions, concentration on agricultural periodicals, where those most knowledgeable about cotton cultivation expressed their views, would offer a more balanced and informed perspective. Second, research into yield per acre both in 1860 and later in the nineteenth century should clarify the quality of land planted in cotton, for the yield figures would surely testify to the productivity of the soil. Should the inquiry result in optimistic experts and postbellum yields per acre matching or exceeding antebellum ones, that outcome should settle the "exhaustion" issue. Then, the motivation for expansion would have to lay elsewhere. In 1975 I published the findings in an essay in Agricultural History.[1]

By the mid-1850s the antebellum South faced a cotton crisis—modern historians, while not inventing that conclusion, have certainly contributed to it and refined it. Some years ago Charles Ramsdell argued that the cultivation of cotton had reached its geographical limits by 1860. Because of climatological conditions, he claimed, the cotton culture simply could not go beyond its 1860 frontier, central Texas. Also no expansion could occur in the older states, for few productive acres remained unclaimed. The economic result of that limitation, Ramsdell went on, would have meant an economic decline in the South followed, in turn, by the demise of slavery.[2] Of course war intervened so events did not take their natural course.

More recently Eugene Genovese, while devastatingly critical of Ramsdell's thesis, also asserts that slavery needed fresh lands to survive.[3] Genovese's conception of expansion, however, envisions more than new cotton fields; he talks about mines and other enterprises. Still, for him, the crisis was essentially agricultural because wasteful agricultural practices along with inefficient slave labor destroyed productive land at a rapid rate and necessitated expansion. Failure to expand, Genovese continues, would have meant stagnation, disruption of the interstate slave trade, and economic catastrophe, which would have heralded the political and social disintegration of the planter class. Cotton made up a crucial part of this grim equation because it so dominated the southern agricultural and economic scene. Genovese further maintains that southern leaders recognized their plight and acted for expansion to avert collapse. His is no one-dimensional argument, for he "propose[s] to show that economics, politics, social life, ideology, and psychology converged to thrust the system outward."[4] Even so, for him, the economic or agricultural crisis assumes major proportions, for it undergirds the threat of depression and dissolution of the slave regime. In other words, prosperity and a belief in continued prosperity breed confidence, while their absence breeds pessimism and fear.

Genovese's view of the southern rural economy, though probably the most influential, does not stand alone or unchallenged. The new economic historians or econometricians have made intensive investigations of slavery and the southern economy. A dramatic exposition of their work has appeared with the publication of Robert Fogel and Stanley Engerman's *Time on the Cross.*[5] Provocative and controversial, *Time on the Cross* challenges Genovese's conclusions on almost every economic count. Basically it describes a healthy and profitable slave system and a prosperous economy, particularly the agricultural sector. Approaching the agricultural South from the perspective of a cultural geographer, Sam Hilliard has built a persuasive case against any inferiority or weakness based on food scarcity and puny animals.[6]

None of these scholars, however, has looked in depth at two fundamental aspects of the crisis issue. No one has tried to discover what southern agriculturalists and planters thought about the presence or absence of an agricultural crisis. For his procrisis brief, Genovese relies overwhelmingly on the public statements of politicians and professional expansionists. Nowhere does he show conclusively that planters foresaw doom; rather the inexorable logic of his own argument places them in that position.[7] Rejecting any crisis outlook, Fogel and Engerman use an index of sanguinity based on the relationship between the purchase price of slaves and their hire rate to argue that, during the late 1850s, planters had "a buoyancy of expectations."[8] An examination of agricultural periodicals of the antebellum South will provide a more precise idea of how those most concerned and knowledgeable about southern agriculture assessed the agricultural situation.

Also no one has really tested the conflicting hypotheses regarding the limits of productive cotton land. Ramsdell said no more land remained, while Lewis Gray, the great historian of southern agriculture, asserted much more remained but did not develop his case.[9] Fogel and Engerman simply state, without any attention to levels of productivity, that the number of acres in cotton increased greatly after 1860.[10] Genovese implies, without treating the question directly in detail, that the best lands had already come under cultivation; thus few acres were left anywhere in the South (outside of Texas) that could support cotton at sufficiently high production levels.[11] A comparison of the antebellum acreage, production, and yield-per-acre figures with figures from the postbellum years down to 1890 should help settle this question of exhausted lands.

These two investigations will help determine whether or not southern agriculturists believed a crisis existed and whether or not one in fact did exist. If the evidence from the agricultural journals points away from any crisis mentality, that will raise serious questions about the belief in a crisis. At the same time, if the comparison figures indicate that ample good land remained for a generation of expansion, that will raise serious questions about the actuality of a crisis.

Although no claim can be made that an exact one-to-one relationship existed between the actual views of southern agriculturists and the views expressed in and by the agricultural periodicals, they do provide a valid vehicle for attempting to get at the thinking of the planters. All farmers and planters did not read them, and the journals did not give exclusive coverage to cotton. Still these journals did enjoy a broad circulation. The influential *De Bow's Review,* published in New Orleans, had over one-half of its subscribers in Mississippi, Alabama, and Louisiana, all important cotton states.[12] Published in Montgomery, Alabama, the heart of the cotton belt, the *American Cotton Planter* claimed a circulation of some 10,000.[13] Such numbers did not define the limits of readership in a rural society, for these journals, like newspapers, passed from reader to reader and often formed the basis of conversation on farm and courthouse square. The farmers and planters who thought about cotton and agriculture were certainly more likely to read and contribute to these journals than those who did not. If any substantial number of southern agriculturists thought a crisis existed in southern agriculture, evidence of that attitude would undoubtedly appear in these journals.

Using journals from across the section precluded getting the outlook of just one editor or one set of readers or one part of the South. In addition to *De Bow's Review* and the *American Cotton Planter,* four other periodicals formed the basis for this investigation: *Soil of the South* (Columbus, Georgia), *Southern Planter* (Richmond, Virginia), *Southern Cultivator* (Augusta, Georgia), and *Southern Agriculturalist* (Laurensville, South Carolina).[14]

One word characterizes the agricultural and particularly the cotton outlook in all of the journals: optimism! An 1851 editorial in the *Southern Cultivator* set the tone for the 1850s: "Since the demand for cotton bids fair to exceed the supply for many years to come, . . . it is no longer a matter of doubt our readers have a bright future, and a brilliant career before them, in the last half of the nineteenth century."[15] At the end of the decade, *De Bow's Review* carried numerous articles with descriptive titles such as "Brilliant Prospect for Cotton Planter" and "Production and Consumption of Cotton; Great and Increased Prosperity of the South and the Brilliant Future Which Is Opening Upon Her."[16]

Writers in these journals had few doubts that ample productive cotton land remained within southern borders. A contributor to the *Soil of the South* asserted that an abundance of fertile land lay unplowed in Georgia.[17] Editor Daniel Lee, in *Southern Cultivator,* claimed that "the South now has as large a territory as she can possibly occupy advantageously until her population is greatly augmented."[18] Writers in the *American Cotton Planter* echoed this fear that the slave population might indeed be too small to put the plow to the huge, unused acreage.[19] As late as 1860 *De Bow's Review* carried an article exulting over the "millions of acres" remaining in the South for southern farmers and planters to develop and improve.[20] The agricultural surveyor of North Carolina reported in 1853 that much good, uncultivated cotton land remained in western North Carolina.[21] During the 1850s, various writers remarked not only upon the rich lands of Texas but also spoke of vast, uncultivated sections of Mississippi and Arkansas as well as the excellent prospects for new land clearance in Florida and South Carolina.[22]

Without doubt optimism prevailed—and by a wide margin—on the question of the cotton future of the South; even so, a few pessimists did challenge the predominant opinion. Speaking in Macon, Georgia, in 1852, Colonel A. G. Summer of South Carolina deplored the chains that he felt limited slavery. He prophesied that failure to expand beyond existing frontiers would mean death for slavery.[23] As early as 1854 an editorial in *De Bow's Review* warned that cotton lands in South Carolina had been exhausted.[24] Occasionally even Daniel Lee became discouraged about the possible exhaustion of southeastern cotton lands.[25]

Regarding this seeming disagreement between the optimists and pessimists, two facts stand out. First, in sheer numbers the optimists dwarf the pessimists. A catalogue for any of the journals gives a clear and substantial majority to those writers who paint a bright picture rather than a gloomy one. Second, most of those who expressed concern about the debilitation of productive lands remained convinced that reform would set right all difficulties.[26] Urging planters not to despair at the disappearance of good lands, an editorial in *Soil of the South* assured them that reclamation and improvement could and would return fertility.[27] In each journal almost every writer who bemoaned the illness of exhaustion invoked the remedy of reform.[28] Those contributors who saw holocaust, and no way of avoiding it, numbered but a handful.

Often the question of reform revolved around fertilizer. Debates on fertilizer pervaded all the journals; always the debates turned on what to use and how to use it, not whether fertilization should or could be done. Individual contributors had their own pet theories, but all agreed that fertilization worked and was completely feasible.[29] Individuals who despaired that expense would obviate use of fertilizer or who felt that slaves could not distribute it simply did not contribute to agricultural periodicals.

This overwhelming unity still does not meet all the arguments of the crisis scenario. It maintains that inefficient slave labor and the cost of application (here the large size of plantations played a significant role) made fertilization theoretically impossible, whatever the opinion and success of reformers and innovators.[30] Frankly, incomplete and haphazard antebellum statistics do not permit a final answer on usage and cost. And the investigator who looks hard enough can find planters who confidently assert fertilization will never work.[31] But, as the evidence presented in this essay demonstrates, many planters (including probably those who thought most about it) felt otherwise.

A way does exist to resolve this seeming dilemma. Although there are no good fertilizer statistics for the antebellum period, they do exist for the latter decades of the nineteenth century. At that time in the South, black labor on large plantations still cultivated the bulk of the cotton crop. Thus an inquiry into what happened between fertilizer and cotton after 1865 can give an answer to the question—could black labor on large plantations effectively distribute fertilizer?

A positive answer would cast yet another vote against the doomsday school. Certainly no one can assert unequivocally that, but for the war, the development of the slave society would have paralleled the postwar regime. But if similar conditions of labor and size failed to preclude fertilizer after the war, then one cannot dismiss, in obiter dictum fashion, the probability that slave plantations could have successfully applied fertilizer and reaped its benefits.

Demonstrating that antebellum agriculturalists viewed the future of cotton optimistically does not prove that their optimism had a sound basis. A simple statistical comparison between antebellum and postbellum production can help determine whether or not that basis did exist. Historians have often noted, and mourned, the great expansion in acreage and bales that followed the Civil War.[32] This increase allegedly led, in large part, to the agricultural depression that gripped the South toward the end of the nineteenth century.[33] While recitation of production and acreage totals is common, no one has discussed yield per acre, certainly the critical item.[34] If yield went up along with acreage, then southern cotton farmers were cultivating new land capable of producing yields equal to the cotton lands of the prewar period. Even if yield, failing to leap upward, managed to hold its own, that fact would puncture the theory of limited productive cotton land.

An intensive study of four states—Georgia, an old cotton state; Alabama and Mississippi, the heart of the antebellum cotton kingdom; and Arkansas, a new state—tested yield figures. In every case but one, production and acreage increased notably. Between 1860 and 1890 both acreage and production doubled in Georgia. Although, in these same years, production fell off a bit in Alabama, the number of acres jumped by almost 500,000. And the tremendous and consistent upswing in production after the trough of 1870 indicated that the 1860 figures would soon be passed. Mississippi equaled Alabama's acreage gain while, simultaneously, pushing production up significantly. By 1890 both acreage and production exploded in Arkansas, with the former up some three times the 1860 figure while the latter also shot up (see tables 3.1 and 3.2).

That upsurge in acreage and production did not reduce yield. Generally yield in 1890 exceeded the 1860 rate. A noticeable drop in yield, along with acreage and production, accompanied the unsettled times following the war, but after 1870 the trend is unmistakable. To be sure the vicissitudes of weather and insect infestation caused annual fluctuations; still, the twenty years from 1870 to 1890 found yields steadily creeping upward. Of the four states, Arkansas had the highest 1860 yield, 240 pounds of lint per acre; in 1890 the yield reached 290 pounds. At the other end of the scale, Georgia had a yield of 170 pounds in 1860 and 197 in 1890. The figures for Alabama totaled 175 and 165, for Mississippi 195 and 230 (see table 3.3). Although these results came from only four states, every reason exists to expect the same story in other cotton states. These yields clearly demonstrate that the South could expand, as most of its cotton men believed, to productive cotton lands within the frontiers of the 1860 South.

While the production increase did not wound yield, neither did it precipitate a drastic decline in the price of cotton.[35] It remained relatively stable over the thirty-year period. It did decrease by 2.5 cents per pound, but that slight drop was probably mitigated by three factors:[36] (1) the increase in production; (2) the general deflation of prices in the 1880s;[37] and (3) the increasing value of cottonseed. Cottonseed, of little commercial value in the antebellum period, had become a valuable com-

Table 3.1. Cotton Production in Four Southern States, 1850–1890 (in Bales)

	1850	*1860*	*1870*	*1880*	*1885*	*1890*
Alabama	564,429	989,955	429,482	699,654	760,447	915,210
Arkansas	65,344	367,393	247,968	608,256	610,666	691,494
Georgia	499,091	701,840	473,934	814,441	960,025	1,191,846
Mississippi	484,292	1,202,507	564,938	963,111	1,019,470	1,154,725

Sources: Figures for all years but 1885 can be found in *Eleventh Census of the U.S., 1890: Statistics of Agriculture,* 96, 104 (the pre-1890 figures come from earlier censuses); for 1885, see U.S. Dept. of Agriculture, *Report of the Commissioner of Agriculture, 1886,* 389.

Table 3.2. Cotton Acreage in Four Southern States, 1850–1890

	1850	*1860*	*1870*	*1880*	*1885*	*1890*
Alabama	1,723,447	2,262,754	1,437,272	2,330,086	2,795,760	2,761,165
Arkansas	155,072	612,322	711,734	1,042,976	1,348,048	1,700,578
Georgia	1,597,091	1,651,549	1,330,491	2,617,138	3,047,698	3,345,104
Mississippi	1,182,312	2,466,681	1,644,512	2,106,215	2,535,004	2,883,378

Sources: 1850 and 1860: See tables 3.1 and 3.3; 1870: U.S. Congress, Senate, *Report of the Committee on Agriculture and Forestry,* 53rd Cong., 3rd Sess., Sen. Rpt. 986, pt. 1, vol. 2, p. 355 (serial 3290); 1880 and 1890: *Eleventh Census of the U.S., 1890. Statistics of Agriculture,* 96, 104; 1885: U.S. Dept. of Agriculture, *Report of the Commissioner of Agriculture,* 1886, 389.

Note: Figures for 1850 and 1860 can be determined only by multiplying yield per acre by production (in pounds). Acreage totals for 1870 and after can be located in various government publications.

Table 3.3. Cotton Yield Per Acre in Four Southern States, 1850–1894 (in Pounds of Lint)

	1850	*1860*	*1870*	*1880*	*1885*	*1890*	*1894*
Alabama	131	175	120	154	125	165	208
Arkansas	175	240	139	215	209	290	227
Georgia	125	170	142	163	146	197	206
Mississippi	163	195	137	172	175	230	208

Sources: 1850: E. J. Donnell, *Chronological and Statistical History of Cotton* (New York, 1872), 370–71 (Donnell gave average yield in seed cotton; to convert that to lint, a 3-to-1 seed-to-lint ratio was used); 1860: *Report of the Commissioner of Agriculture, 1867,* 415; 1870: The yield was calculated by dividing production (in pounds) into acreage; 1880 and after: A. C. True, comp., *The Cotton Plant,* UDSA, Office of Experiment Stations Bulletin 33 (Washington, 1896), 269.

Note: I make no claim that these yield figures are precisely correct to the pound. Still, they do show a trend, and that suffices for the purposes of this paper. Probably the later figures are more accurate than the earlier ones, but even for 1880 and after, government sources differ on yield. I chose figures from *The Cotton Plant* because they covered a span of years and because the publication was prepared by recognized cotton experts of that period. For other versions, see *Eleventh Census of the U.S., 1890. Statistics of Agriculture,* 45, 47, 49, 53; and USDA, Agricultural Marketing Service, *Cotton and Cottonseed,* Statistical Bulletin 164 (1955), 10, 13, 14–15.

modity by the nineties. Farmers used it as a fertilizer and they sold it; in 1890 the total income from cottonseed sales from the four states reached $8,400,000.[38] Either way it added up to a plus for cotton growers.[39]

Fertilizer probably played an important part in maintaining yields at a high level. Impressionistic evidence indicates that cotton men knew its value, though some demurred, and all did not rush to it.[40] Census data make clear the dramatic increase in its use.[41] Of course these figures alone do not prove that the fertilizer went to cotton fields. Both in Georgia and Alabama, however, the counties that had the largest yield gains between 1880 and 1890 were counties that had greatly increased fertilizer expenditures.[42]

The crisis script asserts that fertilizer could not be used in the antebellum period because of inefficient slave labor and the size of plantations. In the postbellum period plantations remained large, and in all probability a given plantation had a greater percentage of its land in cotton in 1890 than back in 1860.[43] The labor force remained black, and Fred Shannon found free black labor just as "inefficient" as Genovese found slave labor.[44] The overwhelming majority of postbellum rural blacks lived in conditions not unlike those they or their slave fathers experienced before emancipation.[45] As George P. Rawick has put it: "The plantation system did not change drastically for most ex-slaves after the end of slavery, and many continued to live and work on the same plantations where they formerly had been slaves." Rawick concludes that an "important continuity between slavery and freedom" characterized the life of southern blacks.[46]

These facts lead to only one logical conclusion. One cannot cite the inefficiency of slave or free labor as an argument to prove that planters could not use fertilizer. Of course if one accepts Fogel and Engerman's case for the superb efficiency of slave labor, then fertilizer utilization before 1860 occurred upon a decision of need.[47] No one, however, has made such claims of efficiency for postbellum free labor; yet the amount of fertilizer used increased sharply. Obviously the free labor was efficient enough.

Coming back to the original question, no crisis existed—either in men's minds or in their cotton fields. Most antebellum southern cotton men looked to the future eagerly, not with foreboding. And the facts of postwar cotton cultivation show they had good reason for their optimism. In 1860, antebellum cotton culture and the society based on it stood poised for a generation of growth and expansion within southern boundaries.

4

Daniel R. Hundley, Interpreter of the Antebellum South

I first became acquainted with Daniel Hundley's Social Relations in Our Southern States *while researching my* The South and the Politics of Slavery, 1828–1856 *(1978). Both author and book fascinated me. An Alabamian, Hundley earned a law degree at Harvard and in 1860 lived in Chicago, where he managed property owned by his father-in-law, a Virginian. Initially opposed to secession, he followed his native state out of the Union, joined the Confederate army, and became a prisoner of war, spending the final nine months of the war in a Union prison camp on Johnson's Island in Lake Erie. After the conflict he returned to Alabama and led a quiet life until his death in 1899. He hoped that* Social Relations, *published in New York City in 1860, would serve as a moderating force in the heated political atmosphere of that year. Though a loyal and proud southerner, he insisted that he presented an honest description of his section. He depicted a complex social order with seven classes, even dividing the planters into three separate groups, some with quite unattractive characteristics. While he left no doubt about the importance of planters, he gave the central role to the rural yeomen and the town-dwelling middle class. He never dodged the slavery question, defending the peculiar institution as basically good, with white southerners engaged in what he termed the laudable mission of racial uplift. At the same time he admitted serious flaws, such as the breakup of families by sale. Even so, he maintained that positive reform could occur as soon as the zealous antislavery attack on the South abated. Yet his hope for the positive effect of* Social Relations *was doomed; it received practically no attention. What he saw as its message of moderation and toleration had few hearers in a nation teetering on the brink of disunion and soon immersed in a brutal war. Since its original publication,* Social

Relations *had never been reprinted. As part of its Library of Southern Civilization, LSU Press agreed to publish a new edition, for which I wrote an introduction. That book came out in 1979.*

Daniel R. Hundley set a special mission for his *Social Relations in Our Southern States.* He wanted to provide an accurate picture of the South that would dispel erroneous notions derived from "intemperate newspapers and exaggerated romances of Uncle Tom school." According to Hundley, objectivity was sadly lacking in accounts of the South because they had been written "in praise or blame—generally the latter—of Southern peculiarities." As a result most Americans "remain to this day in profound ignorance of the Summer land." Instead of following this pattern of egregious partisanship, Hundley asserted that he would "endeavor to portray, truthfully at least, what has been presented to my own mind, from my present standpoint." Acutely aware of his assault on partisanship, Hundley announced that he had no intention of whitewashing southern faults. On the contrary, he was determined to "state the plain, unvarnished truth" even though "it may occasionally scratch."[1]

Hundley declared that he possessed a unique perspective for accomplishing his self-appointed task. He claimed for himself a notable objectivity—an objectivity based on his travels in nearly every state, his residence and education in both South and North, and his financial interests in the two sections. He told his readers that his special background would enable him to overcome the simplistic and polarized attitudes that had dominated previous descriptions of the South and southern society.[2]

I

Daniel Robinson Hundley is an elusive figure. The *Dictionary of American Biography* does not include him; nor does any other major biographical dictionary of nineteenth-century men such as *Appleton's Cyclopedia of American Biography, Lamb's Biographical Dictionary,* or the *National Cyclopedia of American Biography.* Only in two old publications dealing specifically with Alabama do biographical sketches on Daniel Hundley appear, sketches most notable for their brevity.[3] No Daniel R. Hundley papers exist in any manuscript depository, though his descendants possess a diary.[4] Hundley and his writing have been the subject of three published articles, but only one has more than rudimentary biographical information.[5] His own publications provide the chief source of biographical material, with supplementary data available from several different sources.

The youngest of six children, Daniel R. Hundley was born on December 11, 1832, into a landholding and slaveholding family of north Alabama. His father, John H. Hundley, a Virginian, migrated to the Huntsville area in 1818, then in 1824 went back to his native state to marry Malinda Robinson. Returning to Alabama with his new bride, John Hundley continued his farming activities. Later he turned away from active farming to the ministry and the practice of medicine, though he retained his land.[6]

We have no information on Daniel Hundley's youth before he left home for college. His father's religious convictions probably played a substantial part in the choice of Bacon College in Harrodsburg, Kentucky, where Hundley received an A.B. degree in 1850. Named after Sir Francis Bacon and chartered in 1837, Bacon College grew out of the religious dissension that wracked Baptist-dominated Georgetown College. Plagued by money problems, Bacon had been its healthiest before Hundley arrived, but it survived precariously until 1855, when it "no longer showed life." Although the name was lost forever, the college was resurrected in the late 1850s as Kentucky University. After the Civil War it became one of the building blocks that went into the construction of the University of Kentucky. All of his life, Hundley retained a definite loyalty to his alma mater, where he delivered the alumni address at the 1860 commencement.[7]

From Bacon, Hundley moved on to the study of law at better-known educational institutions. First he studied at the University of Virginia for a year; then in 1852 he registered at Harvard University. At Harvard he completed the law requirements in one year. The law faculty recommended the LL.B. degree after only one year for Hundley and four other students because the five had attended another law school for at least six months. Accordingly, on July 20, 1853, Hundley was awarded his law degree.[8]

Upon graduation from Harvard, Hundley did not return to the land or to the law of his native Alabama. In November 1853 he married his first cousin, Mary Ann Hundley of Virginia, whose father, Elisha E. Hundley, had considerable wealth and wide financial interests, including real estate in the Chicago area. To that city the young law graduate moved in order to manage his father-in-law's holdings. Details of Daniel Hundley's business activities are unknown, but family tradition gives him poor marks for business acumen. As for Hundley, he liked his northern home. "I had many warm friends in Chicago," he remembered, "and I preferred living there to living in Alabama." Even so, he kept in close touch with his first home. The Hundley clan still had property in Alabama, and his own family wintered there every year.[9]

No evidence suggests that Hundley took an active role in politics prior to the crisis of 1860–1861. Claiming to "subscribe to no party creed or shibboleth," he condemned "party shackles" while professing loyalty only to "the constitution and laws of my country." There is no reason to doubt his assertion that his first political post came during the presidential contest of 1860, when he was an election judge in Chicago.[10] Although Hundley was not active in the political wars before 1860, that inactivity did not mean that he had no interest in public affairs.

Not only did he have a keen interest; his interest had an outlet. In the late 1850s he contributed two articles to *Hunt's Merchants' Magazine.*[11] In one of them he extolled the "national freedom" and the "commercial prosperity" enjoyed by the United States, both North and South. This happy state of affairs he attributed to "the *virtue* and *manhood* of our fathers." Hundley believed that losing the priceless legacy of character would endanger American political and economic health, notwithstanding the country's material advantages. To prove his contention that moral corruption would engulf the unwary, he pointed to the fall of previous commercial empires, from ancient Phoenicia to the Hanseatic League. He thought his argument unanswerable. Hundley's second article berated "the pharisaical spirit" that permitted "philanthropists" in England and the North to denounce southern slavery while remaining silent about a much greater evil. In Hundley's view the transportation of nonwhites to labor in the British West Indies wrecked many more lives and was far crueler than slavery in the South. He urged the enemies of evil to train their weapons upon their own devils rather than spend all their time assaulting the South.

Following the Panic of 1857, Hundley wrote a thoughtful pamphlet on the danger posed by unemployment and the urban poor.[12] The deprivation visited by the panic upon sincere, hard-working men moved and frightened him. To alleviate the plight of the unemployed and the hungry, he called for a tax to create "a charity fund," which could provide essential financial support during emergencies. Hundley contended that failure to act would mean permanent pauperism in American cities. If such a condition ever came to pass, Hundley maintained that social upheaval would threaten the country. He was not censuring urban America; he praised American society for being "as near perfection now in our own social organization as we need ever expect to be." But he insisted that Americans had to preserve the virtue of all citizens, a virtue that underlay social contentment. Otherwise a desperation born of a terrible fear could vitiate the virtue America spawned and Hundley cherished.

These pieces served as a preface to *Social Relations in Our Southern States,* which Hundley published early in 1860. In *Social Relations,* he touched upon some of the themes discussed in his previous writing. More important, in his first book he strove to cool the rapidly warming sectional passions by merging his self-proclaimed special objectivity with an appeal to the moderation and good sense of all Americans.[13]

This attitude presaged Hundley's stance during the secession crisis. Identifying himself as one who "has loved this Union," he took a public stand against what he defined as extremism. With that epithet he branded both southern secessionists and northern antislavery zealots, among whom he included the Republican party. Not surprisingly, Hundley vigorously advocated the presidential candidacy of Stephen A. Douglas, "who used the most superhuman exertions to enlist conservative men of all classes in his support." His dedication to Douglas's cause brought about his first political post, service as an election judge in Chicago, "to prevent the Republicans from committing frauds upon the ballot-box."[14]

After Abraham Lincoln's election Hundley gave up on the Union. Returning to Alabama, he cried that the Republican victory had destroyed "the *fact*" of the Union. He called for "a united South" and "a defiant South" to "secure her rights *out of the Union* now" or forever lose them.

When a business trip in Chicago in April 1861 turned into a nightmare, including a narrow escape from antirebel vigilantes, Hundley became an evangel of secession.[15]

He directed his special efforts toward Kentucky, then holding to an uneasy neutrality. In a public letter addressed to the "Citizens of Kentucky," Hundley admitted that he was not a native son but insisted that he shared much with Kentuckians—his college days, his political conservatism, and his devotion to "one of the loveliest regions in the country." His message offered Kentucky a clear choice: either align with her sister states of the South or be ground down by the despotic North. He preached a gospel both urgent and militant: "Do not deceive yourselves with the delusive hope that we can ever have peace until it is won by the sword. You must strike now and strike as freemen only strike, whose liberties are endangered. Strike, then, and God defend the Right!"[16]

Hundley was obviously prepared to fight, and fight he did. He raised a company in his north Alabama neighborhood, was elected its captain by acclamation, and took it off to Memphis to join the Confederate army. The new soldier cut a dashing figure; he was tall, six feet two inches, with dark eyes and complexion. This martial effort led to temporary marital distress, because Mary Ann Hundley wanted the new captain at home, not on the battlefield. To his diary he confessed, "I feel that duty calls, honor calls, my country calls and I must obey."[17]

Thus Daniel Hundley went to war, and by all accounts served honorably. In April 1862 he became colonel of the 31st Alabama Infantry. With his regiment he fought in East Tennessee, in the Vicksburg Campaign where he was wounded, and in the battles to defend Atlanta. In the great effort against William T. Sherman's southward plunge into Georgia, the 31st Alabama belonged to Edmund W. Pettus's brigade of John B. Hood's corps in Joseph E. Johnston's Army of Tennessee. Engaged constantly during the Confederate retreat from Dalton toward Atlanta, Hundley fought for the last time on July 15, 1864, when he was captured in open battle near Big Shanty. Colonel Hundley was transported to Johnson's Island in Lake Erie, where he remained a prisoner for the duration of the war.[18]

For his time as a prisoner, Hundley left a full record—a detailed diary—which he published in 1874. In the aftermath of a daring and exciting, albeit unsuccessful, escape attempt in January 1865, his diary was confiscated. He did not see it again until early 1874, when it was returned to him under mysterious circumstances. Having taken the oath of allegiance just prior to his release from Johnson's Island, Hundley proclaimed himself resigned to Confederate defeat.[19] Even though he had accepted the defeat, he believed the diary should appear unaltered.

The diary is certainly a war document. In it he condemned his captors as well as the treatment he received. Phrases such as "coldblooded despot and human butcher," "the vulgar dictator at Washington" (both referring to Lincoln), and "the bloody monster" (referring to a Union general) abound. "I have learned pretty thoroughly by this time," Hundley railed in October 1864, "how to conjugate the verb *to hunger* in all its moods and tenses. I am hungry all the time." But through all the hardships, Hundley affirmed that he and his compatriots retained an almost unbelievable optimism about Confederate fortunes. Not until the end was at hand did he acknowledge the ultimate failure of his cause. The prison diary is a monument to man's struggle to overcome adversity.[20]

Upon his release from Johnson's Island on July 25, 1865, Hundley journeyed to the ancestral acres in Alabama, where he spent his remaining years. He seems not to have taken a very active part in the drama of Reconstruction. His models were the great Confederate general and the great Union president. In 1874 he wrote: "Since the end of the war, taking for my example noble and spotless Robert E. Lee, I have endeavored faithfully to perform the humble duties of my private station with 'malice toward none and charity for all.'" Those tasks included practicing law, serving once as county solicitor, and briefly editing Huntsville's *North Alabama Reporter.* According to family tradition, however, his income in the postwar years came neither from legal practice nor newspaper work but from the family farming operations managed by his brother. Hundley did announce a "work on the results of the Rebellion," but it never appeared.[21]

A local editor stated that ill health forced a quiet life on Hundley. Whether that is true or not, Daniel R. Hundley was not a public person and had not been one for many years when he died at home in Mooresville on December 27, 1899. Even in Alabama his death did not make news outside his immediate neighborhood; newspapers in neither Birmingham nor Montgomery noticed it.[22] And today Daniel Hundley is remembered not for the whole of his life but for a book he wrote at age twenty-eight, *Social Relations of Our Southern States.*

II

Daniel Hundley published *Social Relations in Our Southern States* in 1860. Although no evidence reveals his thoughts about its reception, I do not think they were joyous. He hoped that an analysis of the South by a southerner who admitted "there is much in the Slave States to call forth either unqualified approbation, or equally unqualified denunciation" would spark northerners and Englishmen to view the South rationally and to realize they had nothing to fear from it. He believed that an identical generalization could be made "with equal truth and pointedness" about any other society, "free or slave," as well as the South.[23] But few paid any attention either to his hopes or his book.

There was practically no reaction—in the South, in the North, or in England. Searching for reviews of *Social Relations,* I went through almost twenty periodicals, such as the *Southern Literary Messenger, De Bow's Review, North American Review, Harper's Monthly, Atlantic Monthly, Hunt's Merchants' Magazine, Edinburgh Review,* and *Blackwood's.* All of them noted and reviewed many books, but only *De Bow's Review* printed a review of *Social Relations.* That review was generally positive, though it expressed strong reservations about Hundley's treatment of the southern upper class. Most of the review, however, did not deal with *Social Relations* at all; instead the reviewer, J. T. Wiswall, spent most of his space discussing his own theories of the origin and value of an aristocracy.[24]

One can only speculate about the reasons for the inattention to Hundley's book. Most of the major periodicals in 1860 were basically literary journals; they noticed and reviewed mostly *belles lettres* and history. *Social Relations* fit neatly into neither category. This selectivity could explain its inclusion in *De Bow's Review* but not in the *Southern Literary Messenger.*[25] Yet such selectivity could not account for the exclusion from *Hunt's Merchants' Magazine,* especially since Hundley had been a recent contributor to its pages. Probably more important than the genre of *Social Relations* was the timing of its publication. Appearing at a time of increasing sectional tension and polarization, its call for moderation had little appeal. Hundley's literary fortunes matched the political fortunes of his hero, Stephen A. Douglas. Hundley called for the North to understand a South that deserved both praise and blame. In 1860 these views were not especially popular anywhere in the United States.

Although contemporaries paid little attention to *Social Relations,* it has become an invaluable source for students of the antebellum South. Even so, historians did not always recognize its worth. The first serious notice of *Social Relations* came from the first great historian of the antebellum South, Ulrich B. Phillips. In an essay prepared for *The South in the Building of the Nation,* Phillips described *Social Relations* as "a general treatise upon social types," which "stands alone among the productions of Southern writers." Phillips thought that Hundley made "particularly useful contributions" with discussions of social class among whites and general conditions among slaves.[26]

Phillips's comment did not, however, lead to the immediate widespread use of *Social Relations.* Phillips himself employed it little in his major books on slavery and southern society. Among his fellow historians of the South, probably the most important was William E. Dodd, who used *Social Relations* not at all in his two influential studies, *The Cotton Kingdom* and *Statesmen of the Old South.*[27] This pattern of neglect set by Phillips and Dodd was followed in the 1920s and 1930s by other scholars of the antebellum South, including Jesse T. Carpenter, Francis P. Gaines, and William S. Jenkins.[28]

Since 1940, however, *Social Relations* has been widely used by historians. They have heeded Phillips's early appraisal rather than the example of their predecessors. This turnabout occurred in part because historians began writing a new kind of social and intellectual history that drew upon a wider variety of sources. Certainly the rediscovery of Hundley and *Social Relations* has enriched the study of the antebellum South. Even more impressive than the number of historians utilizing *Social Relations* is the variety of uses to which they have put it. Examples abound. For Clement Eaton, *Social Relations* underscored the importance of the yeoman in antebellum southern society. Carl Degler recently called Hundley "the antebellum South's prime contemporary commentator on social mobility." Although W. J. Cash found *Social Relations* full of enthusiasm for "the Southern gentleman," William R. Taylor discovered that Hundley gave other groups more force than the gentleman. Bertram Wyatt-Brown gave *Social Relations* high marks for its discussion of family pride, but he asserted that Hundley "shamelessly romanticized southern life." In direct contrast to any romantic ideal, Kenneth Stampp drew upon *Social Relations* to help make his case for the maltreatment of slaves and the evils of slaveholding.[29]

Obviously Daniel Hundley did not write a simple book setting forth a simple view of the South.

III

In writing *Social Relations* Hundley strove to keep his pledges; in large part he avoided both emotionalism and simplism. The society he described was far from simple; the South that emerged from the pages of *Social Relations* was complex and complicated. Throughout his discussion of white society, Hundley juxtaposed the seemingly opposite themes of unity and diversity. He depicted a society greatly influenced by the power and pretension of social class, but simultaneously he insisted that the watchword of the society was democracy. While he praised the worth inherent in an agricultural society, he eagerly welcomed industry to the South. He called slavery a noble institution but acknowledged that an ugly reality often violated his ideal formulation. A curious mixture of traditional values and contemporaneously modern ideas informed his analysis of southern society.

No claim about the South aroused Hundley's ire more than the assertion "that in the south, aside from the negro slaves, there exist but two other classes—Poor Whites and Cavaliers." This gross misrepresentation, which had "misle[d] the mass of Free State citizens," Hundley attributed to "windy Northern demagogues."[30] Hundley's proper denial of that charge and his effort to correct it became the chief organizing principle of his book. His chapter titles point to a dramatically different analysis of the white South. Instead of two different classes he found seven, and he spent 75 percent of his pages describing them.

Hundley divided southern whites on the basis of their moral values, their personal and social mores, and, generally, their *weltanschauung.* In his scheme wealth or economic status occupied a singularly unimportant position.[31] Wealth obviously separated the rich from the poor, but, except in that very broad sense, Hundley had little use for it. Occupation assumed greater importance for him; for example, it was crucial in differentiating the middle classes from the yeomen. The former were engaged in town or urban as well as in agricultural jobs, while the latter were solely farmers. Although occupation provided a partial help in describing different classes and groups, it did not explain behavior.

Hundley's discussion of the planter class clearly revealed his limited use of occupation as an explanatory tool. His treatment of the planters emphasized his perception of the mainspring of social organization and behavior. Hundley cataloged the planters into primarily three groups—the southern gentleman, the cotton snob, and the southern yankee.[32] All three clearly had the same occupation, though he found southern yankees in other areas as well. Although the three groups had more or less the same economic standing, Hundley argued that the three were composed of very different people who had radically different values. Hundley, then, did not bequeath his interpretation of the planters to their most influential modern student, Eugene Genovese, who groups them together and gives them a common world view.[33]

Of all Hundley's planters, his ideal was the southern gentleman. And in him Hundley anticipated the ideal of a later, equally perceptive interpreter of the South, for Hundley's gentleman shares much with W. J. Cash's Virginian. Hundley's gentleman was "a man every inch, bold, self-reliant, conscientious; knowing his own convictions of duty, and daring to heed them." Like the Virginian, the southern gentleman possessed all the characteristics of conventional gentlemen, but in addition was "peculiarly the outgrowth of the institutions of the South." With an aristocratic heritage, he acted according to his own code and refused ever to become "the SLAVE OF PUBLIC OPINION." Motivated by gentility and warmth of spirit, the southern gentleman never allowed financial gain or garish display to corrupt his values. Education for education's sake, a deep respect for religion and family, abiding concern for slaves—these qualities underscored his distance form ordinary men. A man of the outdoors, the southern gentleman was a magnificent physical specimen. "Good size" and "graceful carriage" highlighted his "faultless physical development," which led to "remarkable powers of endurance." Hundley, again like Cash, made no claim that these gentlemen pervaded the South; on the contrary, they were "not quite so plentiful as blackberries in summer-time, or New England robins in spring."[34]

In direct contrast Hundley condemned the southern yankee and the cotton snob for lacking all ennobling characteristics. The southern yankee "invariably boasts but one armorial motto, and that is, *vincit omnia* AURUM." Besides love of money, cruelty to slaves, meanness of temperament, and disregard for family marked the southern yankee as a disreputable inhabitant of Hundley's "Summer land." Unpleasant physical characteristics complemented character faults. With phrases such as "heavy-jawed" and "beetle-browed," Hundley dramatized the southern yankee's physical inferiority to the southern gentleman. The cotton snob stood alongside the southern yankee in Hundley's lineup of social criminals. Ill bred and the personification of *nouveau riche,* the cotton snob flaunted his new wealth. Vulgar display, debauchery, disdain for religion and proper education, and a total lack of concern for others, including his own family, denoted a "ridiculous and contemptible" class, which brought reproach and obloquy upon the South.[35]

The origin and history of the values that Hundley used to distinguish his three groups of planters provide the key to Hundley's own values. For Hundley, one source chiefly accounted for the radical differences among southern gentlemen, southern yankees, and cotton snobs. Because of their ancestry, these three types confronted the world in their own particular ways. Hundley took pains to spell out the genealogy of the planters.

He drew the family trees in some detail. The southern gentleman always derived from "good stock . . . usually of aristocratic parentage," which gave him a "faultless pedigree." In the southeast his European ancestors were English cavaliers and the better class of French Huguenots; farther to the west "the progenitors of the Southern Gentleman were chiefly Spanish Dons and French Catholics." The less fortunate southern yankees and cotton snobs had to make do with a considerably less impressive family tree. The former "[sprang] from all manner of forefathers, though in most cases from persons of the middle class." The latter carried an even heavier burden, for "in nine cases out of ten he is the son of the Southern Yankee."[36]

Throughout Hundley's analysis of these three types of planters, he made clear that in his mind each was either blessed or cursed from birth. Both the values that Hundley cherished and the characteristics that he abhorred were intimately associated with family and blood. He "contend[ed] there is a great deal in *blood,*" and the family was absolutely critical, for it held and passed on traits, both noble and ignoble.[37] It served as the agent of transfer: the dead bequeathed; the living inherited. For Hundley, this law was immutable. Change had little place in his scheme—once a gentleman always a gentleman, once a snob always a snob. Although Hundley made no provision for yankees and snobs to move up to gentlemen, and allowed little room for changes in values, his system did not preclude social and economic mobility. He believed that in southern society a man could advance his social position and his financial fortune. But such improvement rarely entailed any fundamental shift in moral values.

The physical and emotional characteristics were static; combined they composed Hundley's iron law of social organization, which included physical description, personality, and values. He extended its sway throughout southern society. Although Hundley's emphasis on ancestry and his insistence on the immutability of inherited values appears terribly antiquated, his outlook fitted perfectly with the work of contemporary European students of society. The European social scientists, ethnologists they called themselves, classified virtues and defects of people and races just like botanists and zoologists defined the particular characteristics of flora and fauna.

Such diverse fuels as physiology and nationalism propelled European ethnology. By the midcentury, ethnologists shared a general belief in the efficacy of explaining personal as well as cultural values by specifying physical and social characteristics, characteristics handed down from generation to generation. Probably the most influential scientific statement advocating this ethnology was Count Arthur de Gobineau's *Essay on the Inequality of Races,* published in the mid-1850s. Gobineau concluded that he found "in the physical nature of men themselves the factors of race that explain men's minds and institutions." These attitudes spread far beyond the books and conversations of the ethnologists. Even men of letters became imbued with the theories propounded by Gobineau and his scientific brethren. When Stendahl described Italians as "slender, almost thin, very dark, with blazing eyes and a sallow complexion; he lives on coffee and a very few abstemious meals," he gave expression to the power of the new science. Talk of Celtic, Nordic, and Mediterranean characteristics permeated the continent; for the disciples of ethnology, physical characteristics as well as inherited cultural traits explained everything from political success to artistic genius.[38]

Although no direct evidence indicates that Hundley ever read the European ethnologists or even their American followers, like Dr. Josiah Nott of Hundley's own Alabama, he had a great deal in common with them. Except for anatomical measurements that fascinated the ethnologists but held no interest for Hundley, a striking similarity marks Hundley's analysis of personality and society and the work of the ethnologists. Both shared a penchant for classification as well as the conviction that classification permitted the separation of man into various types. In this separation physical traits identified social groups and provided clues to values.

Of his three groups of planters, Hundley clearly preferred the southern gentleman but never allowed favoritism to blind him. As William R. Taylor has noted, Hundley recognized that in the South of 1860 his beloved southern gentleman was an endangered species. Both the southern yankee and the cotton snob had greater numbers and more force than the idealized gentleman. To the southern yankee in particular, Hundley awarded the prize for energy and drive. The yankee had "contributed no little to the present unprecedented prosperity of the Slave States." From clearing new ground for planting, to promoting the use of fertilizer, to building railroads, the southern yankee operated at the center of southern material progress.

The southern yankee had even "stimulated the Southern Gentleman to activity and enterprise." Hundley granted the southern yankee that role while condemning the motive: the southern yankee had "only sought to make money and to advance his private interests." In contrast, the southern gentleman, reacting to the example of the southern yankee, had been "influenced by public spirit and patriotic pride." Still, Hundley gave the devil his due; the southern yankee had "ever been foremost" in southern economic growth. Admitting southern yankee's contribution, Hundley not only revealed his belief in the power of strength and energy, he also identified himself with the social manifestation of Charles Darwin's biology. Yet perhaps the southern gentleman was not doomed to extinction. Because Hundley believed so strongly in ancestry and family as shapers of values, he could imagine the gentleman becoming more energetic while also retaining his nobler qualities. Possibly, then, Hundley thought the gentleman could survive along with the yankee.[39]

Although the planters occupied the highest level in the southern social system, they did not compose the central class in southern society. Long before Frank L. Owsley, Hundley bestowed that honor upon the yeoman and the middle class. Determined to correct the widespread notion that a social vacuum existed between planters and poor whites, Hundley emphasized the importance of the overlooked middle. The "poor white trash," as Hundley called the lowest order of whites, he relegated to a negligible role in the South. In his scheme the middle classes "constitute[d] the greater proportion of [southern] citizens, and [were] likewise the most useful members of her society," while the yeomen were "most deserving of esteem." For Hundley, two separate groups existed in the middle. The middle classes engaged in a variety of occupations, including farming and planting, but many of them lived in towns, where they followed nonagricultural pursuits. In contrast, the yeoman lived on the land, where they were the staple of southern agriculture. Hundley pointed out still another difference; the middle classes enjoyed slightly more economic success than the yeomen.[40]

Emphasis on difference does not, however, explain satisfactorily Hundley's treatment of the two groups. As I have previously noted, Hundley never put much stock in either financial status or occupation as molders of character and shapers of values. The sources that generated character and values for Hundley indicate not differences, but marked resemblances between the middle classes and the yeomen. These resemblances are so pronounced that the two groups can be merged into one for discussion. Both groups descended chiefly from the middle ranks of English colonists. Hundley depicted the middle classes as appearing in all shapes and sizes, but he stressed "broad shoulders and angular outline." At the same time he noted that "physical heartiness" set yeomen apart. Describing the social characteristics of the two, Hundley used a common language. Hospitable, civil, God fearing, independent of mind—for possessing these qualities in plenitude, Hundley praised the middle rank of southern society.[41]

The importance of the combined middle class stemmed chiefly from its contribution to the South, not merely from its numbers. Hundley's middle classes were certainly not mindless men following wherever the planters led. Quite to the contrary, as men of the "stoutest independence" they acted as equals with the planters in managing southern society. No yeoman, Hundley declared, "had learned to fear mortal man"; nor would he "under any circumstances humiliate himself to curry favor with the rich or those in authority." Politics, a politics dominated by a pervasive interest and a broad suffrage, gave the middle class its influence. Extremely well versed in "the lore of politics," the middle class participated actively in that southern passion. Hundley commented favorably on their significant contribution to the roster of southern political leadership. He also believed that the middle ranks of southern society as well as the upper ranks were much more involved in politics than their northern counterparts. Phrases such as *comprehensive knowledge, clearer perception,* and *better versed,* governed Hundley's account of these men in the middle and politics. From my own work in the antebellum southern political history, I am convinced that Hundley knew of what he spoke.[42]

The numerical majority and the political activity of the middle class ensured that without its concurrence the issues of the planters could never dominate southern politics. Hundley recognized that political harmony prevailed because the middle class and the upper class viewed politics through an identical lens. Ties formulated by economic interests, political culture, and race pride merged the two great components of southern white society into one. Thus, unity, not diversity, was the benchmark of the society. The unity drew a firm strength from a political system that allowed the meaningful participation of all white males. In Hundley's mind this unified white society had one overriding mission—to defend slavery.

The slaves were at the bottom of southern society, but they also formed the foundation for that society. Hundley simply could not envision the South without slavery. And without doubt he bowed before the southern myth; Hundley's slaves were happy, well-fed "simple creatures." In fact much of his long discussion of slavery could fit perfectly into any traditional defense of the peculiar institution. He also castigated the self-righteous opponents of slavery who "damn incontinently" a people and an institution of which they know nothing. Hundley styled them "the latter-day Popes, from whose decree there is no appeal."[43]

While Hundley did follow the conventional road on slavery and abolition, he simultaneously gave his account his own stamp. In the southern slave system he found imperfections and admitted evils. And he dealt with both publicly, a rare phenomenon in the South of 1860. In Hundley's story Simon Legree, with his "crime and oppression," could be found in the southern countryside. On the plantations of an evil slaveowner, especially the southern yankee, "the crack of his whip is heard early, and the crack of the same is heard late, and the weary backs of his bondmen and bondwomen are bowed to the ground with over-tasking and over-toil." Then there was "the most utterly detestable" slavetrader, whom Hundley pilloried with abandon—"a coarse, ill-bred person, provincial in speech and manners, with a cross-looking phiz, a whiskey-tinctured nose, cold, hard-looking eyes, a dirty tobacco-stained mouth, and shabby dress." Hundley scorned this villain who "habitually separates parent from child, brother from sister, and husband from wife."[44]

In spite of these horrors Hundley insisted upon the morality and essential humanity of southern slavery. He argued that abuses could not destroy the legitimacy of noble institutions. Holding to his Calvinist heritage, Hundley wrote that abuses would never totally disappear because of the essentially evil nature of man. Refusing to accept the doctrine of perfectibility, he asserted, "There is in every man a private devil of his own, who can turn his bosom into a hell or heaven." Drawing analogies with institutions generally beloved in mid-nineteenth-century America, he asked if Christianity should be abandoned because of the tortures of the Spanish Inquisition, or if marriage should be cast aside because of divorce? Hundley answered his own questions with a resounding negative.[45]

Although Hundley vigorously defended slavery, even with its admitted abuses, he advocated placing the peculiar institution "upon a more humane basis than it rests upon at present." He especially wanted to alter laws "allow[ing] families to be broken up and sold to separate masters." And he was "persuaded that the Southern people, if left to themselves," would accomplish just such reforms. But first "all apprehension of intermeddling from outsiders" would have to disappear. To effect that end, Hundley called upon all true friends of the slave to cease their warfare upon the South's peculiar institution. Then, but only then, maintained Hundley, the condition of the slave would improve.

To Hundley, the only valid inquiry regarding slavery concerned whether or not the blacks themselves had been improved and uplifted. Arguing in the affirmative, Hundley repeated the traditional southern story. Savage and heathen blacks had been civilized and Christianized; moreover they were engaged in productive labor that benefited the entire world, not only their masters and the South. To prove his contention, Hundley contrasted the well-being of the southern slave to industrial laborers and free blacks in the North, but especially to black Africans. He drew a bleak picture of factory workers, the "weak, hollow-eyed women and sickly hued men" who suffered from "lack of nourishment, and proper rest" in their "miserable tenant houses." The northern free blacks Hundley described as weighted down with the yoke of discrimination. "*We heap upon them,*" he cried, "*moral obloquy more atrocious than that which the master heaps upon the slave.*"[46]

Even though Hundley made the usual southern bow to the plight of industrial workers and of northern blacks, he devoted considerably more attention to Africa. He presented a grim catalog of savagery, despotism, and ignorance pervading black Africa. In his own mind his case was irrefutable because his evidence came from "the latest and most reliable travelers," such as Heinrich Barth, David Livingstone, and James Richardson. These men were simultaneously exerting a powerful influence on British and European opinion regarding Africa. In view of the barbarism dominating black Africa, Hundley called on all antislavery men in the North and in England to reassess their condemnation of southern slavery.[47]

In his appeal to northerners and Englishmen, Hundley urged the general recognition of race mission. Making a Darwinian case, he asserted that the specific black-white relationship in the South was simply one manifestation of the cultural superiority of the white race. For him, as for many of his contemporary students of society, race equaled culture, and racial superiority meant cultural superiority. Claiming correctly that northerners and Englishmen shared his views on white supremacy, Hundley spelled out the similarities between slavery and other forms of cultural supremacy. For the North, it was the treatment of free blacks. For England, it was the treatment of the natives in India as well as the coolie traffic in which the English transported Indians, Chinese, and Africans to their West Indian islands to serve as peasants. Both the northern and the English practices Hundley chastised as far crueler than southern slavery, though he understood them as examples of racial-cultural superiority.

Notwithstanding his dislike for practices in India and the coolie traffic, Hundley envisioned England as standing on the brink of its great opportunity. He called for England to take over Africa, and he was convinced "in time" the English, in conjunction with the French, would do so. To Hundley, such an eventuality was inevitable. It would signal a magnificent chapter in English history and in the destiny of the white race. As Hundley saw it, the English would turn the wilds of Africa into a prosperous garden just as their kinsmen had changed the forests of the South into an agricultural showplace. This great work by England—its sharing in shouldering the white man's burden—did not necessarily mean enslavement of the Africans. On the contrary, Hundley maintained that it might be accomplished "in the name of Freedom, as the English now rule the Indies." Offering that alternative, Hundley made his major point. It mattered not whether the inferior race was enslaved; total domination by the stronger was the critical requirement. He willingly accepted different methods of attaining the goal, which he regarded "as certain as fate."[48]

Despite the sincerity of his invitation, Hundley never understood that the antislavery forces in England and in the North made their fundamental opposition exactly where he thought he had been so generous. Racial domination most antislavery men readily accepted, even, as

Hundley noted, in cruel forms. But slavery they viewed as qualitatively different from any other kind of discrimination or domination. Apostles of free-labor ideology, they demanded the maintenance of the form of voluntary choice, a condition symbolized by a joint contract and the payment of a wage, even if the contract and the wage mocked free choice and resulted in "nearly absolute subordination." Such an argument totally perplexed Hundley, who found it thoroughly artificial. For him, it created a difference where none existed.[49]

With his paean to the white man's burden, Hundley placed the South in the vanguard of the great work charged to the white race—to uplift the lesser races. He predicted that effort would increasingly occupy the attention and talents of the white nations, to their everlasting credit. Did this faith in uplift mean that Hundley envisioned a slaveless South at some future point? The answer is yes, but only at some incalculably distant time. Although "the negroes in the Southern States have been improved almost beyond computation," Hundley still found them "totally unprepared for emancipation." Emancipation, then, was so far away that white southerners did not have even to contemplate the possibility.[50]

Inviting the North and especially England to join the South in a world dedicated to racial uplift through domination, Hundley hoped to guarantee the safety of the South. He believed an objective description of his society to be the surest way to persuade reasonable northerners and Englishmen that the South was no more evil or dangerous than their own societies. Although Hundley cared passionately for the South, he did not camouflage the sores disfiguring it. Although he was convinced that unity overpowered division in southern society, he did not deny the existence of division. Thus, in large part Hundley achieved his goal of objectivity. He presented a more realistic account of the antebellum South than did any of his contemporaries, or have most subsequent historians.

5

The Politics of Slavery Affirmed

THE SOUTH AND THE SECESSION CRISIS

I first began seriously thinking about the secession crisis when working on what became Liberty and Slavery: Southern Politics to 1860 *(1983). My previous book,* The South and the Politics of Slavery, 1828–1856, *had concluded with 1856, when region-wide competition between two major parties that had dominated southern politics since the late 1820s disappeared. My major theme in that volume had centered on the content and thrust of the clash between the parties, especially Democrat and Whig. This contention had consisted principally of one side trying to present itself as the champion of the South and its interests, chiefly slavery in various manifestations, while condemning its opponent of failing or being unable to do so. Then, the second side would return with an identical assault. I termed that political combat "the politics of slavery." Confronting secession, I wanted to see if the same dynamic defined southern politics even without two major, organized parties. In 1981 an invitation to participate in The Citadel Conference on the South of that year provided an opportunity for me to present my argument that, during the contest over secession, the politics of slavery did indeed continue to prevail.*[1]

Secession, the separation of the American Union in 1860 to 1861, remains one of the most vexing questions that confronts American historians. Like other major historical events, the secession crisis was characterized by a multiplicity of causal forces and clouded events that make assessment and judgment extremely difficult, even perilous. But the secession crisis compounds that interpretive difficulty because a satisfactory interpretation of secession must explain not just one phenomenon but rather three phenomena. In the crisis that shattered the Union, the fifteen slave states reacted in three distinct ways: the seven states of the lower South, from South Carolina to Texas, seceded in the winter of 1860–1861, after the election of the Republican, Abraham Lincoln; the four states of the upper South, from Virginia across to Arkansas, joined the secession movement only after the bombardment of Fort Sumter and the onset of war in April 1861; the four border slave states, Delaware westward to Missouri, never seceded.

An endless variety of interpretations, beginning in 1861, have attempted to explain why the Union broke apart when it did. In fact an imaginative scholar could write a book on the historiography of secession alone.[2] For the purposes of this essay, it is essential to notice briefly the major arguments that historians have employed to explain secession.

The first is slavery. Surely slavery as a cause is both obvious and critical. In the crisis of the Union, the states basically divided along slavery lines, those with the institution and those without it; moreover, neither secession nor the resulting Civil War is at all imaginable without the institution of slavery. The existence of slavery alone, however, does not explain secession. Two serious disabilities hobble it. If slavery stands as the cause of secession, why did not the fifteen slave states secede in unison? Simply invoking slavery does not clarify why Georgia or Alabama or Louisiana went out with the initial group, but Virginia, which had more slaves than any other state, rejected secession before Fort Sumter. With the institution of slavery used in this causal fashion, no connection is made to the political process, and secession was a political act. Politicians planned, organized, and presented their positions to the voters, who chose many of those politicians as delegates to the conventions that considered secession. Any satisfactory explanation of secession must be connected to the political process.

Those same two shortcomings bedevil three other major interpretations of secession—those emphasizing the constitutional viewpoint, emotions, and economics. Southerners did speak a great deal about the Constitution and its subversion by the Republicans, but such speech cannot be translated into an explanation for the particular course of secession. Although southerners certainly became excited or emotional over the existence of the Republican party, not to say its victory in 1860, it is impossible to prove that Floridians or Texans feared Republicans more than North Carolinians or Arkansans. In the sense that slavery was in part an economic system, economics certainly contributed immensely to secession, but scholars who make economics the paramount cause of secession by insisting that the South faced an economic Armageddon by 1860 because of the slave-labor system confront three unbridgeable chasms: first, the fact of three different secession policies and the politicalness of secession; second, the overwhelming evidence that southerners perceived no economic crisis in the late 1850s;[3] and third, the indisputable truth that a number of those most closely tied to slavery, the large planters, opposed immediate secession.

The most recent major interpretation of secession, that its course depended upon local political patterns, especially the viability of opposition parties, does have its virtues.[4] Cognizant of three different slave-state responses to the crisis of the Union, it offers a seemingly plausible explanation for them, namely the potency or impotence of such local party divisions. Moreover, the emphasis on local political patterns clearly binds secession to the political process. Even with these strengths, this apparent solution has two fatal flaws. First, and most obvious, it divorces secession from slavery, which is folly. Second, it employs state and local political patterns to explain a desperate crisis on the national level. Whether or not an opposition party could elect legislators in Georgia or in Virginia had precious little to do with the southern reaction to Republicanism or the triumph of Republicanism.

Because none of these leading interpretations provides a complete or totally satisfactory explanation of the secession crisis, it is necessary to develop another one using parts of these arguments where they are appropriate.

Secession was a supremely political act prompted by the values most cherished by southern white society and fashioned within the southern political arena. The politics of slavery offer the best possibility for illuminating this quintessentially southern phenomenon. I will give here only a brief definition of the workings of the politics of slavery. The term "politics of slavery" designates "the world created by the interaction of the four major forces in antebellum southern politics: the institution of slavery, southern parties and politicians, the southern political structure, and the values of southern white society."[5] The result of intermixing these four forces placed a political premium on the vigorous, unceasing commitment of southerners to protect southern interests. Neither politicians nor political groups could escape the need for constant, public affirmation of southern loyalty. As public men they understood that such rhetoric charted the way toward political victory, while silence led to defeat. Moreover, as southerners they realized that the rhetoric of affirmation involved more than mere incantation. It simultaneously plumbed and revealed the core of southern values. Turning to the task at hand, it is necessary to look again at the secession crisis from the perspective provided by the politics of slavery.

In his inaugural address as provisional president of the Confederate States of America, Jefferson Davis equated the southerners of 1860–1861 to their grandfathers and the fledgling southern nation to the old Union. "The Constitution framed by our fathers," he assured his audience, "is that of the Confederate States." That same Constitution formed the bedrock for southern independence. Equally important to Davis was the fathers' "exposition" of the Constitution, which gave southerners "a light which reveals true meaning." No dimension of that truth, no purpose of the Constitution had more importance than preserving the blessings of liberty. But, mourned Davis, southerners no longer enjoyed a secure liberty because the Constitution "had been perverted from the purposes for which it was ordained." Refusing to acquiesce meekly in that perversion, southerners, according to Davis, "labored to preserve the government of our fathers in its spirit." As Davis saw it, by continuing that great work southerners would vindicate secession and secure liberty.[6]

This dirge for the Constitution and for liberty did not originate in the mind of Jefferson Davis. Quite the contrary, such lamentations had pervaded the South throughout 1860, especially during the fateful winter of 1860–1861. In midsummer the *Charleston Mercury* admitted, "The Union of the Constitution, we presume nearly all men in the South, desire to be perpetuated." As far as the *Mercury* was concerned, however, that Union no longer existed because "usurpation and encroachment" by the North had "virtually destroyed" it. In the aftermath of Lincoln's election, the *New Orleans Daily Crescent* announced, "the spirit of the

Constitution, the only valuable part of it, has been utterly violated and destroyed."[7] Thus, in his inaugural Davis merely added what might be termed the closing paragraph to the eulogy that numerous southerners had pronounced over the bier of the Constitution.

Preparing themselves to meet what they perceived as a mortal threat to their most precious possession, liberty, southerners called on the memory of their grandfathers. "Let us follow the example of our ancestors and prove ourselves worthy sons of worthy sires," cried a Georgian before his legislature. Chorusing the refrain "Resistance to . . . tyranny . . . is the cherished birth-right of every citizen," southerners saw themselves emulating the heroic stance of their forebears in 1775–1776. Using the famous Boston Tea Party as a symbol of the revolutionary struggle for liberty, the *Richmond Enquirer* placed the South squarely in that tradition when it noted that furious resistance to the tax on tea "created an independent people and built up a nation." The *Enquirer* went on to claim that the South of 1860 had to protect itself against the tyrannous designs of the new oppressors. In this vision the new engine of oppression, the reconstituted perfidious England, was the new central Union created from the subversion of the Constitution by those who wanted to master the South.[8] Of course, to master meant to shackle liberty.

In its political definition liberty had always meant control of one's own affairs and institutions, of one's destiny. Southerners believed absolutely in this formulation of liberty, just as many northerners did. This commitment added nothing new to the political firmament in 1860, for total devotion to liberty had been a central feature of southern political culture since the colonial era. It had been massively reaffirmed during the Revolution and iterated frequently thereafter. For southerners, the Revolution and the Constitution along with southern-dominated or influenced political parties had ensured the shaping of their own destiny. Of course, for the white South, that destiny was inextricably caught up with black slavery and had been so on a conscious level since the Revolution. For white southerners, the institution of black bondage provided a constant reminder of precisely what the loss of liberty entailed—dependence and utter degradation.

The contest of 1860 was traumatic for southerners because the rise and triumph of the Republican party first threatened, then palpably jeopardized the local control that denoted liberty. The emergence and the success of the Republican party obliterated the traditional arrangements that southerners believed secured their liberty. The Republican party was the first major party without a significant southern component. No southerners (except a few in the border states) ran for office as Republicans, and none helped formulate party policy. Moreover, with their appeal aimed solely at the North, the Republicans planned a strategy for victory that did not need the South at all. The party had concerned southerners from its birth and frightened them from its first national campaign in 1856. From the southern viewpoint the Republican party loomed like a giant tidal wave ready to crush their finely crafted political world. The devastation wreaked upon that world would leave their liberty shattered. In fact, a Republican victory mocked the essence of liberty—local control. Accordingly, southern eyes saw in a Republican victory a mortal threat to their cherished liberty. As a conservative editor in Nashville, Tennessee, pointedly concluded, "The universal Southern mind is in antagonism to the Republican party and its candidates."[9]

For southerners, the Republican threat to their liberty was made even more unbearable because the Republicans simultaneously insulted them. The insult so clearly felt by southerners was derived from both the rhetoric and the politics of the Republican party. The combined Republican attack on the South and on slavery cast southerners in an un-American light. Although there has been debate among historians over the centrality of antislaveryism in the Republican party, southerners themselves agreed with such historians as Eric Foner who give it cardinal importance. This Republican assault on the South and its major social institution made white southerners pariahs in their own land because, in the Republican lexicon, slavery and those involved with it violated the American creed. But, as David Potter has forcibly reminded us, southerners proudly identified themselves as Americans. They wore their American heritage as a badge of honor. The Revolution, the Constitution, Washington, and Jackson they honored as American glories and heroes. Knowingly and with malice aforethought, Republicans besmirched the escutcheon of southern Americanism. Southerners felt this to be an unforgivable slander. With their good name thus slandered, southerners believed their liberty already was endangered, for in the South good name and integrity of reputation were the personal hallmarks of free and honorable men. In the words of a moderate congressman, living under a Republican administration "would degrade & disgrace the South beyond all measure."[10]

When the Republicans won the election of 1860, few southerners believed their liberty was still absolutely secure. Believing their liberty endangered or even destroyed by oppressive Republicans, southerners saw themselves left only with slavery. By definition, the absence of liberty meant the presence of slavery, which for southerners equated with degradation, the very opposite of honor. In this gloomy vision the white South would become enslaved to the tyrannical Republicans. Such an outlook explains why so many southerners framed the overriding issue of 1860–1861 in terms of submission. Submission was a primary characteristic of degraded slaves but spurned by honorable men in full possession of their liberty. Mary Jones, wife of the well-known minister-planter Charles C. Jones, could see no reason for civil war even after Lincoln's election, but she told her son, "even that, *if it must come,* would be preferable to submission to Black Republicanism, involving as it would all that is horrible, degrading, and ruinous." Emphatically rejecting submission, Alabama congressman David Clopton informed a close friend that he could face the hazards of war because he would "rather die a freeman than live a slave to Black Republicanism." To stress his conviction Clopton added, "I would be an equal, or a corpse."[11] The sentiment expressed so forcefully by Mary Jones and by David Clopton was felt by millions of their fellow southerners.

In 1860 the Democratic party ruled over southern politics. Half a decade earlier the Democrats had finally vanquished their rivals, the Whigs, after a long battle fought under the banner of the politics of slavery. That Democratic triumph in the mid-1850s was complete; the defeated Whig party disintegrated and disappeared.

The political destruction of the southern Whigs did not mean, however, that every southerner joined the dominant Democrats. Thousands of anti-Democrats fought their old foe in a variety of political formations with different names, such as the Opposition party. Even though the anti-Democrats never made a national connection to reach for national power, they faithfully adhered to the politics of slavery. In the political furor that developed in 1857 and 1858 over Kansas and the Lecompton constitution, the Opposition press accused the Democrats of disloyalty to the South and of failing to guard southern interests. Addressing the proposed congressional compromise on Lecompton, which had the blessing of most Democrats, the *Montgomery Advertiser* in late March 1858 condemned politicians who "could stoop to the miserable acts of the compromiser. How harshly does the word grate upon the Southern ear. With that unctuous sweetness does it roll from the lips of aspirants for federal position."[12] With such editorial and rhetorical cannonades, anti-Democrats accused their opponents of selling out southern rights and honor and beseeched southern voters to turn to them for political salvation.

In 1860, when the anti-Democrats banded together in the Constitutional Union party, they remained devotees of the politics of slavery. As John Mering has shown conclusively, Constitutional Unionists practiced the politics of slavery with a vengeance.[13] Their appeal to southerners in the canvass of 1860 was couched in strident language: the Democrats would betray the South; only the Constitutional Unionists could be trusted to preserve the two-sided southern holy of holies—slavery and liberty.

Although anti-Democratic parties existed and flourished locally and although the Constitutional Union party made a vigorous effort in 1860, no group, apart from the Democrats, possessed major political influence at the end of the 1850s or during the cataclysm of 1860 to 1861. That position of political notableness went to the so-called Fire-Eaters, or secessionists, or radicals. A new and potent force in southern politics, the Fire-Eaters had sprouted during the crisis of 1850. With the widespread acceptance of the great compromise in that year, they became dormant during most of the decade, only to blossom at its end. These Fire-Eaters added a new dimension to southern politics. While Democrats and Opposition men struggled with each other over who could better protect the South in the Union, the Fire-Eaters aimed to destroy the Union. They pictured the Union as a dagger poised to plunge into the southern heart.

The presence and influence of the Fire-Eaters were connected with the pervasiveness and strength of slavery. Although no census of Fire-Eaters exists, and probably none is possible, they flourished only in those states that had a substantial percentage of slaves in their populations. The three states in which the Fire-Eaters were most prominent included South Carolina, the most densely slave of all with 57 percent; Mississippi, second only to South Carolina with 55 percent; and Alabama, with 45 percent of its population slave.[14] Fire-Eaters operated on a smaller but still influential scale in Florida, Georgia, Texas, and Virginia. They were scarce elsewhere, even in Louisiana, where slaves numbered 47 percent of the population.

While we know too little about these Fire-Eaters, we do know that they were not simply the large slaveowners. In fact, much of their local leadership seems to have come from relatively young town dwellers in the midst of plantation counties. Undoubtedly, the intimate southern relationship between the possession of slaves and the passion for liberty helps explain the citadels of Fire-Eaters. Because of that unique intimacy, white southerners living in the center of black slavery would be extraordinarily sensitive about their liberty. Their immersion in the sea of slavery would prompt them to cry out constantly about the precariousness of liberty. When these whites perceived the destruction of slavery at hand, the possibilities assumed terrifying proportions because, according to the southern calculus, that destruction would necessarily include the extermination of liberty. In 1860 the Fire-Eaters evinced no doubt that the future of slavery was at stake; in the trumpet blast of their leading newspaper, the *Charleston Mercury:* "The issue before the country is the extinction of slavery."[15] This general hypothesis, however, does not lead directly to an understanding of the psychology that propelled individual southerners, even those living in slave-dominated areas, into political radicalism. We need to know a great deal more about the Fire-Eaters, and the lack of a notable book about them forms one of the most glaring gaps in the historiography of the antebellum South.[16]

Fire-Eaters fervently believed that the South faced a simple but momentous choice "between secession and submission to abolition domination." According to the Fire-Eaters, southerners often failed to recognize the starkness of their alternatives because political parties and party politicians clouded the issue. Fire-Eaters poured out some of their harshest rhetoric on what they denominated the venality of party and party loyalists. "The truth is," asserted the *Charleston Mercury,* that party activities "are, more or less, fraudulent in their incipiency and practices." In the view of the *Mercury,* parties certainly did not serve the southern people who "have very little to do with them."[17]

To overcome the party-inculcated torpor that made southerners lethargic to their danger, Fire-Eaters took as their mission what they called the life-and-death southern predicament. In the midst of the presidential contest of 1860, Edmund Ruffin of Virginia sent to the governor of each slave state a pike he had obtained from John Brown's cache of weapons. On each pike Ruffin affixed the label: "SAMPLE OF THE FAVORS DESIGNED FOR US BY OUR NORTHERN BRETHREN."[18] While such dramatic acts did not make up the bulk of Fire-Eater activity, still speakers and editors, especially in the lower South, constantly thundered the Fire-Eater gospel: only secession can save southern slavery and southern liberty. Expounding their text, Fire-Eaters denounced southerners who opposed them as infidels and traitors who would stand idly by while the South was manacled and dragged to social and political perdition.

Through their public onslaught, the Fire-Eaters were responsible for the promulgation of two important ideas. Their solution to all southern problems was secession, and they continually and forcefully preached its necessity. Although others had spoken about secession, its possibility, and its legality, the Fire-Eaters gave form, emphasis, and attractiveness to the concept. By 1860 few southerners denied the legitimacy of secession, though many disputed its efficacy. Turning to the obverse of secession, the Fire-Eaters constantly warned southerners that the Union held great danger for them. Because of the Fire-Eaters' rhetorical blitz, many southerners began to balance the protection afforded by the Union with its potential for harm. Beset by the Fire-Eaters, the southern Democrats had to defend their claim that it was their influence in the Union that always ensured a balance tilted toward safety, not danger.

As Mills Thornton has noted, because the Fire-Eaters advocated drastic and unprecedented action, their success depended largely on outside events.[19] Most southerners believed themselves to be patriotic Americans; they believed in America. They had no eagerness to destroy what their grandfathers had helped create, their fathers had helped nurture, and they had helped guide. Secession required a great leap into the political unknown. As a result most southerners were unlikely to heed the call of the Fire-Eaters, unless outside events gave it gleaming salience. Thus John Brown's raid, the breakup of the Democratic party, and especially Abraham Lincoln's election were bountiful gifts to Fire-Eaters from the gods of politics.

Lincoln's election provided the essential catalyst that enabled the Fire-Eaters to precipitate the political reaction they craved. The Republican victory undermined the southern Democrats' pledge that they and their party guaranteed the liberty and safety of the South in the Union. Southern Democrats certainly shared the general southern view that the electoral triumph of Lincoln and the Republicans signified the culmination of more than a decade of increasingly shrill antisouthern rhetoric, attitudes, and politics. Southerners of almost every political persuasion shared the outlook of the moderate New Orleans editor who described Lincoln's win as "incontrovertible proof of a diseased and dangerous public opinion all over the North, and a certain forerunner of further, and more atrocious aggression." To the conservative Daniel R. Hundley, who had adamantly opposed the Fire-Eaters, Lincoln's victory had destroyed the old fraternal America. Hundley could plot only one course for the South: "You must strike now and strike as freemen only strike, whose liberties are endangered." Practically every southerner looked upon a future Republican administration with combined apprehension and anger, or in Don Fehrenbacher's perspective description, rage.[20] The political unknown of the Fire-Eaters' secession was matched by another political unknown, Republicans in power.

Reaction to the election created in the lower South, the stronghold of the Fire-Eaters, a volatile mixture that could explode, given a spark from sectional radicals. Governors called legislatures into session, and legislatures called for prompt elections to conventions that would meet in December 1860 and January 1861 to consider appropriate action. Nothing foreordained the decisions of these conventions. Ultimately they decided for secession, a decision greatly influenced by the tactics of the Fire-Eaters, who understood the opportunity Lincoln's election had given them and hurried to apply the inexorable pressure that would ignite the explosion of secession.

For the Fire-Eaters, timing was critical. If they could accomplish secession in any one state, then the basic question would be cast differently and to their advantage. After even one state went out, other states would not decide simply to secede or to remain in the Union, but would be drawn into the more complex question of joining or opposing a sister state. Recognizing the importance of immediate action and realizing that back in 1850 to 1851 the quest for unity entailed delay and ultimately defeat, the secessionists moved in the one state they controlled absolutely. On December 20, 1860, the South Carolina convention voted unanimously to sunder all ties to the old Union. At the actual secession of the state, Fire-Eaters everywhere rejoiced. Before the Alabama convention, Andrew P. Calhoun, son of John C., thrilled at the event: "At this point the accumulated aggressions of a third of a century feel like shackles at her feet, and free, disenthralled, regenerated, she stood before her devoted people like the genius of liberty, beckoning them on to the performance of their duty."[21]

Everyone, secessionists and their opponents alike, understood the critical need of momentum for the secessionist cause. Joseph E. Brown, the prosecession governor of Georgia, believed that the secession of South Carolina was a prerequisite for rapid action in his state. South Carolina out, he wrote, "will cause a thrill to pass through the great popular heart of Georgia" and line her up behind South Carolina. On the other side of the political fence, Congressman Zebulon Vance of North Carolina acknowledged the political acumen of the secessionists, who were "acting wisely for their ends" when they "scorn every suggestion of compromise and rush everything with ruinous and indecent haste."[22]

No one felt Fire-Eater pressure more sharply than the Democratic leaders in the lower South. The pressure illustrates the politics of slavery in bold relief. A glimpse at the reaction of two very different men from two very different states dramatizes the political interaction between the regulars and the Fire-Eaters.

United States senator Jefferson Davis lived in a state in which the Fire-Eaters enjoyed considerable political leverage. Although Davis had been associated with advanced southern positions in the 1850s, he was not of the Fire-Eater breed, who camped on his left in Mississippi politics. In fact, after Lincoln's election he counseled a leading South Carolina Fire-Eater against any drastic move. But the intense activity of secessionists in his own state along with the secession of South Carolina caused him to make it clear that he did not oppose separate state action. From his Senate seat he advised the governor of Mississippi on arms purchases and other matters. At the same time he indicated his willingness to support an acceptable congressional compromise.[23] The Fire-Eaters had placed Davis in the classic quandary of the politics of slavery. As a southerner he felt and expressed outrage at the Republican victory like innumerable other southerners, but he was unsure about secession. But when the secessionists forced his hand, he joined them because refusal would have undermined his power base in Mississippi. If Mississippi were to go out, Davis had no intention of losing influence or authority in his own state. Because he wanted to retain his power and because he could not present a sure plan to preserve southern liberty, Jefferson Davis responded to the Fire-Eater challenge by acting with them. He had no viable ideological or political alternative.

John Slidell, United States senator from Louisiana, also responded to the politics of slavery, but in a slightly different configuration. The Fire-Eaters had less strength in Louisiana than in any other state of the lower South, so Slidell, unlike Davis, did not have to worry about an influential force operating on his sectional left. Moreover, Slidell largely controlled the Democratic party apparatus in Louisiana. In addition, as a quintessential political realist and pragmatist, Slidell had never been closely associated with southern extremism, or, for that matter, with any other ideological stance. He did not advocate secession. Just before the election of 1860, he answered a Louisiana supporter, "I agree with you fully as to the necessity of avoiding any precipitate action in Louisiana." As far as Slidell was concerned, his state was "not prepared to take the initiative in any measure of resistance in the event of Lincoln's election," and he was not ready "to counsel such a course." Shortly after the election, however, he announced to President James Buchanan, his close friend, "I see no probability of preserving the Union, nor do I consider it desirable to do so if we could." "Louisiana," he made clear, "will act with her sister States in the South."[24]

Slidell then became a major force in convincing Louisiana to adopt secession. He became convinced that South Carolina and other states would secede and create a southern government. Louisiana, therefore, would have to side with or against her neighbors. If Alabama, Mississippi, and Texas went out, Louisiana might be isolated, with her Mississippi lifeline cut. To Slidell, the choice he and his state had to make really required no choice. Louisiana would have to stand with her own kind. Accepting that eventuality as a fact, Slidell wanted Louisiana to secede promptly so that both he and his state could participate in the making of a southern government. He wanted neither Louisiana nor John Slidell left behind by events.

The relationship among Fire-Eaters, the process of secession, Davis, and Slidell raises the question of popular support for secession and the unity behind secession. Secession was a public issue; no closed-door conspiracy broke up the Union. In every state speeches, editorials, and campaigns engaged the voting South. Initially, the Fire-Eaters led the crusade, for Lincoln's election gave them multitudes of followers; then, the traditional leaders like Davis and Slidell quickly took charge. In South Carolina, Florida, Mississippi, and Texas, a substantial to overwhelming majority favored immediate secession, and the outcome was never in serious doubt. In the other three states of the lower South—Georgia, Alabama, and Louisiana—the contest was considerably closer because of the strength of those who called themselves cooperationists rather than immediatists. Both the popular vote for delegates to the conventions and the early convention votes themselves revealed substantial public backing for the cooperationist position. But too great a distinction can be drawn between immediatists and cooperationists. Immediatists obviously were for immediate secession, while cooperationists preferred a cooperative effort. They did not, however, oppose secession. Thus, the debate in campaign and convention focused on tactics, and while tactical differences can be significant, in this instance they did not separate two adamantly opposed groups. Not all cooperationists belonged to the same camp; for some, cooperation meant a southern convention, for others, a joint statement by more than one state, for still others, simply the secession of another state. Almost every cooperationist in every state quickly and sincerely signed the ordinance of secession before the convention adjourned. These cooperationists warned in the language of one of their major newspapers, "it may prove a fatal, an unretrievably fatal error" should their stance "be misconstrued into *submission,* or delay designed eventually to lead to submission."[25]

In the midst of the furor dominating the winter of 1860–1861, cooperationists could have said nothing else. They agreed that the South had to guard her liberty, which had been jeopardized by the Republican victory, and in order to oppose fundamentally the immediatists, they had to offer a believable alternative to secession. They had none, at least none that more than a few could agree upon. The most striking characteristic of the cooperationists in the crisis was confusion. In contrast to the purposefulness of the immediatists, the cooperationists could not decide whether or not to campaign and could not agree upon a political goal to articulate before the voters. While it cannot be proved absolutely, it is almost as if in the depths of their being they thought the immediatists correct.

When delegates from the states of the lower South congregated in Montgomery, Alabama, in February 1861 to create the Confederate States of America, the initial phase of secession had run its course. Seven states, from South Carolina to Texas, now pledged their allegiance to a new nation. Even so, the bright hopes of the Fire-Eaters had not been realized; fifteen slave states did not stand as a phalanx, stalwartly opposing the oppressive Republican party. In fact, not even one-half of the slave states had heeded the siren call of secession. Yet these eight states that did not cannot be considered as a unit; they must be divided into two parts: the upper South, four clearly slave states, and the border, where the actual involvement with slavery in economic, social, and political terms was often tenuous.

The upper South, stretching more than one-thousand miles from Virginia westward to Arkansas, did not secede upon Lincoln's election, not even upon his inauguration on March 4, 1861. The paucity everywhere and the absence in many places of the Fire-Eaters made the political pressure for immediate secession considerably less intense. In Virginia, the one state where the Fire-Eaters did have a noticeable voice, their influence was offset by the countervailing force of the strongly antisecessionist transmontane region, most of which became West Virginia during the war. While the shortage of Fire-Eaters and their unending insistence on direct action did give regular politicians more operating room, the extra room did not signify that the upper South looked upon the rise of the Republican party and the election of Lincoln as normal political occurrences. The rhetoric in the upper South matched that in their more southerly neighbors. The Constitutional Unionists were strong in all of these states, but like southern Democrats, they too attacked Republicans and supported southern liberty. This rhetoric, however, did not propel the upper South into rapid secession because the political equation lacked the crucial multiplier, the Fire-Eaters. Leaders in the upper South asserted that southern liberty, although challenged, would remain unvanquished until the nefarious Lincoln moved directly against it by either prohibiting slavery in the territories or interfering with interstate slave trade or some other equally heinous act.

Despite tangible differences with the lower South, the upper South could not escape the snares of the politics of slavery. Just as the quick secession of South Carolina and the rapid pace of elections and conventions powerfully affected the course of the lower South, the fact of seven secessions and the formation of the Confederate States of America greatly affected the upper South. At this juncture states and a combination of states replaced political parties and groups as the motivating forces behind the politics of slavery. Those politics fundamentally influenced the course of the upper South, even though a majority of voters in these states probably opposed secession. While such opposition had spawned a political realignment that enabled antisecession Democrats and Opposition men to join together in a new Union party that blocked secession in conjunction with the lower South, as a recent, careful historian of this Union movement has concluded, "the apparently commanding position won by the Union party in the Upper South in early 1861 was illusory." Although the Unionists had become a stronger political force than the secessionists, they "well knew that they were in hostage to circumstances beyond their control."[26] They would have to respond to the baton of the lower South.

With the lower South on an independent tack, the critical question facing the upper South changed slightly but fundamentally. The question no longer was just whether or not to secede but whether or not to aid southern brothers. Theoretically, this question could stand forever without an answer, but in reality an answer was required. If in any way the new Confederacy and the old Union came into confrontation, then the upper South would come face to face with its ultimate decision. Its hand would be forced, and the antisecessionists in the upper South did not relish this prospect at all. "We entertain towards South Carolina the most bitter resentment," railed a vigorously antisecessionist Virginia newspaper. The *Charlottesville Review* accused South Carolina (read, the lower South) of "precipitately throw[ing] down the bulwark of the Union . . . with the full knowledge—aye, the intention—to hold Virginia and the border states between her and the Storm, and to carry out her caprices . . . while relying on them."[27]

Confrontation between the Union and either a seceded state or the Confederacy, no matter the cause or fault, meant the choice for the upper South between slavery and liberty. In the vocabulary of southern politics, coercion by the federal government entailed enslavement for the coerced states and the destruction of liberty for their citizens. The *Charlottesville Review* spoke bluntly: "[A]n issue has been made. The subjection of South Carolina or any seceding state, in consequence of their determination not to submit to the policy of the Republicans is a blow at the entire South—subjection to all. We are, thenceforth, humiliated. We are conquered. We could not hold up our heads in that Union any more."[28] Thus, when the guns roared at Fort Sumter and President Lincoln called for troops to suppress rebellion, Virginia, North Carolina, Tennessee, and Arkansas said no. As they saw it, rejecting that call meant rejecting slavery and embracing liberty. Thus, the politics of slavery underlay this second secession just as surely as they did the first.

In the remaining four slave states, the border states, a different situation prevailed. A small slave population made three of these states slave states primarily in a technical and legal sense. They were certainly not slave states in a political sense. Only Kentucky, where slaves accounted for 20 percent of the population, can be counted as a slave state. Slaves comprised only 13 percent of the population of Maryland, 10 percent in Missouri, and less than 2 percent in Delaware. In addition, the number of slaveowners among the free inhabitants was small—just a fraction over 2 percent in both Maryland and Missouri and no more than one-half of 1 percent in Delaware. Moreover, in all three states the percentage of slaves as well as slaveowners had declined markedly during the 1850s. As recent scholarship makes clear, these states were moving away from the slave South economically, socially, and politically.[29] Unionist sentiment flourished, while Fire-Eaters were rare. This different direction made secession extremely unlikely. In fact, reinforced by the tactics of an antisecessionist governor in Maryland and by the military and political moves of the federal government, it was impossible.

Kentucky requires individual attention. Kentucky had a substantially larger percentage of slaves than any other border state; her 20 percent approached the percentages of Tennessee and Arkansas. And the percentage of slaveowners in Kentucky actually exceeded that in Arkansas. Yet Tennessee and Arkansas seceded, while Kentucky did not. Geography and political tradition help explain its behavior. As in other border states, the northern frontier of Kentucky marked the boundary between slavery and freedom. This proximity to the free states had two important consequences. First, like the rest of the border, but unlike the upper South, Kentucky was home to a powerful unconditional Unionist sentiment. Second, conscious of their physical border location, many Kentuckians wanted to avoid taking sides because they envisioned their homeland becoming a major battleground.

The political heritage of Kentucky further buttressed this desire to steer clear of overt partisanship. Even after Fort Sumter, Kentucky declared neutrality in any conflict between the United States and the Confederate States. Thinking of themselves as conciliators and aware that their great statesman Henry Clay had gained fame as a compromiser of earlier sectional crises, Kentuckians strove to provide a historical encore to Clay's performance. Attempting to emulate Clay, United States senator John J. Crittenden led the major effort to avert secession and conflict through sectional compromise. Despite an untiring struggle, Crittenden failed, and his failure presaged the failure of his state's hopes for neutrality. Onrushing events engulfed compromise-minded Kentuckians. Within months both Confederate and Union armies entered the state. Union military superiority settled the fate of Kentucky.

Secession marked still another triumph of the politics of slavery. Once again southern political leaders in quest of a political goal employed the powerful rhetoric of southern safety cemented to the particular southern view of liberty and forced their issue. Filling the arena of southern politics, this rhetoric expressed exactly the hopes and fears of southern voters, captured the public mind, and supplied the driving force behind southern political action. Used to clarify the complication of three secession policies, the politics of slavery elucidates a crucial event in both southern and American history. But even more important, the course of secession makes it clear that no other interpretive idea so illuminates the form and substance of antebellum southern politics as the politics of slavery.

6

"The Only Door"

THE TERRITORIAL ISSUE, THE PRESTON BILL, AND THE SOUTHERN WHIGS

In the early 1980s, I became a coeditor of a planned festschrift *for David Herbert Donald, my mentor in graduate school who had also taught me as an undergraduate and had become a friend. In addition to my editorial responsibilities, I had to prepare my own essay for the volume. Having just spent more than a decade studying antebellum southern politics, my attention focused there. I had always found most interesting the relationship between the southern Whigs and the territorial issue, particularly the Mexican Cession, the modern Southwest plus California, which the United States had gained in 1848 following the Mexican-American War. This question was fraught for southern Whigs because their northern counterparts almost unanimously opposed any extension of slavery into that area. For southern Whigs, whether they desired to extend slavery or not, such a stance meant political doom, for the southern Democrats would smash them for failing to guard southern interests and rights. This chasm in the Whig party appeared in every congressional attempt to pass the Wilmot Proviso, which would bar slavery in the Cession, or to compromise the issue either by extending the Missouri Compromise line or by turning over the issue to the federal judiciary. While Whigs did win the presidential election of 1848 with Major General Zachary Taylor, a hero of the war, they sidestepped their territorial quagmire by running with Taylor's heroic image, without a platform. Yet thoughtful southern Whigs knew that the problem could not be dodged forever, and they wanted to solve it before Taylor took office in March 1849. Thus, in the second session of the Thirtieth Congress, which convened in December 1848, they devised a strategy that they hoped would remove the territorial issue as a threat to the unity of their party as well as their country. Although this plan had received little attention, they made a strenuous effort, albeit unsuccessful. I decided to write my essay on that ill-fated venture, known as the Preston Bill.*

The inevitable dissolution of the Confederacy"—in February 1849 those ominous words ran through the United States Capitol.[1] That cry was no lonesome wail. In the winter of 1848–49, calculations on the longevity of the Union were legion and loud. The second session of the Thirtieth Congress, which ran from December 4, 1848, to March 4, 1849, witnessed the bursting of sectional tensions that had been festering for almost two years. These tensions were directly related to slavery and its future in the nation, especially in the lands newly acquired from Mexico.

In the second session a vigorous, though little-known, attempt was made to resolve the territorial issue. It proposed to do so with a finality that would have removed the vexed territorial question from the political arena. This endeavor included almost all the ingredients associated with mid-nineteenth-century politics—inventiveness, ingenuity, boldness, caution, fear, partisanship, bipartisan cooperation, sectionalism, nationalism, slavery, and freedom. But after all the politicking, the rhetoric, and the voting, it failed. This is the story of that effort and why it failed.

The question of the new relationship between slavery and the United States had been brought to the fore by the Wilmot Proviso. Introduced in the House of Representatives during the summer of 1846, the proviso prohibited slavery in any territory gained from the Mexican War. The proviso readily passed the House but never made it through the Senate. More important, during 1847 and 1848 it assumed major political importance; in the South it became the chief issue. When the Mexican War ended in 1848, theoretical propositions about slavery in the territories quickly became matters for practical decision. Formally ratified by the Senate in March 1848, the treaty concluding the two-year-old conflict added to the American domain California and the Southwest, more than 500,000 square miles. With the acceptance of the treaty, the slavery issue focused on what stance Congress would adopt toward slavery in the Mexican Cession, permit or prohibit it. Slavery, Vice President

George M. Dallas prophetically recorded in his diary, "will agitate the whole of the session."[2]

From both sides of the Mason-Dixon Line, thunderbolts crashed about the halls of Congress. Resolutions from Florida demanding that Congress recognize the rights of slavery were matched by equally vehement pronouncements from other southern states. The Virginia legislature declared that passage of the Wilmot Proviso would necessitate "determined resistance . . . at all hazards and to the last extremity" by every Virginian. The great sentinel of the South, John C. Calhoun, insisted that the aggression of the North upon the South should be resisted and that the time had come for action. Democrats and Whigs alike spoke the same language. To the Virginia Democrat James McDowell, nothing less than "national safety" was at stake. Henry Hilliard, Whig of Alabama, proclaimed to his fellow congressmen that before he would "surrender one jot or one tittle of the rights or the honor or the glory of the South, 'my right hand shall forget its cunning and my tongue cleave to the roof of my mouth.'"[3]

Northerners did not back away. The legislature of New York passed and forwarded to Congress resolutions urging the imposition of the Wilmot Proviso as well as the abolition of the slave trade in the District of Columbia. The preamble castigated slavery as "revolting to the spirit of the age." Senator John P. Hale of New Hampshire presented to the Senate "a very large number of petitions" demanding passage of the proviso along with abolition of both slavery and the slave trade in the District of Columbia. The Illinois legislature told its state congressional delegation never to permit the extension of slavery into the Cession. To many northerners, such resolutions originated in the conviction that slavery "forever lusts for conquests and expansion." For these northerners, fundamental issues were at stake. On the Wilmot Proviso the cry went out—"The question cannot be compromised."[4]

The territorial issue had become critical. To southerners and northerners alike, the territories represented the future; they ensured the prosperity and permanence of republican government, of the United States. Geographical expansion had been central to the American experience since the colonial period, and during the first four-and-a-half decades of the nineteenth century, the United States was a nation on the march, a march in which southerners and northerners had energetically participated. Southerners viewed the Mexican Cession as a national treasure dearly purchased by blood and money during the Mexican War, much of both theirs. Access to the Cession, which meant no restriction on slavery, they demanded as Americans. In their mind the proviso, an attempt to bar them officially from the Cession, branded them as unpatriotic and castigated them as un-American.[5]

Whether southerners expected or even wanted slavery to expand into the Cession is a difficult question. Southerners both opposed and supported such expansion, but the evidence does not permit a conclusive answer. Among southern Whigs in the late 1840s, however, the dominant view was that slavery would not become established in the territories. Most southern Whigs believed that natural forces, chiefly the climate, effectively barred the growth of slavery in the Cession. But all southerners, opponents as well as supporters, were adamant about southern rights in the territories. They could never accept the absolute prohibition of slavery during the territorial phase. The proviso was anathema to all southerners.

By the mid-1840s, more and more northerners began to perceive the South almost as an errant child, certainly as a section that really did not fit in the new, burgeoning nation. Many saw the South as economically backward and morally deficient, all because of the un-American institution of slavery. Paradoxically, however, in the northern perception the blemished South wielded vast and unjustified political power, a contradiction that mocked American ideals while it restricted legitimate northern power. For those who so described the South, their responsibility was clear: to guarantee national moral and economic progress and simultaneously to bridle southern political power necessitated the restriction of slavery. This outlook had a long history; its birth antedated the nineteenth century, and it was clearly articulated during the Missouri crisis (1819–1821). But after the annexation of Texas and the Mexican War, it loomed increasingly large in northern society.[6]

These divergent northern and southern territorial views had profound political implications. With two great parties competing for votes in the North and South, each actively pursued sectional protection as an appropriate political issue. In the South it gave legitimacy to parties. It was widely employed in the North, especially by the Whigs, and in 1848 it became the keystone of the new Free Soil party. This political reality meant that even those not ideologically concerned about the extension of slavery found themselves caught up in the politics of the territories. Practically no one, certainly not active, ambitious politicians, could stand back and look upon the territorial question as just another political topic. For almost everyone, the meshing of ideology and politics made the territorial issue a powerful, explosive force.

Although Democrats and Whigs as well as antiparty zealots were deeply involved in this territorial crisis, the Whigs had special concerns. Almost every Whig was painfully aware that the proviso had created a broad, deep chasm in the party. The double question of the proper policy toward expansion and a united party front on the issue had plagued the Whigs since the presidential campaign of 1844 and the furor over Texas. The northern Whigs adamantly opposed bringing Texas into the Union, while southern Whigs ranged across the spectrum of opinion, from outright opposition to enthusiastic support. Attempting to find a safe island in this political torrent, the party's paladin Henry Clay pleased few and helped defeat himself. After that disorienting and dispiriting experience, all Whigs became alert to the dangers posed to their party by territorial expansion. Their deep internal division convinced Whigs that the country could not stand the strain if slavery and expansion became one. In this sense Whigs saw their party as a laboratory testing unity and disunity for the nation.

After the annexation of Texas, most Whigs stood foursquare against any more territorial expansion. The Democrats differed totally; they galloped on their steed of expansion. Opposing what they called an offensive policy, Whigs could find little positive in President James K. Polk's ambition for the Southwest and California. When that drive led to war with Mexico, the Whigs protested the president's culpability, though most in Congress felt compelled to vote additional troops and money as long as American soldiers were in combat. But the onset of war did not change the Whig attitude toward expansion; the party generally urged that additional territory not become a spoil of war. Such booty, Whigs feared, would mean desperate trouble for their party and their nation. With the treaty ending the war, Whig opposition to more territory became academic. The Mexican Cession was a reality, and Whigs had to confront what they had so vigorously fought and deeply feared—the merging of slavery and expansion.

The initial consideration of this potent combination occurred in the long first session of the Thirtieth Congress, which lasted from December 1847 all the way into the hot summer of 1848. The result, however, was not a confrontation. The first major effort to avoid a North-South showdown on imposing the Wilmot Proviso in the Cession originated with the Democrats and enjoyed the strong support of President Polk. Even though most Democrats were willing to extend the hallowed Missouri Compromise line from its original western boundary on out to the Pacific Ocean, they could never muster the votes to gain passage. When the Missouri option faltered, a select Senate committee devised another formula. Carrying the name of the Delaware Whig senator John M. Clayton, the Clayton Compromise proposed to turn the question of slavery in the Mexican Cession over to the federal judiciary. The striving of Senator Clayton and other border and southern Whigs, along with the backing of President Polk and many Democrats, enabled the compromise to pass the Senate by a narrow margin. But in another close vote, it failed in the House. Thus, when Congress adjourned in August 1848, it had not found a way around the Wilmot Proviso. As a result, all of the Mexican Cession remained unorganized.[7]

From the failure of the Missouri extension and of the Clayton Compromise, from all the debate and votes surrounding their legislative history, one clear message emerged for the Whig party. Although a substantial majority of southern Whigs were willing to accept either the extension or the compromise, every northern Whig opposed both. On the key issue of solving the Wilmot Proviso, the party was stumped.

Already well underway when Congress disbanded, the presidential campaign did not aid Whig unity. Most Whigs, southern as well as northern, lined up behind Major General Zachary Taylor, a hero of the Mexican War. For the southerners, Taylor was something special, a slave-owning cotton planter who called Baton Rouge, Louisiana, home. That particular southern identity, coupled with his heroic wartime service, caused southerners to flock to his banner. Few northerners felt the same joy about Taylor, but by a variety of routes and for a number of reasons, most supported his candidacy. Only the extreme antislavery men refused to join Taylor's political army. Appalled that a slaveowner headed the ticket, they bolted and helped form the Free Soil party, which made the Wilmot Proviso a political article of faith. General unity on Taylor did not mean, however, that the Whigs had discovered a solution to their territorial puzzle. The party simply dodged the entire question by not adopting a platform expounding principles and goals. This underscored Whig division on the territorial issue, a wide gap already seen in Congress.[8]

During the campaign, there seemed to be two Taylors. Southerners presented him as a native son who would never act against the interests of the South or of slavery. Of course, most southerners did not and could not separate the two. In contrast, northerners depicted him as a nationalist and a good Whig who would surely abide by the will of Congress. If Congress passed the Wilmot Proviso, they insisted that Taylor as president would sign it into law. Although Taylor kept his own counsel throughout the furor, only one valid conclusion can be drawn. On the territorial issue, two different Taylors were presented by Whig enthusiasts on opposite sides of the Mason-Dixon Line. This truth was never more forcefully put than by an angry Democratic correspondent to the *Washington Daily Union.* Notwithstanding the partisan passion of the accusation, it carried a powerful truth: "Louisiana and Massachusetts have joined hands. One urged that safety to the South demanded the election of General Taylor; while the other, with equal vehemence, declared that protection to the North from the encroachments of slave power imperiously required the same result. A very great fraud has unquestionably been perpetuated by the friends of General Taylor, either in one section of the Union or the other. Somebody has been cheated and grossly deceived." Thus on the territorial front, the Taylor victory did not at all signify that the Whigs had overcome their cleavage of two years. But with Taylor's great win, the party would have to govern, which meant it would have to devise a territorial policy or face possible ruin.[9]

That possibility quickly jumped from theoretical to practical. The discovery of gold in California caused great excitement. Throughout the country, newspapers were filled with features on California, discussion of the best ways to reach the new El Dorado, stories about individuals or groups striking out for the goldfields. Few locales escaped or wanted to escape the California fever. Describing attitudes in Washington for former president Martin Van Buren, an experienced political hand underscored that "California occupied every body's thoughts . . . to the exclusion of every thing else." This consuming interest had a most practical political manifestation. California had no civilian government; it was run by the military. To organize the area officially and to set up a civilian government required congressional action, so the question of slavery in the Mexican Cession would have to be confronted—in some fashion.[10]

The solution to the pressing territorial problem was crucial for the nation and for the Whig party. Thoughtful Whigs knew full well the extent of their difficulties. They also recognized that the interregnum—the five months between Taylor's election and his inauguration—comprised a critical time for them, one simultaneously filled with danger and opportunity. Throughout those weeks the Democrat Polk would still occupy the White House, and during most of them the second session of the Thirtieth Congress would be meeting. Two old facts were known: the first session of the Thirtieth had failed utterly to resolve the territorial dispute; James K. Polk would veto any bill containing the Wilmot Proviso. But there was also a new fact. On March 4, 1849, a Whig, not a Democrat, would become president. This new situation did not, however, clarify the territorial issue—nobody knew where Zachary Taylor actually stood. Assumptions abounded, but concrete knowledge was scarce. Thus, absolute certainty about what President Taylor would or would not do could not substantially influence Whig congressmen and senators.

When the second session opened on December 4, 1848, the Whigs were no more unified than they had been during the first session or in the presidential campaign. All Whigs recognized that it was "of the first importance to [them] to 'start right.'" But few agreed on the direction. Ardent Free Soilers had their platform for the newly elected administration: "We declare that there shall be no more Slavery and no more Slave States." The *Albany Evening Journal*, whose editor Thurlow Weed, the kingpin of the Whig organization in New York, had been a mainstay in the Taylor campaign, announced that the election signaled "a boundary line had been fixed for Slavery. The next Congress, with the assent of the president, will carry out the wishes of the People." In contrast, Virginia congressman Jonathan Pendleton wanted to come up with a plan that would attract southern Democrats. He was looking for "something that will carry with us the Southern people." Noting this basic difference, thoughtful party leaders who saw Taylor's victory "not as a temporary triumph but one which if wisely and prudently directed is to . . . the remotest time a decisive and salutary influence in the destinies of our country" were indeed anxious.[11]

None exhibited more concern than John J. Crittenden and John M. Clayton. Crittenden had relinquished his Senate seat to become governor of Kentucky. The protégé of Henry Clay, Crittenden had broken with his mentor to back his old friend Zachary Taylor for the Whig nomination. Viewed as wise and reasonable as well as a confidant of Taylor, Crittenden maintained a correspondence that kept the postal service active between Frankfort and Washington. And no one wrote to him more frankly and thoughtfully than Clayton, the senator from Delaware, who had given his name to the ill-fated Clayton Compromise. Both men were joyous over Taylor's triumph. They believed it augured a brilliant future for both the Whig party and the nation, and they did not separate the fate of one from the other. They also perceived a common danger. "The great [threat]," wrote Clayton in early December, "is the slavery question." Responding, Crittenden agreed, "This question of slavery is the only one that seriously threatens us." Each a moderate border-state man trying to balance ardent proslavery spokesmen with zealous antislavery crusaders, they sought to control emotion and find a middle way. In Crittenden's careful formulation the slavery issue "ought therefore to be dealt with, always, with the utmost coolness and discretion." But the great puzzle remained, "Now upon the slave question what can be done?"[12]

While Whigs wrestled with their dilemma, the Democrats moved. In the aftermath of their defeat in the presidential election, a number of Democrats, in the words of Vice President Dallas, wanted "to try hard to do nothing:—leaving all unsettled questions and especially the free soil one, to harrass [*sic*] Genl. Taylor next winter." Aware of the Whig division, Democrats of this inclination just wanted to let their political enemies sweat. But President Polk did not want to wait at all. Concerned about the ultimate fate of what he saw as the great prize of his administration, Polk was both eager for and anxious about the formal organization of the Mexican Cession. He feared that congressional inaction might lead to any one of several possible disasters, such as an independent California, the reversion of much of the Cession back to Mexico, or a frightful, sectional division in the United States.[13]

In his final annual message to Congress on December 5, 1848, Polk did not minimize the gravity of the issue. He urged the assembled congressmen and senators "at your present session to approach the adjustment of the only domestic question which seriously threatens, or probably ever can threaten, to disturb the harmony and successful operation of our system." Lecturing the lawmakers, he professed that "it is our solemn duty to provide with the least practicable delay for New Mexico and California regularly organized territorial governments." Keenly aware of the powerful reactions engendered by the territorial question, Polk called on "the spirit of compromise," which had "overcome" the slavery-related difficulties of earlier times, all the way back to "the adoption of the Constitution."[14]

The president did not content himself with either platitudes or generalizations. He pointed to the Missouri Compromise line of 36°30′ as possible solution. "Upon a great emergency," Polk reminded Congress, a previous deal had been struck to eliminate a menace to the Union. Congressional action to extend the line westward to the Pacific Ocean would receive his blessing, for he was confident that would cause "peace and harmony [to] again fill our borders." But Polk was not a one-solution man. Should Congress instead "prefer to submit to legal and constitutional questions which may arise to the decision of the judicial tribunals," he and "all parts of the Union should cheerfully acquiesce." That reference to the once rejected Clayton Compromise indicated that Polk was willing to support any feasible compromise plan. Concluding this portion of his message, he "earnestly invoked" Congress, "for the sake of the Union, its harmony, and our continued prosperity as a nation, to adjust at its present session this, the only dangerous question which lies in our path, if not in some one of the modes suggested, in some other way which may be satisfactory."[15]

Another way became the Democratic solution. After the failure back in the summer of both the extension of the 36°30′ line and the Clayton formula, few in Congress felt either could become a legislative success, despite Polk's hopes. The territorial issue was simply too explosive. Minds were set, and the realities of politics in both North and South made practically impossible the legislative give-and-take required to turn either approach into acceptable legislation. President Polk saw only one aspect of the territorial issue when he described it as "a mere political question on which demagogues and ambitious politicians hope to promote their own prospects for political promotion." But he was surely right when he condemned them for "disturbing the harmony if not dissolving the Union itself." The issue simultaneously excited and paralyzed. Realistically, there was no chance for a true territorial compromise.[16]

Polk's wishes seemed doomed, but a young Democratic senator from Illinois was determined to prevail. Thirty-five-year-old Stephen A. Douglas was just emerging as a major Democratic and national figure, a position he would occupy for the next dozen years. Convinced that territorial expansion was necessary for national greatness, and especially that the immediate organization of California was essential, Douglas strove to find some legislative path that the country and Congress could safely follow through the political minefield created by the Wilmot Proviso. On the first day of the session, he indicated his strategy—the prompt admission of California as a state. Then on December 11 he staked out his path. Acknowledging the political impossibility of territorial action, Douglas declared it unnecessary. Taking another tack entirely, he presented a bill that would bring in all of the Mexican Cession as one state, California. Because California was so huge, Douglas's bill reserved for Congress the right to create later additional states from the area that lay east of the Sierra Nevada. Douglas argued that passage of his bill would simultaneously guarantee American control of the Cession, meet the critical need for governmental organization in California, and destroy the proviso as a dangerous political issue. His was a bold initiative and absolutely unprecedented.[17]

Douglas's new thrust did not generate an overwhelmingly positive response. Even among fellow Democrats doubt was widespread, and outright opposition was present. Some argued that such a giant state as Douglas's California would be impossible to govern. Others asserted that Mexicans living in the Cession were unfit to become immediate members of the American congregation; they needed a period of tutelage, not provided for in Douglas's plan. Then, certain senators raised procedural points over the proper committee to consider the bill. Douglas wanted it assigned to his own Committee on the Territories, which was dominated by friendly colleagues. Several southerners insisted that the bill be referred to the Committee on the Judiciary, chaired by Andrew P. Butler of South Carolina and unfriendly to Douglas's plan. These senators argued that statehood bills had always been sent to Judiciary. Douglas replied that policy had been followed only because no Committee on the Territories had existed; it was relatively new. This contest involved both policy and rules. And Douglas failed. By a margin of one, the Senate sent his California bill to Judiciary. The vote was sectional, not partisan. Every senator voting in favor of Judiciary was from a slave state, while all but one for Territories were from free states.[18]

This lack of enthusiasm was symptomatic of the major negative reaction among Democrats. Butler was a disciple as well as a colleague of the other senator form South Carolina, John C. Calhoun. And Calhoun opposed Douglas's statehood scheme. Calhoun and his followers blasted the plan as the Wilmot Proviso under another rubric. "The object [of immediate statehood]," they declared, "is manifestly to exclude slavery" just as surely as Wilmot's proviso would have. As the Calhounites interpreted the issue, "it is a matter of little importance . . . practically, how we are deprived of the common conquest and purchase." They vehemently denounced Douglas's initiative as "a sneaking, crawling expedient, to surrender every thing to the North."[19]

This attack prefaced Calhoun's major initiative during the session. Calhoun sensed that the genuine rage southerners felt about the proviso could provide the foundation on which he could build the southern unity he had cherished for so long. Among southerners in Congress that rage deepened when on December 21 the House passed New Yorker Benjamin Gott's resolution instructing the House Committee for the District of Columbia to report a bill outlawing the slave trade in the district. On the very next evening some eighteen senators and fifty-one congressmen representing both parties and every slave state but Delaware met in the Senate chamber. To Calhoun this conclave offered the opportunity he so wanted and believed essential for southern unity. He planned a published address specifying southern grievances and calling for a southern convention, which would present the southern position—perhaps even an ultimatum—to the North.[20]

At this dramatic moment Calhoun recognized that his success depended upon nonpartisan support. He had to bring both Whigs and Democrats to his banner. His personal strength among southern Democrats and the close ties many of his lieutenants maintained with the party prompted substantial Democratic backing. In fact, when Calhoun's Southern Address was formally adopted in January 1849, the signers included every southern Democratic senator except the two Texans and more than two-thirds of the southern Democratic congressmen, an impressive achievement indeed. The southern Democrats who failed to participate were notable in their solitude.[21]

Calhoun also united southern Whigs but not quite as he had hoped. Southern Whigs shared the distress of Calhoun and the southern Democrats over the militant antisouthern stance taken by numerous northerners, many in their own party. But at the same time they perceived Calhoun's move as a threat to the bright political future they envisaged with Zachary Taylor. From the southern Whig vantage point, the Calhoun–southern Democratic combine was attempting to undo the Whig presidential victory. That alliance, as the prominent Georgia Whig congressman Robert Toombs put it, had mounted "a bold stroke to disorganize the Southern Whigs and either destroy Genl. Taylor in advance or compel him to throw himself in the hands of a large section of the democracy of the South."[22]

Determined to prevent what they saw as a poorly disguised campaign to sabotage their actual and potential success, southern Whigs torpedoed Calhoun's hopes for unity. Initially many attended the southern caucus, and some actively participated. The southern Whigs, however, were not there to help the caucus but "to control and crush it." And with various techniques they succeeded. Despite vigorous attempts to attract the Whigs, Calhoun failed. His long-cherished unity went aglimmering. A saddened Calhoun wrote that "the [southern] Whigs . . . are opposed to any activity; they rely on General Taylor."[23]

Calhoun's failure had not been for want of trying. He strove to woo the southern Whigs. "We have done all we could do here to unite the South," he informed a South Carolina friend. Even so, Calhoun "found it impossible to draw the supporters of Genl. Taylor beyond a very limited extent." "I conversed freely with them," Calhoun reported, "and gave every assurance that our object was to support [Taylor], if he would support the South, by rallying with his supporters and uniting the whole South in support of him and his administration." "But," as Calhoun lamented, "it all proved in vain."[24]

Rejoicing over Calhoun's failure, the southern Whigs congratulated themselves on their political prowess and lauded their hero, Zachary Taylor. Their faith was in the future, not the present. They "did not expect an administration which [they] had brought into power would do any act or permit any act to be done which it would become necessary for our safety to rebel at." Because of Taylor, southern Whigs feared neither the antislavery North in general nor the internal Whig conflict over sectional issues in particular. The diminutive, forceful Alexander Stephens captured this mood exactly—we "feel *secure* under General Taylor."[25]

Although supremely confident, indeed overconfident about Taylor, the southern Whigs were under no delusion about their northern comrades. Many believed with a North Carolina congressman that the northerners had "a fixed determination" on the territorial issue as well as other slavery-related matters. After all, the spark that led to the specific timing of the southern caucus was lit by a northern Whig, Benjamin Gott of New York. Northern Whigs voted overwhelmingly for Gott's resolution, an action that helped prompt southern Whigs to join the southern caucus. By moving toward Calhoun, the southern Whigs had more in mind than influencing the outcome of the caucus; they also wanted to use that affiliation to press northern Whigs to pull back on Gott's resolution. They succeeded on the latter front as well as on the former. Only six days after passing the resolution, the House refused to lay on the table a motion to reconsider. Although the vote on December 27 did not specifically defeat Gott's resolution, it did block any positive action. This effective revocation of the resolution angered certain northern Whigs who criticized their comrades for supporting reconsideration. Even among those who stood by Gott, some believed that northern Whigs were "not acting wisely on the slavery question." Men like Nathan K. Hall of New York felt that too often northern Whigs were "improperly & unnecessarily offensive" to the southerners.[26]

That attitude along with the reversal on Gott's resolution prompted one important southern Whig to think that the party could find unity on slavery. Robert Toombs believed that his northern comrades would "come up to safe ground." As he viewed intraparty relations, "the temper of the North is good & . . . I think we can work out the present troubles, preserve the Union & disappoint bad men & traitors." Referring to what he called "these legacies of Polk's administration," Toombs foresaw "nothing desperate in settling [them] . . . unless we have treason in our ranks."[27]

Toombs's optimism augured well for the party and for the country, if he and his colleagues could turn it into reality. That would not be easy. Just as the southern Whigs would not and could not accept the Wilmot Proviso, many northern Whigs had adopted it as their issue. Early in the session an important Cincinnati editor urged Indiana congressman Caleb B. Smith "to push it to an issue at once." Thomas B. Stevenson wanted the proviso forced in the House even if it was destined to fail in the Senate or to be vetoed by Polk. Should failure or veto occur, Stevenson was sure "it will raise such a storm in the north that it *must* go hereafter and add to the inducements to Taylor and the South to acquiesce in the bill in the following session." A close congressional friend of the vice president–elect Millard Fillmore told his fellow New Yorker that Taylor and the southern Whigs must "submit to the prohibition of slavery in the territories [or] his administration will be in a minority in Congress & with the people." And the zealous pro-proviso northerners who inclined toward the Free Soil party wanted nothing more than "to arouse public sentiment at the North" behind the proviso.[28]

If an open battle took place over the proviso, the Gott reconsideration would evaporate in the heat of vicious intraparty fighting. Many southerners tried to assure their northern comrades that they did not demand or expect slavery to migrate to the Cession, though certain northerners still feared "a plot" to plant slavery in the new lands. A key southern Whig editor told Fillmore that "not the first slave will go there, if no such proviso or restriction is enacted." The proviso, he went on, "is needless as a practical matter and will certainly place the Southern Whigs in a hopeless minority." Daniel Lee's prescription was: "Let the Northern Whigs evince their good sense by forbearance on so excitable a topic and all will be peace, harmony, and continued success." Congressional southerners echoed the sentiment that slavery could never flourish in the Cession. Do not wreck the fortunes of the party on the abstraction of the proviso, they implored their northern colleagues. "Why in the name of common sense," asked the *Louisville Daily Journal,* "do [northern Whigs] insist upon the actual Congressional prohibition of slavery?" According to the *Journal,* the South was "willing" to let the territories "follow their destiny," but southerners would never consent to the congressional violation of their rights by enactment of the proviso.[29]

It seemed, then, to many perceptive, moderate Whigs that room did exist for party rapprochement on the crucial territorial issue. Experienced politicians such as Crittenden and Clayton believed that agreement on the territorial question was not only opportune but essential. They feared that the longer the delay in settlement, the greater the likelihood that the issue would tear apart the Whig party. They, along with others, concluded that a solution ought to be found before Taylor's inauguration on March 4, 1849. To postpone or to avoid or to neglect dealing with the territories would leave a potentially dangerous threat to the success of the Taylor administration and, thus, to the well-being of the Whig party.

These Whigs moved directly. Although the evidence does not permit a precise charting of the course they followed, it is clear where they landed—Douglas's California bill. Before the end of 1848, the *Richmond Whig* found Douglas's statehood bill the best chance to provide "equality and justice to all the States." Even those who really cared little for Douglas's proposal thought it had to be carefully considered, given the serious difficulties presented by expansion and slavery. As early as December 13, Senator Clayton had assured Crittenden that "Taylor shall have no trouble with [the proviso]." Clayton was confident that "we will saw round that knot." Acknowledging the failure of his own compromise proposal back in the summer, Clayton insisted, "But now I have another project which I think will succeed." Douglas's specific bill Clayton called "a failure," but, he went on, "if any chance should offer, we will use it to settle the matter at once." By the words "any chance," Clayton obviously meant the fashioning of a Whig agreement. By marking his letter "confidential" and by telling Crittenden that he would not use his franking privilege because he feared the envelope might be opened, Clayton underscored the delicacy of his position and the fragility of his hopes. Crittenden himself believed that coopting Douglas's approach would bring to the Whig party and to the country "certain success."[30]

With Whig unity, a reasonable hope for success did exist. Whigs controlled the House by a narrow margin, 117 to 111. But that majority had a gross sectional imbalance; there were twice as many northerners as southerners. Clearly, the party rapprochement that Toombs described was critically important. The Democrats enjoyed considerably more sectional balance; free-state men outnumbered their slave-state colleagues by only 5. In the Senate the Democrats dominated, 36 to 22.[31] In Democratic ranks the southerners edged out northerners, while the Whigs broke evenly along sectional lines. If the Whigs could forge any kind of unity and attract Democratic support, there was indeed an opportunity for the Clayton-Crittenden approach to succeed. Success, however, would require Democratic backing, which did not at all appear impossible.

Douglas's bill certainly had not died. The energetic Illinois senator never slackened in his determination to push it to a vote. And during December, President Polk made a slightly different version of Douglas's original bill an administration measure. After repeated conversations with Douglas, his cabinet, and other influential senators, Polk decided that the statehood plan was the safest way around the proviso and the surest way to organize the Mexican Cession before he left the presidency. The cabinet, however, believed that the entire Cession was simply too large for one state. As a result, Polk urged Douglas to alter his bill so that it called for two states—California, and the land east of the Sierra Nevada organized as New Mexico. After some thought, Douglas agreed to modify his bill.[32]

This new plan became Douglas's proposal as well as the administration's way around the noxious Wilmot Proviso. And Polk put all of his effort and authority behind it. In his mind it took on the character of a compromise solution in the manner of both the Missouri extension and the Clayton bill. No one pushed harder for passage than Thomas Ritchie, editor of the administration's newspaper voice, the *Washington Union*. A major Virginia Democratic leader who had edited the *Richmond Enquirer* for four decades before going to Washington to take charge of the

Union, Ritchie focused considerable attention on the southern Whigs. Warning that Zachary Taylor would not protect them from the Wilmot Proviso, Ritchie urged the southern Whigs to work with their Democratic counterparts to eliminate forever the threat of the proviso. He told them that Taylor's friends in the House had the power to settle the Cession issue. He challenged them to meet "the great duty which now calls upon [you] to act in behalf of the South, or rather in behalf of the Union." And he assured them that the Democrats stood ready to cooperate in the critically important cause of southern safety and national unity. Ritchie argued that the strength of proviso sentiment in Congress made the statehood alternative "all that is left." He warned southern Whigs that if they refused to support statehood and brought on the proviso, "how *then* can [you] excuse [yourselves] to [your] indignant constituents?" No idle threat this—in southern politics accusations that a party failed to guard zealously southern rights could easily mean political disaster.[33]

The advocacy of Douglas, Polk, and Ritchie had two crucial meanings for southern Whigs. First, it indicated that the votes might be there to pass some kind of statehood plan, if the southern Whigs could unite behind it. Second, general support among southern Democrats would provide assurance that the statehood solution would not end up haunting the Whigs. The southern Democrats could never attack them for giving away the possibility of slavery in the Cession. Both parties would have joined forces behind a measure that everyone knew would preclude the introduction of slavery. No one doubted that California would enter the Union as a free state. Calhoun and his loyalists would surely cry foul, but with the Whigs and Democrats marching arm in arm, the Calhounites would cry in vain.

For both southern Whigs and southern Democrats, immediate statehood also guaranteed that southern honor could escape the territorial tangle unscathed. Everyone agreed that a state could make its own decision on slavery. Thus, southern rights would not be threatened or disregarded should California and possibly New Mexico request admission to the Union as free states. Southern rights, which ultimately meant southern honor, only became involved with proposals to shut slavery out of the common national possessions, the territories. That potential outcome, of course the goal of the Wilmot Proviso, the South could not and would not accept. Southerners saw the proviso as an assault on their Americanism and an insult to their honor.

The Whigs behind the Clayton-Crittenden strategy went on the offensive in the House. Their majority made this move logical. Besides, despite Douglas's energy and determination, his bill was still bottled up in the Senate. William B. Preston took the lead, introduced the bill, and made the key speech. A forty-three-year-old Virginian, Preston was serving his first term in Congress. He was neither a major force in the Whig party nor even a widely known southern Whig. Although the evidence is unclear on why Preston took or was assigned his primary role, his specific proposal was too close to the designs of Clayton and Crittenden for mere coincidence. Clearly, he represented the border and moderate southern Whigs who wanted to solve the territorial issue with statehood prior to Taylor's inauguration. Preston's bill harked back to Douglas's original proposal; it would bring in all the Cession as one state, California.[34]

There are several possible reasons for the choice of Preston. From early in the talk of presidential candidates, he had been a vigorous Taylor man. Using Preston could easily imply that the president-elect himself favored the statehood approach, which might bring in some wavering Whigs. Nothing concrete indicates precisely where Taylor stood in early February, though he did adopt a variation of the statehood approach when he became president. Then, Preston hailed from Virginia, not a border slave state but also not a deep southern state. An appeal from a reasonable upper South man might entice some moderate northerners and could undoubtedly be counted upon to attract substantial votes from the lower slave states, Whigs for sure and possibly even some Democrats.

William B. Preston addressed his fellow representatives on February 7. In his speech Preston made a valiant and largely successful effort to omit nothing pertinent. He announced that he intended to propose a remedy for "the great question of the age." He would shun discussing "the merits or demerits of our peculiar system in the South, or the merits of those principles which gentlemen of the North propose to lead in by Congressional legislation here upon us." He maintained that he advocated solution, not argument. Acknowledging that others had pursued a similar goal, he noted Douglas's bill. With his praise for Douglas as "very patriotic and determined," Preston angled for Democratic support. Time and time again through the long speech, he stressed the nonpartisanship of his bill, and he called for help from "the good men and the calm men and the wise men of all parties." He denied his proposal as "a bill under which neither party is victorious, and neither party overcomes." He described his purpose as embracing the "spirit of republicanism, [which] is but the spirit of the Revolution." Asserting that Washington was no closer to California than England was to the colonies, he called on Congress to uphold the sacred American tradition of letting the people govern themselves. For Preston, that was the supreme principle, not the presence or absence of the institution of slavery.

In Preston's depiction this loyalty to the greatest American virtue would spare the country "perpetual agitation" over the territorial issue. He argued that his bill was "*no compromise at all.*" Possible compromises, like extending the Missouri line, Preston asserted, only guaranteed future battles. Those contests would occur, he predicted, each time a new state carved from the Cession asked for admission to the Union. Thus, in his scenario the sectional dispute took on a quality of endlessness, precisely what Preston wanted to preclude. "I want the question ended," he announced. In his mind his bill would provide just that. Echoing the call of many moderate Whigs, certainly those troubled by events since 1844, Preston cried out, "I want repose." And as he put it, "*The bill now offered gives finality to the question.*"

Preston also turned his attention to zealous supporters of the proviso, many of whom claimed allegiance to the Whig party. In an attempt to win their support or at least quiet their opposition to his statehood proposal, Preston repeated the moderate southern Whig refrain that slavery would never flourish in the Cession or in his new state. According to Preston, the forces of nature decreed against the success of slavery. That reality, Preston insisted, made pressing for the Wilmot Proviso at best unnecessary and at worst dangerous. The result, freedom in the Cession, would come from either approach. Why, then, he questioned the provisoists, demand something so bitterly and deeply opposed by the South when the goal could be achieved without such animosity?

But Preston hurried to declare that his legislative initiative in no way violated the honor of the South. Emphasizing the "great, abiding, solemn question of honor that every southern man, who does not stand up to, is recreant to himself and forgetful of his ancestors," Preston thundered, "Now, I yield to no man on these points." To Virginia, with "my eyes full upon her," and to his fellow southern congressmen he declaimed, "I do not, as a southern man, surrender anything to [the North]." Because southerners as well as northerners agreed that a state had the authority, in fact it rested nowhere else, to decide about slavery for itself, Preston did not believe there could be any possibility of blemished honor or bartered rights.

In conclusion Preston invoked the good sense and patriotism of all Americans. Calling his proposal "the only door" through which the new territories could safely be incorporated into the Union, he urged his listeners to think solely about the benefits of its passage—benefits that, he assured the House, could be gained in no other way. He reiterated this claim along with all that went before in a florid peroration: "Recognize this principle—adopt the remedy imbodied [*sic*] in this bill, and it will come over this House and over this nation like the sweet breath of spring to the chamber of disease—healing, strengthening, renovating all of us, so that we shall take up our beds, like the man of old, and run the great and glorious republican course which lays so full before us."[35]

In the immediate aftermath of Preston's impassioned oratory, the inner circle of planners expressed pleasure and optimism. Toombs informed Crittenden that Preston's speech "was a very good one and its effect happy." Reprinted in a national periodical such as *Niles' National Register,* the speech itself was carried far beyond Capitol Hill. An inveterate optimist on the party-sectional issue throughout the session, Toombs pronounced "the question for all practical purposes as now settled." He reached that conclusion even though he knew that both the Calhounites and the antislavery extremists were dead set against Preston's proposition. He also noted that New York and New England Whigs wanted to hold off passing Preston's bill until the Thirty-First Congress. In Toombs's interpretation that hesitancy was politically, not ideologically, motivated. "Their object," he reported, "is unmistakable to make themselves necessary to the [Taylor] adm. in carrying it, and demanding terms for their service." Despite that possible barrier, Toombs exuded confidence: "We shall bring them in I think, but not if we can carry it without them."[36]

Toombs had good reason for his buoyant mood. In Preston's native state his effort brought forth lavish praise. Calling his plan the proper solution and printing the speech, the *Richmond Whig* congratulated Preston for proposing a measure that "compromises neither the honor nor the interests of any portion of the confederacy." According to the *Whig,* it would "restore tranquility to the country and peace to the national councils." Both Democrats and Whigs cheered Preston. To one senior Virginia Whig, former United States senator William C. Rives, Preston's performance "look[ed] like the revival of the glories of our earlier history, when the statesmen and the patriots of Virginia were also the statesmen and patriots of the Union." Governor John B. Floyd, a Democrat, added his accolades. In Congress Preston's Democratic colleague James McDowell called the statehood plan one "of mediation and peace." In McDowell's mind all other considerations paled beside "what [statehood] may fairly hope to accomplish—the pacification and perpetual union of more than twenty million freemen!"[37]

In the House McDowell's was not an isolated response. Border-state Whigs were emphatic in their support. Preston's bill called for an unusual state, a Marylander admitted, but critical times overrode conventional thinking. Alabama Whig Henry W. Hilliard insisted that statehood would preserve southern honor. He underscored his loyalty to the Union and to the South: "I will cling to both." Preston's effort even gained congratulations and tentative support from Deep South Democrats. Albert G. Brown of Mississippi viewed statehood as a possible way to preserve the "harmony and peace of the Union." He was ready, he told the House, but "I want to know whether our opponents [the provisoists] are ready to meet us in a corresponding spirit." Certainly, the House allies of Stephen A. Douglas were, but, then, they had never been vigorous crusaders for the proviso. Ominously, this chorus of enthusiastic or, even, qualified support for Preston's bill included no northern Whigs.[38]

Not everyone liked Preston's bill. Some Democrats, North and South, saw grave difficulties in it, though from dramatically opposite perspectives. A close observer of Georgia politics wrote to his state's most prominent Democratic congressman, Howell Cobb, that the statehood idea simply would "not suit the present state of the public mind in the South." In his view both Douglas's and Preston's bill were "founded upon a mere quibble." To accept either would be "a fatal indication" of southern weakness. To North Carolina congressman Abraham Venable, Preston's bill gave away too much: "To vote for this bill is to seal forever the question against the South." A congressman from Douglas's Illinois condemned his colleagues for supporting statehood "for the purpose of avoiding this vexed question of slavery." He wanted to meet it head on, "boldly and fearlessly."[39]

Although Preston did not persuade all Democrats, the most vigorous opposition arose within his own party, among his northern colleagues. Congressman Horace Greeley of New York denounced Preston's proposal as "contrived" to deliver the Cession to slavery. As such, Greeley announced that he would oppose it to the utmost. His newspaper, the popular and widely read *New* York *Tribune,* rarely missed an opportunity to excoriate anything or anybody opposed to free soil. Thurlow Weed's *Albany Evening Journal* wanted the proviso attached to any California bill. Condemning slavery as "insidious," the *Evening Journal* declared, "Better that the whole of government should be stopped—better recede the Territories acquired, or permit them to be formed in an independent Republic—than that the majority in the popular branch of our National legislature should again succumb to the chicanery or threats of the South." John Gorham Palfrey of Massachusetts thought the entire statehood scheme "a plot" to slip slavery into the Cession, but he felt sure that Preston's bill could get nowhere in the House "as a distinct proposition."[40]

Events on the Senate side of the Capitol certainly gave credence to Palfrey's opinion. To no avail, Douglas had tried through January and into February to get his revised California bill brought to a vote. Then on February 20, John Bell, a Whig from Tennessee, attempted to push California statehood before the Senate. He, like Preston, emphasized the disastrous potential of the proviso, of the unending battle over slavery in the territories. He asserted that Congress must make an "irrevocable" decision, statehood, in order to "close up this breach forever." "Cut off the head of the hydra," Bell pleaded. Despite the similarity to Preston's approach, not a shred of evidence even suggests that Bell was the Senate spearhead of a two-front Whig advance on California. The outcome of Bell's effort also implies that he acted on his own. When the Senate on February 21 buried his proposal by 39 to 4, Bell was the lone Whig voting aye. None of his southern Whig colleagues joined him. He was supported only by Douglas, ever willing to back any statehood initiative, along with two of his Democratic friends, a northerner and a southerner. Of the other slave-state Whig senators, 5 voted with the majority and 5, including Clayton, did not vote. Although Bell's location in the Crittenden-Clayton design cannot be pinpointed, the Senate decision did not augur well for Preston, who was awaiting House action on his bill.[41]

In the House the northern antagonism toward any substitute for the proviso had a tangible impact. On February 27 the House resolved itself into the Committee of the Whole to consider California. Congressman Preston moved the adoption of his bill, technically a substitute for a territorial bill. George Ashmun, a Massachusetts Whig, and William Collins, a New York Democrat, proposed amendments. Collins's specifically added the Wilmot Proviso to the bill; the Collins amendment forbade slavery in the proposed state of California. Preston had anticipated the possibility of a proviso-type amendment. During his major speech, he argued that his bill precluded the proviso because Congress could not dictate to a state. Evidently, the members felt that all had been said that needed saying because no debate followed the introduction of Collins's amendment. Immediately, tellers were appointed, and the question was called—91 congressmen voted for the amendment; 87 voted no. The Wilmot Proviso now adorned the proposal that was designed to avoid it. And the adoption of the Collins amendment killed the Preston bill. In the vote on the bill with the proviso attached, not a single aye vote was cast. With no ayes reported, the noes were not even counted. The Preston bill was dead.[42]

Exactly who would have voted for the pristine Preston bill, the bill without the proviso, is impossible to ascertain. A vote on it never occurred. Whether or not Toombs had carefully counted votes or exaggerated wildly, we will probably never know, though the second possibility seems likely. It is even impossible to be precise about either the sectional or the partisan division on Collins's amendment. Neither the *Congressional Globe* nor the *House Journal* provides a roll call for the 91 to 87 tally. It is a reasonable assumption, however, that almost every southerner voting was in the minority, for later on the same day 87 congressmen, including every slave-state representative voting but two Kentuckians, opposed unsuccessfully a California territorial bill with the proviso included. And without question the 91 congressmen favoring the Collins amendment included both Democrats and Whigs, though possibly more northern Democrats than Whigs did not cast a ballot. That surmise rests on the support initially provided to Preston by certain northern Democrats.[43]

The shutting of Preston's "door" ended any possibility of solving the territorial problem during the Thirtieth Congress. Provisoists rejoiced over Preston's failure, but they kept up their guard lest some legislative trick be played against free soil at the very end of the session. An attempt was made to permit President Polk to appoint territorial officials without formal organization, but it went nowhere.[44]

In the South the voice of opposition to Preston's statehood strategy became louder and louder. Southern Democrats took the lead in denouncing immediate statehood as no more than the proviso by another name. Building through the late winter and spring, this attitude attracted widespread support. The result even affected the relentlessly sanguine Robert Toombs. Back in Georgia after Congress had adjourned, Toombs took stock of public opinion. He was surprised. In mid-May he informed his friend William Preston, by then a member of Zachary Taylor's cabinet, "It is an undeniable fact that the public feeling in the South is much stronger than many of us supposed. It is now my deliberate opinion," he went on, "that the passage of the Wilmot Proviso would lead to civil war." Toombs said he did not base his somber conclusion on excitement or emotion but on "something infinitely more dangerous a settled resolute determination in all classes not to submit to it." According to Toombs, the admission of California as a state would be accepted only "with bitterness of feeling & without cordiality, if slavery was in turn excluded."[45]

The increasing southern Democratic campaign against statehood made it more and more unlikely that statehood could remain a viable political platform in the South. Responding to the southern Democratic cry and to the unyielding northern Whig stance, southern Whigs backed away from statehood. By the autumn of 1849, a meaningful southern constituency for statehood had disappeared. When President Taylor in December proposed his version of statehood to the Thirty-First Congress, he found practically no support among southern Whigs for a plan most had been willing to accept ten months earlier. Taylor's insistence led to a fundamental break between him and those who had so lauded and counted upon him. Vigorous animosity replaced enthusiastic friendship.[46]

Preston was right. His plan provided "the only door" through which the territorial problem could be solved; statehood would have eliminated the proviso as a political issue. The ungainly size of Preston's California would have undoubtedly led to future questions, but they would not have possessed the emotional and political force of the proviso. And politicians could probably more easily have dealt with them. The supporters of Preston's bill saw a moment of political opportunity and tried to capitalize on it. They failed. They were unable to withstand the force of the territorial issue, which the Compromise of 1850 would check only briefly. The issue became more and more furious until it could be neither managed nor put off. Cataclysm resulted.

7

Edwin Forbes and the Civil War

In 1991 LSU Press decided to bring out a new edition of Edwin Forbes's Thirty Years After: An Artist's Memoir of the Civil War, *originally published in 1890 and never reprinted. Fortunately for me, I was invited to write the introduction. I say fortunately because doing so introduced me to a subject I had never before investigated—the pictorial reporting of the Civil War. And I found it fascinating. The Civil War was the first war widely reported with illustrations, mostly engravings that originated with pictorial reporters termed "special artists." For reasons my essay makes clear, overwhelmingly these special artists accompanied the Union armies. They joined print reporters to form what contemporaries identified as the Bohemian Brigade because in 1860 reporters existed on the margins of the journalistic world. Heretofore, newspapers and magazines had been largely equated with editors. Special artists made sketches in the field, then sent them back to their home periodicals, where engravers redrew them and made metal copies.* Harper's Weekly *was undoubtedly the best known, but there were others like* Frank Leslie's Illustrated Newspaper, *Forbes's employer. The special artist who gained the most renown as a serious artist was indisputably Winslow Homer. Notable neither before nor after the war, Forbes concentrated his art on his wartime observations. He made two major contributions—*Life Sketches of the Great Army, *a collection of forty etchings that he exhibited in 1876 to critical acclaim, and* Thirty Years After, *a unique Civil War memoir, for no other special artist produced such a book. The narrative in* Thirty Years After *recounts Forbes's time with Union forces while the sketches capture the range of soldiers' experiences, from the tedium of camp life to the terror of the battlefield. Finally, the page numbers cited in parentheses below refer to quotations and illustrations in the 1993 edition of* Thirty Years After.

Edwin Forbes went to war in 1862, just as tens of thousands of other young northerners and southerners did early in the Civil War. He did not, however, shoulder a rifle or wear a sword, or even carry a pistol. Instead he was armed with a pencil and a sketch pad. The twenty-three-year-old Forbes marched to war under the banner of *Frank Leslie's Illustrated Newspaper.*

When young Edwin Forbes started south, he was a member of the Bohemian Brigade, the name given collectively to the multitude of reporters who followed the northern armies into the South and into battle. The name derived from the appellation *Bohemian* given around 1860 to reporters centered in New York City. At that time the profession of reporting was basically new; American newspapers had been chiefly editorial. Reporters were generally considered on the margin of both the newspaper business and respectability. Many of them thought of themselves as vagabonds and free spirits.[1]

Forbes was a new recruit for the Bohemians. Although information about his early life is quite scarce, no evidence indicates that before 1860 he had anything to do with newspapers, much less with reporting. He was born in New York County, New York, in 1839 and given the name John Edwin Forbes, but early on he dropped "John." Traditional sources indicate that he began to study art in 1857. Trained in classical fashion, Forbes painted animals, landscapes, and genre. In 1860, while living in Hoboken, New Jersey, a suburb of New York City and in the mid-1850s and 1860s a popular art colony, Forbes had a painting accepted at the National Academy of Design.

The outbreak of war in 1861 turned Forbes's artistic career in a completely different direction. In 1862 Frank Leslie, the owner of *Frank Leslie's Illustrated Newspaper,* hired Forbes to join the corps of artists he was sending south to provide illustrations for his paper. These pictorial reporters were known as "special correspondents" or "special artists." Forbes immediately left for the front in Virginia, where he would remain until the autumn of 1864.

The youthful Forbes headed to the South for what would become the pivotal experience of his life. In the two-and-a-half years Forbes covered the war, he spent most of his time with the Army of the Potomac, though his initial campaign experience occurred in the Shenandoah Valley in the spring of 1862. From then until the fall of 1864, he observed most of the major battles in the eastern theater of the war, including Cedar Mountain, Second Manassas, Antietam, Chancellorsville, Gettysburg, the Wilderness, and Petersburg.

Forbes had a straightforward mission—to sketch scenes of the war that would end up as illustrations in *Frank Leslie's Illustrated Newspaper.* He had to learn his craft quickly, for he had not previously done any commercial artwork. His artistic ability along with his energy and determination enabled him to become proficient rapidly. Like so many other new soldiers, Forbes discovered that battles were not exactly what he had imagined. He remarked that he had expected to accompany troops into battle and "seat myself complacently on a convenient hillside and sketch exciting incidents at my leisure."[2] Forbes found that strategy to be impossible, however. At his first battle, Cross Keys, in the Shenandoah Valley on June 8, 1862, he heard musket fire and wanted to watch the infantry charge. But he quickly learned that Confederate artillery raked the ridge which offered the best view of the fighting. In addition, Forbes admitted that the sight of wounded soldiers being moved toward the rear did not serve to drive him forward. He did know about combat, however. At Second Manassas he found himself in the midst of heavy fire, and he spent the final day at Gettysburg just on the rear side of Cemetery Ridge, the point assaulted by Confederate major general George Pickett.

Forbes did not make many sketches of actual fighting. The etching in *Thirty Years After* entitled *The Distant Fighting* gives a good sense of the perspective from which he felt safe. Although he did not usually chronicle the fighting from up close, he did sketch from personal observation such combat scenes as a battle line forming, an artillery section going into action, and a cavalry charge. Forbes concentrated, however, on scenes he could witness close at hand. The bulk of his sketches deal with the everyday life of the soldiers, and their variety makes clear that he could do almost as he pleased in observing the army and following its movements. His employer liked the action coverage the best, and because of that preference, fewer than half of Forbes's wartime sketches ended up being produced in *Frank Leslie's Illustrated Newspaper.*[3]

Forbes departed the army and returned to New York City in the autumn of 1864. Precisely why he left his position and the war at that time is not at all clear. In a real sense, however, he never left; the war and his experiences in it remained central to him for the rest of his life.

Details about Forbes's postwar life and career remain almost as murky as those of his youth, except for his artistic endeavors that focused on the war. The story of his first marriage is a mystery. By 1875 he was a resident of Brooklyn, where he lived until his death. Sometime in the early 1880s he married for a second time. His second wife, Ida Batty, a schoolteacher, survived him. There were children, probably a son and a daughter, the former most likely with Ida Forbes, and the latter most likely with his first wife. Almost immediately upon his resettling in New York City, Forbes reclaimed his original sketches from his employer and began work on a project that would become his greatest artistic achievement. Between 1865 and 1868, he completed drawings of forty scenes based on his wartime sketches, which were then transferred to ground-copper plates. In 1876 he exhibited the resulting etchings as *Life Studies of the Great Army* at the Philadelphia Centennial Exhibition.

Life Studies received considerable critical acclaim. For it, Forbes won an award from the Centennial Exhibition. A contemporary critic called *Life Studies* "the first notable example of etchings as yet produced in this country." Forbes sent a portfolio of the etchings to the London Etching Club, which named him an honorary member, and he also belonged to the French Etching Club. Without question, *Life Studies* was a major achievement that represented a notable step forward in establishing etching as a fine art in the United States. Twentieth-century historians of etching consider Edwin Forbes a founder of etching as art in this country.[4]

Forbes was eager for *Life Studies* to become a commercial success as well as an artistic triumph. To sell it he published a catalog that also contained favorable comments from leading war figures, including President Ulysses S. Grant, to whom he had sent editions of the portfolio. William T. Sherman, commanding general of the United States Army, bought the original portfolio to decorate his office. The outcome of Forbes's promotional campaign is not known, but in 1884 a bill was introduced in Congress to purchase Forbes's collection of sketches and drawings for $100,000. It failed. The collection survives today because in 1901 Forbes's widow sold it for $25,000 to J. P. Morgan, who donated it to the Library of Congress in 1919.[5]

While trying to market *Life Studies,* Forbes busied himself with other artistic enterprises. In the 1870s and 1880s he produced a number of oil paintings, including war scenes. Most have disappeared, though the Library of Congress possesses twelve small canvases of the Battle of Gettysburg. In addition, Forbes provided illustrations for several books—three children's books, one of which his wife wrote, and a novel and a war memoir, both by a New York veteran.[6] The quality of the pictures in these five volumes does not match that of Forbes's other illustrative work. His final major project is not at all inferior, however. In 1890 he produced *Thirty Years After: An Artist's Story of the Great War.* In it, with his own words and pictures, he recounts his experiences in the great war of his generation.

Although Forbes devoted his life to art, he made one noteworthy contribution in a quite different area. He had always liked horses, and he enjoyed painting and drawing them. He also became an avid devotee of horse racing. A few years before he died, he invented a starting-gate apparatus that was adopted by some race tracks. Edwin Forbes died in Brooklyn of Bright's disease on May 6, 1895.[7]

The Bohemian Brigade and the Civil War had a great influence on each other, and in a fundamental way the war transformed reporting. Before 1860, American newspapers were identified chiefly with editors and editorials. Existing on the periphery of both the newspapers and society, reporters had largely unsavory reputations as "ne'er-do-well[s]," as "key-hole-snooper[s]."[8]

Reporters brought war news to the homefront, to a civilian population eager for information about the conflagration and the men engaged in it. Every substantial newspaper assigned reporters to cover the war. In the beginning, southern newspapers, like the northern, dispatched reporters to the front, but in the face of advancing Union armies and massively increasing shortages of essential materials, like paper, they could not sustain their effort. The leading scholar of the Confederate press turned up ninety-four reporters who at one time or another chronicled the war for southerners. In contrast, about five hundred reporters followed northern armies through the South, reporting back news of the armies and the soldiers. The public looked to the press not just for opinion but for information about great events.[9]

The reporting of war news in pictures as well as words helps account for its impact. Artists along with reporters belonged to the Bohemian Brigade. The two groups thought of each other as colleagues: each was involved in telling the story of the war to the readers back home. The reporters wrote their stories. The special correspondents, or special artists, drew theirs.

Pictorial reporting assumed significance because of the illustrated newspaper, which was introduced in the United States by Frank Leslie. Leslie was born in England in 1821 with the name Henry Carter. Trained as an engraver and having worked for the *Illustrated London News,* Leslie arrived in this country in the late 1840s and started out as an engraver in New York City. In the early 1850s he had several different partners in various illustrated-newspaper ventures. Finally, in 1854 he published *Frank Leslie's Ladies' Gazette of Fashion.* The next year *Frank Leslie's Illustrated Newspaper* appeared. Leslie's paper found a place between the staid traditional press and the florid penny press. Still, Leslie devoted considerable space to sensational events and stories; his *Illustrated Newspaper* did have a certain tabloid characteristic. The paper, a weekly, succeeded. By 1860 it had a circulation of more than 150,000, with special issues sometimes selling over 300,000 copies.[10] Leslie's success generated competitors. *Harper's Weekly* came out in 1857, and the *New York Illustrated News* followed two years later.

When war broke out, Leslie and his competitors determined that they would provide their readers with pictures of the conflict. All three illustrated newspapers hired artists and sent them to the South. Leslie himself employed as many as twelve at a time.[11] Most of these special artists were young men in their early twenties who were not yet sure of their life's work. Edwin Forbes worked only for Leslie. The most prolific and best-known special artist, the English-born Alfred R. Waud, covered the war from First Manassas to Appomattox. Beginning with the *New York Illustrated News* in 1861, he moved over to *Harper's Weekly* the next year. Undoubtedly, the special artist who went on to the greatest renown as a serious artist was Winslow Homer, who made excursions in the South for *Harper's Weekly.*

The Confederacy did not have the resources, either human or technological, to equal the coverage provided by the three northern illustrated newspapers. A modest amount of pictorial reporting did take place from the Confederate side, however. In the late summer of 1862 the *Southern Illustrated News* was established in Richmond, Virginia. Although consciously modeled on the pictorial papers of London and New York City, it was a poor imitation. The lack of qualified engravers along with dwindling supplies of paper and of the wood essential for the engraving made for an all-but-impossible task. The *Southern Illustrated News* contained only a few illustrations, most of defective quality, and never a single battlefield scene. By the winter of 1864, the newspaper began shrinking in size, and by the end of the year, it had disappeared. In addition, Frank Vizetelly of the *Illustrated London News* ranged across the South. Even though Vizetelly sympathized with the Confederacy, many of his sketches involuntarily ended up in northern newspapers. They were confiscated from captured blockade runners and pirated by the northern press, who credited only an English artist.[12]

The war presented these special artists with a marvelous opportunity despite the advent of photography. Although the camera had been present in the Crimean War, the Civil War marked the first conflict in which photography became important. It was the most-photographed war to that time. Nevertheless, technical problems severely restricted its role. The size and weight of cameras and tripods hampered movement. The necessity of having portable darkrooms presented a distinct handicap. The long exposure time precluded photographing anything in motion. Also, costs were quite high for field photographers, and before the development of photoengraving, newspapers did not cover these expenses.

In contrast, the special artists used minimal equipment, which permitted great mobility. They usually carried a large portfolio suspended from a strap over the shoulder which contained paper, pencils, crayons, pens, brushes, and at times a few watercolors. They generally used pencils for battle sketches, but for camp scenes they often preferred crayons and charcoal.[13]

Like the regular reporters, the special artists lived with the army and depended upon it for subsistence. They were the comrades of the soldiers. They knew the rigors of campaigning in the field; they endured exhaustion; they shared the range of emotions that stretched from the tedium of the camp to the terror of the battlefield; they faced the possibility of being captured or wounded or even killed. To convey their impressions realistically to the public, they had to cope successfully with military life in all its guises.

The sketches drawn by Forbes, Waud, Homer, and their compatriots had to undergo a transformation in New York City before they reached newspaper buyers. The engravers redrew every field sketch on wood, cut away the inked sections, and then made a metal impression. The skill of the engraver affected the fidelity with which the sketches were reproduced. In this instance Forbes was fortunate to work for Leslie, who, as a former engraver, understood the critical importance of the engraver's role better than anyone else in the business. He personally supervised the preparation of each illustration for his *Illustrated Newspaper.* Most of Forbes's sketches were faithfully copied by engravers, though they were sometimes adjusted in size or perspective to fit the layout of the paper.[14]

Leslie devised a system that greatly expedited the process of turning an artist's sketch into a newspaper illustration. Larger engravings required numerous blocks of wood, which were bolted together. For his large engravings, Leslie had the blocks unbolted and the sections distributed to individual engravers to complete portions of the engraving. Then the blocks would be rebolted. In this way large engravings could be produced in almost the same time it took to complete one small engraving.[15]

Through their work, the special artists certainly made the war more realistic for newspaper readers of the 1860s. They also left a significant pictorial record for history. Their illustrations enable those who study the war to understand it more fully. That these sketches, drawings, and etchings grace so many books on the war testifies eloquently to the enduring worth and value of the contribution made by the special artists.

Edwin Forbes brought out *Thirty Years After: An Artist's Story of the Great War* in 1890. *Thirty Years After* is a war memoir, just like scores of others written by both Union and Confederate veterans, especially in the final two decades of the nineteenth century. *Thirty Years After,* however, contains more than just Forbes's reminiscences of his own experiences. While his personal recollections make up an essential part of the narrative, they do not form the central thrust of the book. He used them chiefly to give himself credibility, to give authority to his assessments of the army, the soldiers, and battle. Forbes focused on the army and the soldiers who constituted it. Although he rarely identified a particular army, he generally referred to the Army of the Potomac, his military home for most of his tour. In fact, Forbes often did not specify locations or indicate precise times. Instead, he strove to emphasize the universality of the soldiers' experience. He used pictures and words to tell the story of men at war.

Illustrations surely abound. Almost three hundred etchings taken from Forbes's field sketches, including those in *Life Studies of the Great Army,* dominate *Thirty Years After.* To these Forbes added twenty half-tone equestrian portraits from original oil paintings. They include obvious choices like Grant, Sherman, Philip H. Sheridan, and George H. Thomas. But to get his twenty, Forbes padded with such figures as Don Carlos Buell, Quincy A. Gillmore, and Joseph Hooker. Although these portraits do not materially aid Forbes in accomplishing his major purpose, he obviously thought they would help him sell his book.

Even though Forbes was known as an artist and designated his occupation in the subtitle, thus underscoring his own conviction about its importance, his words do help him. His word-pictures evoke mental images, which the etchings then often confirm. Forbes described the constantly hungry soldiers as "a kind of human locust" (p. 17). He graphically recounted the scene on Cemetery Ridge at Gettysburg after Pickett's Charge: "A great convulsion of nature could not have made more universal destruction; everything bore the mark of death and ruin" (p. 178).

Picturing a night march during the Battle of Chancellorsville, Forbes employed striking language: "Fires were blazing on every side, which, with the pine trees that had been ignited, so lit up the road that objects were as discernible as in the day; and surging through it all was a mass of earnest, determined men who were intent only on reaching the line of battle where they could be of service to their struggling comrades" (p. 34). On the facing page is one of Forbes's most effective etchings, *Through the Woods at Night.* In a nearly ghostly scene, soldiers march resolutely through the darkened forest with their way lit by flaming trees.

Forbes wanted his readers to understand what it meant to be a soldier in the Union army. For him the army was a living, breathing organism, whose inner workings he desired to reveal. He would accomplish this goal by illuminating almost every possible area of soldier life. To meet this end he divided *Thirty Years After* into eighty brief chapters, or more accurately snapshots, because the illustrations make up such a critical part of the book. They impart the essence of particular activities, whether feeding the troops or withstanding a charge.

Forbes concerned himself chiefly with the private soldiers, not the generals. Readers will find very little about any general, or for that matter any officers. He does give, however, an illustrated eyewitness account of President Abraham Lincoln reviewing the Army of the Potomac at Falmouth, Virginia, in April 1863. Forbes succeeded in portraying the reality of military life largely because he understood that the soldiers did not exist in a one-dimensional world. He correctly perceived the astonishing juxtaposition of activities, circumstances, and emotions that made soldiering in wartime a unique experience.

Forbes's soldiers spent much time tending to the same tasks that would occupy a civilian. Activities such as cooking, eating, washing, and leisure pursuits fill many pages in *Thirty Years After.* The etchings provide memorable concrete visual images: lining up to eat (p. 51), washing clothes in a tub and hanging them on a line (p. 170), shoeing a mule (p. 142), whiling away the hours reading newspapers (p. 135), playing cards (p. 166), fishing (p. 214), and even making and then playing a violin (pp. 266, 267).

The soldier confronted the elements in a way that a population still largely rural or with keen memories of the countryside could identify with. Marches in the rain turned into contests for survival. The cold and wet were exacerbated by roads that became quagmires swallowing up man and beast. In the marvelous etching *A Tough Pull,* the viewer can almost taste the dominating mud that clings to everything and has already put down one artillery horse (p. 211).

This kind of exercise could result in utter physical exhaustion, which Forbes vividly depicted. In one etching a tired soldier slumps against a tree (p. 210). In a larger illustration a soldier sits against a tree with his head bowed while his companion stretches out on the ground (p. 203).

Civilian types of undertakings as well as tedium and exhaustion could suddenly turn into what made being in the army different—the terror of combat. Then fury and violence reigned. In *The Halt, for Reforming the Line,* the surviving infantrymen standing just behind their dead comrades prepare to face the enemy once again (p. 75). An artillery section moves forward into the billowing smoke and the resulting darkness of battle in *Pulling into Position* (p. 179). *A Cavalry Charge* evokes the ferocity of mounted men in collision (p. 11). While the main body hurtles forward, in the foreground the dead riders and horses attest to the horror of battle. *Charge and Check,* though somewhat stylized, presents the face-to-face, personal character of so much Civil War fighting. Union soldiers, with one of their group already killed, defend a cannon at point-blank range against oncoming Confederate cavalry. The charging horses, with legs outstretched, nostrils flared, and eyes wide with fear, transmit the fierceness and violence of the impact (p. 255).

Forbes realized that the two worlds of tedium and terror coexisted in the closest proximity. His wonderful rendition of a moving clothesline—drying clothes hanging from the rifle barrel of a marching soldier—captures that reality (p. 171). At one battle Forbes observed a field hospital with severely wounded men and blood-stained surgeons almost next to a reserve artillery battery whose troops were sleeping, making coffee, and playing poker. He expressed a great admiration for the individual soldier who inhabited and even mastered this strange world. Convinced that these men had determined "to do what they had undertaken," Forbes forcefully delineated this belief in *Infantryman on Picket,* which could just as readily be entitled "A Study in Resoluteness and Solidity" (p. 127).

Forbes knew that battles were dangerous affairs, even for observers like himself. Getting close enough to see what was actually happening necessitated putting oneself in jeopardy. Forbes found the destruction at the point of contact between two armies appalling, in his words "so storm-swept with bullets and shell" (p. 258).

All battles did not present the same scene or spectacle. From Forbes's vantage point, Second Manassas offered a grand panorama of rolling hills and fields over which men fought. The tangle of the Wilderness made it impossible "to catch the faintest gleam" of the battle, even though over one hundred thousand troops were locked in combat. To Forbes, Antietam provided "a dramatic and most magnificent series of pictures" as two veteran armies collided with each other throughout the day (p. 258). No matter his perspective on a particular battle, Forbes understood that the average fighting man only knew what occurred in his immediate vicinity. He learned of the general outcome only after the shooting had stopped.

Forbes did not try to put forward every soldier as one of his resolute heroes. He faithfully recorded the presence of shirkers, or in the colorful phrase of his army days, "coffee coolers." These men found somewhere else to be when their units were ordered into action. Then, as soon as the danger had passed, they turned up claiming that they had gotten lost or had ended up fighting with a different outfit. A telling illustration, *Under the Bank,* shows five "coffee coolers" sheltered around their coffeepot while in the background their compatriots march into battle (p. 67). There were also common thieves who, when convicted, were literally drummed out of the army, as *A Bitter Lesson* strikingly renders (p. 303).

One of Forbes's most powerful etchings conveys the awful grandeur of the ultimate penalty for one of the gravest military crimes, desertion. According to Forbes, by 1863 desertion had become a growing problem because of the army's reluctance to enforce the supreme punishment and because of the increasing number of draftees and hired substitutes, but by the end of that year, the army was becoming stricter. Once, Forbes witnessed the execution of five deserters. His pictorial account is vivid and forceful. Facing the firing squad, the five condemned men sit blindfolded on the edges of their coffins, with their fellow soldiers massed to watch in the background. Forbes's etching captures the definitive moment, with smoking rifle barrels signaling the sentence in the act of being carried out (p. 155).

A Union patriot, Forbes concentrated on the Union army. He did take note of the Confederate enemy, however. To Forbes, the Confederates believed in and fought for their cause just as the Union soldiers did. During the early summer of 1863, while visiting Union pickets along the Rappahannock River, he saw Confederates on the opposite bank, some even bathing in the river. This shared humanity led to what he saw as an almost eerie fraternization between pickets on opposing sides. At times they chatted and exchanged coveted items, as in the swap of southern tobacco for northern coffee pictured in *Coffee and Tobacco Trading—A Truce* (p. 163). Then, of course, in nearly the next moment these temporary friends would be trying to kill each other.

Forbes also admitted and admired the military talent of Confederate leaders like Thomas J. "Stonewall" Jackson. After all, Forbes's introduction to the war had been on the losing side in the Shenandoah Valley in 1862. But he evinced even greater admiration for the average Confederate fighter, whose "soldierly qualities were very remarkable" (p. 173). And the "dashing bravery" that impressed him was forcefully illustrated in the stylized *A Gallant Deed of Arms,* which depicts the conclusion of Pickett's Charge at Gettysburg on July 3, 1863 (pp. 173, 175).

Forbes's summation of Confederate soldiers touched upon the sectional politics of the late nineteenth century. He told his readers that when they heard a northerner "breathing out particularly hot talk about the South or 'Confederate Brigadiers,' two to one you will find that during the war he was snugly at home making money or earning promotions in politics." These "self-seekers," according to Forbes, could not imagine "the fraternalism that grew up even between opposing armies after hearty fighting, followed by the fellowship of traffic between the lines" (p. 162). Traveling along the road to reunion, Forbes respected the courage and devotion to cause exhibited by the Confederate veterans. They shared much with him; all veterans belonged to the same band of brothers.

For Forbes, however, the war entailed more than the human drama that had produced a powerful bond among participants. The war also had concrete results for the United States. The Union had been preserved, and what he termed "The Reliable Contraband" had become free. Forbes discerned that the black Americans enslaved in the South had been at the center of the difficulties and antagonisms that had brought on war. He states directly that slavery was "the cause of the great rebellion" (p. 233). In *Thirty Years After* he dedicated considerable attention to the people who became contraband of war and refugees on their way to freedom. But like the overwhelming majority of white Americans of his time, northerners and southerners both, he believed that blacks were inferior to whites. He called blacks the "unfortunate race" (p. 233).

Although he clearly thought blacks less than whites and certain of his comments sound condescending to our ears, Forbes recognized their dignity as human beings and also their value to the Union army. He praised blacks for their trustworthiness as guides and for the help they gave to sick and wounded Union soldiers. They were responsible for much of the "daily industry-domestic work" (p. 149). *A Warm Breakfast—Winter, The Chief Cook,* and *An Evening Meal—Summer Camp* picture cooking activities (p. 150). Forbes maintained that only blacks could successfully manage the mule teams so crucial to the supply trains without which the army could not function. An evocative etching, *The Army Mule Team,* shows them in action (p. 243).

Forbes regarded blacks as almost always cheerful, even in "the most laborious duties," and he thought he knew why (p. 149). Two secondary reasons had merit. They were no longer under the control of their former masters, and they could earn a few dollars. But from personal observation, Forbes was persuaded that blacks were committed to doing their very best for the soldiers who were fighting to end slavery. He noted many instances of individual bravery, including a cook's service at a cannon at the Battle of Cedar Mountain until killed. And Forbes reported that later in the war blacks gave a "splendid account" of themselves as combat troops (p. 234).

The last chapter of *Thirty Years After* underscores Forbes's conviction that the slaves he encountered during the war recognized their allies. He commented on the "unceasing streams of slaves" entering Union lines wherever Union armies appeared (p. 289). Illustrations on pages 290 and 291 show refugees on foot and in a wagon moving into the Union position. Both the slaves and Forbes comprehended that the Union army furnished the slaves refuge and that their freedom depended upon its success. The final etching, *The Sanctuary,* which represents a scene that Forbes said he had witnessed, dramatizes this truth. In the foreground a black man, woman, and child, with a dog—a family—emerge into a clearing. They have obviously found what they left home for. They manifest a deep gratitude—the woman on her knees with arms upraised in thanksgiving, the man with uncovered head—for what stands in the background, a fort flying the Stars and Stripes (p. 319).

8

Jefferson Davis Confronts a Changed World

It pleased me immensely when Dr. Lynda Crist asked me to write the introduction for volume twelve of The Papers of Jefferson Davis. Editor of the Papers, Lynda had been a stalwart for me since the beginning of my travels with Davis. Moreover, she had become a friend. Besides that personal connection, I saw this particular volume as covering pivotal years in Davis's life, from 1865 to 1870. The documents published in its pages deal with a formerly powerful and wealthy man having to cope with powerlessness and poverty. The defeat of the Confederate States of America, to which as its president Davis had totally committed himself, left him not only bereft but also a prisoner of the United States facing possible trial for treason. Uncertainty about his fate dominated his time in prison. But the "state prisoner," as he was known, found refuge and strength in his family and his God. Finally, in early 1869 the federal government dropped all pending charges against him. Afterward, his main goal focused on finding a way to support his wife and four young children. The outcome of the war, with the destruction of slavery and the loss of his lands, made it impossible for a return to his prewar occupation of planter. A return to politics was out of the question. Unlike many of his peers, Davis had no legal training; thus, he could not turn to the law. His search led in different directions, including an unproductive trip to Europe. He finally ended up as president of an insurance company headquartered in Memphis. In bittersweet terms Davis expounded upon the financial and social reality of his former and current worlds. Still, in 1870 with his family with him, the former Confederate president said that a brave man could not permit himself to be mired in a sad past, but he must forthrightly face the future.

Uncertainty, pain, determination—these three emotions form the core of the five-and-a-half years of Jefferson Davis's life covered in this volume. For the first time in more than two decades, Davis was no longer a substantial planter, no longer a major political figure, no longer a president and commander in chief with a country to preside over and armies to command. His deepest hopes had crashed with the Confederate States of America. He had devoted to the fledgling country his every strength, physical, mental, and emotional. Yet despite his conviction about the rightness of his cause and his absolute commitment to the Confederacy through four years of increasingly brutal and desperate warfare, it had failed.

Taken prisoner by the victorious United States Army in May 1865, Davis found himself utterly powerless, facing an uncertain, even fearsome, future. In the emotional aftermath of Abraham Lincoln's assassination, an angry northern public opinion and an antagonistic, suspicious government assumed Davis's complicity, even to the point of orchestration, in that horrific act. The government determined that Davis would be treated differently from all other former Confederate officials who had been arrested upon the collapse of the Confederacy. Davis was incarcerated in Fort Monroe, Virginia, the prison of only one other ex-Confederate. Termed "the state prisoner," Davis was initially cut off from all communications except with his captors, kept in a casemate cell, watched around the clock, and even shackled briefly.

Although his situation improved over time—night lamp and guard removed from his cell; exercise outside permitted; finally, in the fall quartered in a cell in an officers' building—still his imprisonment was not easy, particularly for a man who for years had been wracked by numerous physical maladies. He had no sense of what would happen to him. As he informed his wife in November, "It is six months since we parted and I know no more of the purpose in regard to me than I did then." The United States government had indicted him for treason, and he probably faced trial. He knew that he had been allowed counsel, but his lawyer could not get authorization to visit him. During these months of uncertainty, Davis found strength and solace in three sources: his wife and family; his religious faith; and his conviction that even though in prison, he still represented the rightness of his failed cause.

In late August 1865 Davis received permission to correspond with his wife, though he could not comment on public affairs. In addition, the letters had to go through the fort commander and the attorney general of the United States before final transmission. For the next eight months, this correspondence became Davis's lifeline to his loved ones. These letters leave no doubt about the closeness between husband and wife that had been forged during the war. In October he confessed to Varina, "You have a key to my heart and know its unuttered feelings." Similar professions occupied almost every letter. Varina, in turn, mirrored his love and devotion in her missives to him. Calling him her first and only love, she blessed God for every day she had borne Davis's name. This forced separation, penetrated only by the mail, brought them closer together. Their letters underscore husband and wife utterly intertwined, spiritually and emotionally.

Davis also expressed great pride in his wife's energy in adapting to unexpected and uncharted circumstances. She had now become the guardian, caretaker, and provider for their four young children, the oldest only ten, the youngest not yet two. That he could not materially aid her frustrated him, but he evinced no want of confidence in her ability. Always his children absorbed him. He wanted to know all about them and constantly commented on Varina's accounts of their activities. He did send advice to be relayed to them, but mostly he wanted love and affection conveyed.

Davis had good reason to be confident about his wife, for since his imprisonment Varina had been in charge of the family. In a hostile environment she performed heroically, finding places for the family to live, including her mother and younger sister. Eventually, she settled them in Canada, believing it best to place them beyond possible interference by federal authorities. To defray expenses, she accepted and managed funds salvaged from the Confederate government that came to her from former Confederate functionaries. At the same time she pled her husband's case before federal officials, including President Andrew Johnson, and the northern public, emphasizing Davis's poor health and what she defined as mistreatment.

In every letter Davis spoke about the comfort he derived from his Christian faith. Although a nominal Christian during most of his adult life, Davis was baptized and confirmed in the Episcopal church only during the trial of war. He thanked Varina for leading him to the heart of the church. Details about his Bible reading and prayers filled his letters. He professed his belief that Christ watched over His flock, no matter the wretchedness of conditions. Then, Davis described an active God, whose wisdom and goodness directed all events. As a result he accepted God's will, even when it led to unwanted results.

Just as Davis never doubted a God ruling over human affairs, he expressed no misgivings about his course since 1861. He spoke of "representing a sacred cause" in which "the South strained every nerve to maintain a separate existence." He felt that in an important sense he represented the entire South. He hoped the northern craving for vengeance would be spent on him, thus sparing the southern people. With this vision of his new service to the South, he told Varina that he could with dignity withstand his trials. The South he cherished returned that sentiment. To white southerners, the imprisoned Davis became their representative man. Convinced that their course had been just with no cause for punishment, they believed Davis unjustly charged and held. This burgeoning unity formed an early, critical building block in the ideology that would come in the next two decades to dominate the white southern memory of the Confederate experience. Although Davis continued to struggle with all involved in his jailing, his spirits brightened and his days became much less onerous when, in spring of 1866, his captors relented and permitted Varina to visit. Arriving in May, she became instead of a mere visitor a resident of Fort Monroe. At the outset quartered in the casemate and allowed to see her husband only during daytime, she and he were living together by autumn in a four-room apartment, with kitchen, in the same officers' quarters building where he had been held.

Yet his legal case had not disappeared. What to do about the country's most famous prisoner became a political issue as well as a problem of law and jurisprudence. President Johnson's cabinet divided over the question of lenient or harsh treatment and over whether Davis should be tried before a civil or military tribunal. Then as strife between the president and Congress began to dominate postwar politics, especially the shape of Reconstruction in the old Confederacy, the ex-president was caught in the political tangle. Neither side wanted to appear soft on the man who had led the Confederacy. Thus, no basic decisions were made; Davis remained in place.

Legal positioning and maneuvering centered on how to handle this unique case. Of course, the attorney general of the United States, with presidential backing, took the lead, with distinguished outside counsel also enlisted. The government finally decided to try Davis for treason in a federal court. The trial would have taken place in Richmond, Virginia, for the Constitution specifies that trials for treason must be held where the alleged crime was committed. And Davis had resided in Richmond, the Confederate capital. A proceeding there meant the involvement of another prominent individual, Salmon P. Chase, chief justice of the United States. At that time the justices still traveled on circuits, where they sat with the local federal district judge, and Virginia was in Chase's circuit.

In preparing for trial, government attorneys envisioned two major problems. The first was Chief Justice Chase, who announced he would never hold court in Virginia until, by his definition, all military authority had ended. Moreover, he had doubts about treason. Then, the lawyers were concerned that but a single Confederate sympathizer on a jury could destroy their case by making it impossible to obtain a verdict of guilty.

Davis's defense team also had worries. It was headed by Charles O'Conor, a prewar Democrat and leading member of the New York City bar. Ten days after Davis was brought to Fort Monroe, O'Conor wrote the secretary of war volunteering his services. O'Conor was informed that he could do so by sending an open letter to Davis through the attorney general. He did, and Davis accepted his offer, even though he and O'Conor were not allowed to meet. While O'Conor led, he had able assistance from other lawyers, both northern and southern. O'Conor did not believe that, in a fair trial with an impartial jury, Davis could be convicted of treason. But he and his colleagues feared a jury in Richmond impaneled by the Republican district judge. They foresaw a jury that would make political, not legal, judgments.

The legal posturing and sparring resulted in no definite outcome. Trial dates were set; attorneys from one or both sides appeared; the chief justice did not; continuances became the norm. Finally, in the spring of 1867, two years after Davis entered Fort Monroe, the two sides agreed to free him on bail. The government would not drop the case but would give

Davis his freedom. Bail was set at $100,000, three quarters of it guaranteed by prominent northerners. On May 13 in the federal courtroom in Richmond, in the same building where Davis's presidential office had been located, the state prisoner was discharged.

Upon release, Davis and his wife, who had accompanied him from Fort Monroe to Richmond, left for Canada to join their children. Now Davis had to turn his attention to providing for his family. Some funds remained from the Confederate sources that had supported Varina, but they would not last. The war had destroyed his way of life and his means of livelihood. From what Davis always termed "the wreck," nothing was left for him. His plantation along with that of his eldest brother and benefactor, Joseph, was now in the hands of former Davis slaves, sold to them by Joseph. As he searched for possibilities, few appeared. Ultimately, he invested some of his scarce dollars in a Canadian copper-mining venture. That, however, did not solve his income woes.

Although earning money was a pressing concern, Davis's life was also governed by the court calendar. His bail arrangement stipulated that he had to appear in federal court in Richmond in November. Accordingly, he returned to the United States for the first time since his release. O'Conor had apprised his client that he did not think a trial would take place at that time. He was right. When court convened, the government asked for a continuance until the spring term of the court, March 1868.

After the postponement Davis went to Mississippi with Varina. He had not been to his home state since the war and wanted to visit family, especially brother Joseph, now past eighty. In that sense his trip was successful, for he visited siblings and other relatives. But his journey saddened him. He witnessed firsthand the devastation wrought by the war. The destruction of slavery demolished the foundation of the Davis brothers' wealth as well as that of their state. Still, the former planter worried about his ex-slaves, now free and coping with a new environment. The ravages of war had blasted the southern economy, resulting in a scarcity of money and plummeting land prices. Davis noted deprivation and poverty.

In Mississippi he made no public statements about Reconstruction or any other political developments. Acutely aware of his status and of his image in the North, he believed anything he said could end up harming southern whites. He refused an invitation to visit the University of Mississippi, which had offered to save places for his two sons, because he feared that even his appearance on campus could hurt the institution.

Public silence did not mean, however, that he had no opinion about the South and Reconstruction. Congressional Reconstruction, with its military districts and political rights for blacks, deeply troubled him. He saw oppression of southern whites; he viewed the South as unjustly punished. His reaction was not unique, for most white southerners of his class and background shared his outlook. From Mississippi he wrote a friend: "My thoughts are ever turned to our oppressed countrymen and my prayers are daily offered for their restoration to freedom and prosperity."

Just as court requirements dictated Davis's travel to Mississippi, they controlled his leaving. When he appeared in court in Richmond in March, the outcome replicated the result of the previous autumn. At the request of the government, his case was delayed. Once again, because of legal doubts and political events, the government wanted postponement.

With his legal situation still in limbo, Davis returned to Canada. His effort to find a steady income was also in limbo. That search led him to think about a voyage to Europe. The major investors in the mining enterprise wanted to sell their property. Concluding that England would be an excellent place to find a buyer, they decided that Davis would go as agent with authority to close a sale. Although selling the mines was his chief goal, Davis tried to diversify by arranging a connection with a British merchant house in Liverpool, the great cotton port. Before sailing, he contacted his friends in an attempt to gain commitments for shipments of cotton consigned to him, but to no avail.

The Davis legal situation and family interests also argued for Europe. O'Conor had reported to him that his trial had been put off to late November. Even more important, for the first time O'Conor expressed confidence that a trial would never occur. Additionally, Davis and his wife thought of Europe as possibly a less expensive place to raise and educate their children. In their decision to cross the Atlantic, money was central.

In late summer the entire family took its fortunes to England. Before 1861 Jefferson Davis was a wealthy and powerful man, but he never went to Europe. In 1868, when he did go, he was poor and powerless. Still, he received a warm, generous welcome from Confederate sympathizers, including members of the aristocracy. While the Davises appreciated their social reception and marveled at the wealth and grandeur of some of their hosts, they realized their financial plight precluded their participating in English society.

In Europe Davis had both positive and disappointing experiences. Reuniting with Confederate comrades, among them Judah Benjamin in England and John Slidell in Paris, gave him great pleasure. Then, in the summer of 1869 he took a marvelous journey to Scotland, where he reveled in the scenery and historic sites. Yet his major reason for the trip ended in failure. He never found any buyers for the mines; he never executed any successful business deals. Summarizing his entire experience, he wrote that he had been asked "to wait until evening when I should see what I should see." He never saw anything.

His business failure necessitated a return to the United States. He still needed a reliable income to support his family. Meanwhile, his legal status had changed fundamentally. In the winter of 1869 the government finally decided that it would never prosecute Jefferson Davis. Still anxious about the outcome of a trial, the government reached its final conclusion when Chief Justice Chase declared that in his judgment the Fourteenth Amendment had ended the Davis matter, with its stipulation that no person could hold office who had sworn an oath to uphold the Constitution and then participated in the rebellion. To him a Davis trial would entail double jeopardy. In late February the attorney general informed Davis's counsel that directions had been given to nol-pros all indictments for treason. For the first time in almost four years, Davis no longer faced the threat of federal prosecution.

When Davis left England for the United States in September 1869, he had not made a decision on employment. His prewar occupations of planter and politician were closed, and unlike many of his political peers, he had no legal background. Employment that he preferred, president of a college or a position with the Southern Pacific Railroad, either offered too little remuneration or never materialized. Although the possibility of a job with the Carolina Life Insurance Company, headquartered in Memphis, had come up before his departure for Europe, yet he made no commitment, in no small part because he knew nothing about the insurance business.

Upon his return, Davis went to Memphis to talk with company officials. Initial intimations had been that the firm intended to open a branch in Baltimore, with Davis as manager. But in Memphis a different decision was made. The directors, after the sitting president stepped aside, offered Davis the presidency of Carolina Life, with an annual salary of $12,000 plus travel expenses. He would live in Memphis. This position had two overriding assets, availability and good salary.

Aware of the relationship between occupation and social status, Davis wanted to make a decision about employment that would not diminish his standing either in his own estimation or anyone else's. He reminded his wife that even if they forgot, "others will not fail to remember the difference, between a man of business, and a Soldier, or a Planter, or a Senator, or a Cabinet minister, or a President, or even an exiled Representative of an oppressed people." Knowing that Varina did not prefer living in Memphis, he told her that he refused to accept proffered private donations and their former property had nothing for them. He said only in Memphis could he earn a living to support his family. He then furnished his own primer on social ranks and prejudices. The differences between classes, he asserted, was greater in London than in Liverpool, just as the gap was wider in Baltimore than in Memphis. He maintained that the upper class in the former would have greater prejudice against the agent of a company than its president, a position he did not have there. "I have compounded with my pride for the material interest of my family, and am ready to go on to the end as may best promote their happiness," he concluded.

At sixty-one Jefferson Davis started down a new road as an insurance executive. As he set about learning the insurance business, he dealt with a wide range of subjects: the mathematics of life insurance, recruiting agents, studying salary structure and marketing strategy. His new post also required considerable travel, for Carolina Life considered the entire South its territory.

Yes, he had a good job, and that was reason for optimism, but a powerful sadness still enveloped him. Although he did not break his public silence, the tribulations of the South, as he saw them, still grieved him, though he rejoiced at the Democratic resurgence in Tennessee. In addition, the increasing feebleness of Joseph worried him deeply. Most important, that his wife and children remained in Europe preyed upon him. His every letter professed his love for them. Varina, in hers, reciprocated. Throughout it all, he wrestled with where life had placed him. He spoke often of sorrow and disappointment.

Struggling in a turbulent world, a lonely Davis found solace in his friendship with Clement and especially Virginia Clay. He had known them since the 1850s, when Clement had served as senator from Alabama and Virginia, Ginnie to him, had enjoyed a prominent social role. Clement, also, for a time was jailed at Fort Monroe, which led to a deepening bond that extended to Virginia. Alone in Memphis, he reached out to them for his emotional lifeline. He saw them at their home near Huntsville, Alabama, and wrote to them often. In turn, letters came from the Clays, but mostly from Virginia, who wrote for herself and for her asthmatic husband. Davis did not hold back his feelings, speaking of "my precious Clays" and recounting his devotion to them. In unusually open and emotional letters, Davis left no doubt about his need for the Clays' friendship. Although he never hid his abiding affection for Ginnie, he always thought of two Clays, not just one. He told them his daydreams for the three of them—a good ship, good cigars, and a good library.

While Davis carried on his duties with Carolina Life, he decided the time had come for his family to rejoin him. In August 1870 he sailed for England and by October had returned with Varina and the children, except for their older daughter, who stayed with a sister of Varina's for schooling. Although having his family reunited pleased him enormously, he mourned the death of Joseph, who had died before Jefferson left England.

For Davis, uncertainty hovered over his world. He was still adjusting to his business undertaking. Bouts of physical illness always seemed close by. Varina, too, was plagued with poor health. His thoughts never wandered far from his beloved, beleaguered South that in his view had been shrouded by "a long dark night." Even so, he faced forthrightly toward the future. As he said to a Tennessee audience, "It is not the part of brave men to brood over the sorrows of the past, but rather to look forward with bright hopes for the future."

9

The Critical Signpost on the Journey toward Secession

While working on my study of the crisis of the Union, which became We Have the War Upon Us: The Onset of the Civil War, November 1860–April 1861 *(2012), I once again had to confront the secession movement. This renewed focus caused me to reassess my earlier views. Looking closely at the timing of the state secessions in conjunction with what was taking place in Congress, I concluded that congressional action or inaction had considerably more influence than I had originally imagined. Yet previous scholars of secession had given little attention to that connection. Yes, all agreed that a national event, the election in November 1860 of the Republican Abraham Lincoln as president, sparked the states in the Deep South to break up the Union, but then they concentrated almost exclusively on what happened in those states. This essay, which originated as my presidential address to the Southern Historical Association in 2010, aimed to redirect attention to the national scene, specifically to Congress, as crucial for the course of secession.*[1]

The Civil War stands out as the most cataclysmic event in United States history. Almost all historians as well as most of the general public agree with that generalization. I do not intend to challenge it, for I certainly concur. Nor am I going to treat the war at all. Rather, I am going to address the secession crisis, or the crisis of the Union, in 1860–1861. Without that crisis there would surely have been no war, at least not at that time. Thus, the crisis of the Union merits careful attention.

I realize bringing up secession in this setting means taking a great risk. I say *risk* because the membership of this organization contains a number of scholars, some undoubtedly here tonight, who have made notable contributions to our understanding of the crisis. Perhaps age has brought me no more wisdom than it did my maternal great-great-great-grandfather, who, as the oldest member of the South Carolina secession convention, made no known effort to halt his and his colleagues' headlong rush over the precipice. My taking this risk calls to mind not only my ancestor but also David F. Jamison, the president of that convention. Imploring his fellows to act, Jamison cried, "To dare! and again to dare! and without end to dare!" Just as I am acknowledging Jamison, he gave due to the French revolutionary Georges-Jacques Danton. Calling on Danton can be extremely hazardous, however; he ended up on the guillotine.[2]

At the outset, I must note that just three years ago the distinguished historian and my longtime friend Bill Freehling brought out his impressive and massive *The Road to Disunion,* volume 2, *Secessionists Triumphant, 1854–1861.* That book filled a critically important void—secession is arguably the least studied major event in American history. Prior to Freehling's volume, the last full investigation was Dwight Lowell Dumond's *The Secession Movement, 1860–1861,* published in 1931. The immediate question is why? In part, I think secession has been subsumed by the larger theme of the coming of the Civil War. Every major study of the onset of the war comments on secession, but none engages in a thorough investigation. Perhaps even more important is that secession is an exceptionally vexing topic. It is easy to say that slavery caused secession, a claim that today draws a practically unanimous chorus from historians.[3] Yet if simply slavery is at fault, then all fifteen slave states should have acted similarly. We know that these states did not. They reacted in three different ways. Seven Deep South, or cotton, states left the Union by the beginning of February 1861; four upper South states followed upon Abraham Lincoln's call for troops after the surrender of Fort Sumter; four border states never seceded.

To explain satisfactorily what happened in the slave states during the secession winter and spring requires accounting for the three different courses taken by the slave states. Then, it is essential to connect secession with the political process across the South, for the decision to secede or not was basically political. Freehling fully understood the complexity of his task, and he successfully completed it. He recognized and accounted for the three separate reactions, pointing to the various political and social forces that influenced events. One does not have to accept completely his interpretation to avow his achievement.[4]

My goal here is neither to challenge directly nor to replicate his accomplishment. I know that latter assertion pleases you, since even to approach replication would keep us here not only all night but at least until Christmas or maybe the New Year. The question, however, remains, what caused secession?

I begin by underscoring Freehling's attainment. No one else has ever done so much work on the phenomenon of disunion or provided such a rich context. With his unparalleled research, it took a book of 565 pages of text even to get to the mid-1850s, and in volume 2 he did not reach secession itself until page 343. Also, I wholeheartedly endorse his insistence that we must strive to see the crisis as contemporaries did. In other words, we must, as much as possible, reject hindsight and embrace contingency. Of course, as all in this room realize, reaching that goal is much easier said than done.[5]

As did the Fire-Eaters, or the immediate secessionists, Freehling understands the essential occurrence as the secession of a single state. I agree, for that event would change the fundamental question from "Do we secede?" to "Do we join a sister slave state that has already seceded?" I also assent to his insistence that the initial act of secession was utterly critical. As a result, Freehling spends considerable time on South Carolina. In his view, once South Carolina opted for single-state separation, the balance tipped. Then, in his account, nothing could stymie the other Deep South states, despite significant opposition to immediate secession in at least three of them: Alabama, Georgia, and Louisiana. And, of course, within six weeks of South Carolina's secession on December 20, 1860, the other six left the Union.

While Freeling's magnum opus stands as the only comprehensive modern history of the secession crisis, there is no dearth of state studies. Of course, almost all of them antedate Freehling's work. A close look at them emphasizes the magnitude of what Freehling did. He surely did not weave a synthesis from the existing scholarship. That is easy to discern, given that the monographs on states offer an almost bewildering variety of explanations for the course of secession in their bailiwicks. Without question, in all of them slavery provided the key in one way or another, but in attaching slavery to the political process, wide differences mark these books. Let me hasten to add that here I am talking only about the Deep South, the cotton states, the initial seven. The political calculation changed notably after the creation of the Confederate States of America in mid-February 1861 and especially after the clash at Fort Sumter in April.

First, consider South Carolina, the state where it began. Within the last generation, four stalwart examinations have been made. For Steven A. Channing, his title, *Crisis of Fear,* says it all—a rampaging fear, probably irrational, of slave revolts and Republicans drove the state out. In *Origins of Southern Radicalism,* Lacy K. Ford Jr. finds Fire-Eaters triumphant because of unity between yeomen and planters stemming from a common devotion to country republicanism that all perceived as threatened by economic shifts in the state and Republican victory in the nation. Stephanie McCurry, in *Masters of Small Worlds,* complements Ford in perceiving yeoman-planter unity, though her explanation rests chiefly on a shared commitment to mastery, whether over slaves, or women or children, or all three. In contrast, Manisha Sinha, in *The Counterrevolution of Slavery,* has reactionary planters forcing secession on subservient whites in order to maintain planter dominion over the state. Aside from agreeing on the urging of the Fire-Eaters, disagreement reigns.[6]

Moving away from the cockpit of radicalism, one discovers no more agreement on why states seceded. The most recent study of Mississippi concentrates on masculinity. To explain the situation in Alabama, J. Mills Thornton III brilliantly discusses republicanism but also points to shifts on state financial policy by the Democratic party that led to yeomen's apprehension about economic and political change, spurring their embrace of disunion. William L. Barney thinks a serious drought had a central role. In the key state of Georgia, according to Michael P. Johnson, arch-conservatives plus bad weather on election day combined to drown the opponents of immediate secession. Anthony Gene Carey, however, finds Georgians overwhelmingly supporting secession. Analyzing Louisiana, a state without strong Fire-Eater presence, John M. Sacher reports that widespread distress over Lincoln's election coupled with the determination of leaders like United States senator John Slidell underlay the narrow margin of victory for immediatists. The most recent attempt to make sense of Texas focuses on mysterious fires in the Dallas region that spawned hysteria spreading through the state. Believing abolitionist activity and slave unrest responsible and fearful of what might be forthcoming, Texans raced for safety outside the Union.[7]

Surveying these books, I can only conclude that producing a synthesis would be difficult indeed. How could we effectively synthesize everything from plotting reactionaries, to enthusiastic yeomen, to weather, at once too dry and too wet, with panic, whether from fires or fear of slaves, thrown in? For myself, I marvel at the extraordinary divergence of opinion coming from such an array of serious historians.

Yet, what baffles me most about the multitudinous causes delineated in the state studies, as well as by Freehling, who devotes so much time and space to South Carolina, is their incredibly sharp focus on the states. Although such a concentration is probably understandable in the volumes on the states, every state responded to a major national event, Lincoln's election. All these scholars acknowledge that fact, but afterward the national scene quickly fades away. I am not saying that what happened in the states lacked importance, for surely those events mattered a great deal. But each of the seven remained in the Union until it actually went out. And most modern students of secession agree that outside South Carolina, probably a majority of citizens and voters were reluctant to go for disunion. The Fire-Eaters really had to push, even in South Carolina. In fact, Freehling maintains that a majority enthusiastic for immediate secession never existed in any of the Deep South states, except for South Carolina, and even there, in his view, it took an especially propitious set of circumstances for the immediatists to vanquish waverers. I concur, and on this point my opinion has changed during the past twenty-five years.[8]

At the same time, throughout the meeting of state legislatures, the holding of special elections for delegates to secession conventions, the convening of the conventions, and even the creating of the Confederate States of America, the United States Congress was in session. Moreover, for the entire second session of the Thirty-Sixth Congress, strenuous efforts took place to fashion an agreement to hold the Union together or, at the least, to restrict secession severely. Of course, all these efforts failed, but contemporaries did not know they would, though radicals North and South prayed for precisely that outcome. Yet the historians I have noted overwhelmingly assume failure. Congressional unimportance is abundantly clear in Freehling's book, which has a single chapter of but twelve pages that covers what he terms "Compromise Rejected." Only nine of these pages deal with Congress.[9]

For the moment, my interest in the congressional session has a single focus—the South and the possibility of compromise. When Congress convened on December 3, 1860, southern members ranged across a broad spectrum on the matter of disunion. At one extreme stood the two South Carolina senators, who had already submitted their resignations from Congress, a contagion that raced through the entire delegation, infecting some men who had just a short time earlier condemned such a rash step as ridiculous. Close to the Carolinians, other Fire-Eaters in Washington hungered for disunion, eagerly anticipating the secession of their states. In contrast, some solons absolutely opposed breaking up the Union. Most of the lawmakers found themselves between those two extremes. One could label them reluctant secessionists or quasi-Unionists. Those appellations do not exactly replicate the immediatist-versus-cooperationist designation signifying views on state action, with the former championing independent state action and the latter advocating either cooperation of one or more states or a southern convention before action.

What I find most striking about congressional southerners in December is not only the divergence of opinion but also how quickly it changed, and then changed again. One day secession seemed absolutely essential, but on the next perhaps not. Although both senators from South Carolina had resigned their seats in November, the opening of Congress found five of the state's six House members in attendance. Senator Jefferson Davis arrived from Mississippi hopeful about a settlement; next he despaired; then he agreed to serve on the Committee of Thirteen created by the Senate to try to come up with a resolution. Later, Davis said he did not give up all hope until the end of the month, when the committee failed.[10]

It is not possible here to discuss every activity regarding the crisis in the second session of the Thirty-Sixth Congress. Yet concentrating briefly on one critical moment during the session can, in my judgment, illuminate the course that events did take. When the Committee of Thirteen deliberated, the major proposal it considered came from one of its members, John J. Crittenden of Kentucky. The primary component of Crittenden's plan revived and extended the Missouri Compromise line westward to California, with slavery protected in the area south of the line in territory possessed by the United States at the time and also "hereafter acquired." He wanted his proposition placed in the Constitution in order to remove the explosive slavery question from normal political discourse and from electoral politics. But before debating Crittenden's or any other possible solution, the committee adopted a crucial procedural rule. For any proposal to receive its blessing, it would have to garner a majority of both Democrats and Republicans. Thus, either side could block any positive action.[11]

Crittenden really believed he presented a reasonable compromise to the embattled southerners and Republicans. The Republicans insisted that no additional territory be open to slavery under any circumstances. In fact, they advocated congressional prohibition of slavery in all territories. That position had been central for the party since its inception. In contrast, southerners declared that as American citizens they had a constitutional right to take their property, including slave property, into any territory owned by their country. In making their case, southerners always emphasized that the United States Supreme Court in its *Dred Scott v. Stanford* decision of 1857 had decided the constitutional issue in their favor. To them the constitutional and legal question had been settled. In their minds, they occupied the constitutional high ground.[12]

A number of important southerners indicated they could accept Crittenden's blueprint or something similar, including the two Deep South men on the Committee of Thirteen, Jefferson Davis and Robert A. Toombs. Ever since Lincoln's election, Davis had been struggling to find some way to avoid dissolution of the Union, an eventuality he desperately wanted to prevent. He found that protecting southern rights, as he understood them, while coping with an increasingly radicalized Mississippi, was no simple task. But, for him, Crittenden offered an acceptable plan that Davis could defend back home. Toombs, the senior senator from Georgia, did not share Davis's outlook. An active proponent of secession, Toombs was a leader of the disunion forces in his state. He also made clear that Crittenden's ideas did not satisfy him personally. Yet Toombs made known his willingness to support the plan because he knew that Georgia would embrace it.[13]

With Davis and Toombs in the aye column, Crittenden's design had the backing of all the non-Republicans on the committee. I say non-Republicans rather than simply Democrats, though all seven of that party were on the pro-side, because Crittenden refused to align with either party, clinging to his memory of his revered Whiggery. There were four Democrats from the slave states and three from free states. The two other southerners, Robert M. T. Hunter of Virginia and Lazarus W. Powell of Kentucky, were stalwart for Crittenden's plan, as were William Bigler of Pennsylvania, Stephen A. Douglas of Illinois, Henry M. Rice of Minnesota, and, of course, Crittenden himself.

While Davis and Toombs signaled their willingness to sign on for Crittenden's proposal, Fire-Eaters in and out of Congress had no use for it. They wanted no compromise of any kind, dreading that any successful move toward a settlement would frustrate their drive for disunion. The southern "ultra men" desired no "redress of . . . grievances"; rather, they strove to block any path to adjustment. They also prayed for Republican intransigence. Nothing would provide more impetus to their drive for disunion than implacable Republican opposition to any congressional attempt at resolution.[14]

We know that the Fire-Eaters got their wish. No settlement was reached; the Committee of Thirteen agreed on no solution. It never approved Crittenden's program or anything else. Just as the Fire-Eaters desired, the Republicans adamantly opposed Crittenden's and all other ideas that permitted even the possibility of slavery's expanding to any territory. In the committee all five Republicans, headed by their congressional leader, William Henry Seward of New York, cast negative ballots. Thus, Crittenden's compromise died in committee because it did not obtain the required majority from both sides. On December 31 the committee reported its failure to the Senate.

Imagine for a moment, however, that the Committee of Thirteen had adopted the Crittenden plan or something comparable. And other possibilities were afloat, including extending the Missouri line and admitting two huge states, one north and the other south of the line, to be named Washington and Jefferson respectively. The northern would prohibit slavery; the southern would permit the institution. With the committee agreeing on a formula for compromise, what would have happened to the march toward secession?[15]

I admit that we cannot know for sure, but strong signs point toward a turn onto a different road. What the committee did clearly did not matter to South Carolina; the state seceded on December 20, even before the committee broke down. But Georgia and Alabama would not have followed the Palmetto State. Even after South Carolina had seceded and the committee had failed, the delegates elected to the secession conventions in those two states were closely divided. In Georgia Toombs's acquiescence in a settlement would have scuttled secession, an outcome secessionists acknowledged. Likewise, Fire-Eaters in Alabama would have been foiled. Davis would have obstructed immediate action in Mississippi. Those actions would surely have deterred Louisiana, where Fire-Eaters had limited impact. There, to follow other Deep South states out, the Democratic party leadership practically forced the decision for secession. With no one but South Carolina to emulate, the Louisiana politicians would not have moved. Likewise, it seems most unlikely that secessionists in Texas could have prevailed, especially given the massive geographical gap between the Sabine and Savannah Rivers. Of the Deep South states, this calculation omits only Florida. Concerning it, I am unsure, but it seems most probable that Florida would have lined up behind Georgia and Alabama, not South Carolina. The scenario of the initial secession crisis that I have sketched has a stark conclusion: a reprise of nullification, with South Carolina alone confronting the federal government. Positing the outcome of that eventuality requires even more speculation than I will contemplate, at least on this occasion.

To return to the committee and what it did not do, I want to make an obvious point. The Republican negative was central. I cannot develop my arguments here on the why of that decision. Yet I do want to point out that the Republican camp was not initially united. In fact, deep divisions on the efficacy of compromise marked the party in and out of Congress, as noted long ago by David M. Potter and more recently by Russell McClintock. Historians who assert, or take as a given, that the party was always a phalanx in opposition to any possibility of compromise have either not looked thoroughly at the record or engaged in wishful thinking. The left of the party, the most zealous antislavery men, constantly and vigorously denounced any thought of territorial compromise; but many others, including notable figures, either wavered or even embraced reaching an equitable settlement with the South.[16]

The most prominent Republican in Congress, Senator Seward, spent most of December marking time while his close political ally and alter ego, the New York party chieftain and editor Thurlow Weed, spoke forthrightly for compromise, publicly proposing the extension of the Missouri line. Most Republicans, however, did not line up alongside Weed. Instead, they huddled with Seward, waiting to see what course the new party leadership would adopt. That meant looking westward to Springfield, Illinois, and the president-elect, Abraham Lincoln.[17]

As everyone knows, Lincoln ended up taking a hard line against any deal on the territorial issue. Time and time again he made clear to Republicans, in and out of Congress, as well as to others that he would condone no arrangement that permitted even the possibility of slavery's expansion into any territory. Before reaching that decision, Lincoln had received advice from both pro- and anticompromise champions. His decision to go with the latter, resulting in his unyielding opposition to any territorial settlement, killed any chance that such an agreement could be reached. In my opinion, it is instructive that Seward did not clarify his position on the territories or in the Committee of Thirteen until after a mid-month meeting between Weed and Lincoln.[18]

A number of Lincoln scholars have praised his firm stance, asserting that he acted properly in his steadfast loyalty to the Republican platform of 1860 and his rejection of any territorial compromise. That outlook is surely a possibility. In the war that eventually resulted, Lincoln prevailed with the Union intact and slavery abolished. Yet that interpretation comes at the study of history backward, with hindsight as headlights. No one in the crisis of 1860–1861, not even Lincoln, could read the future, much less the precise future that unfolded. In my judgment, a key question that remains largely unanswered is why Lincoln, supposedly a conservative, certainly more so than Seward, ended up such a hard-liner. Taking up that question in detail is beyond the scope of these remarks, though I intend to do so elsewhere. Still, in this address, I want to suggest what stands out as a central reason for Lincoln's unbending posture: his ignorance of the South.[19]

Lincoln initially dismissed the seriousness of secession and looked on it as a conspiracy plotted by a small band of radicals soon to be put down by sensible Union men like himself. He found no other explanation possible. In his view nothing he or anyone else in his party had said or done could have motivated secession. That judgment leads inescapably to the observation that he rationalized his famous House Divided declaration of 1858, for in it he bluntly told southerners that the Union of the future had no place for their central social and economic institution. Moreover, the irrepressible-conflict script intoned by many Republicans did likewise. Could Lincoln have been tone-deaf to how southerners would hear such assertions? He must have been, for ten days after the election he told a conservative Kentuckian that neither he nor any other "prominent public Republican had justly made himself obnoxious to the South by anything he had said or done."[20]

Lincoln evidently never stopped to think how he would have reacted had a southern political leader asserted publicly that the free states had no place in a future Union. Yet he did react forcefully to what he claimed was a scheme to nationalize slavery. In his rhetoric, that design was part of the slave power conspiracy. Although Lincoln struck out on the stump against this specter, even suggesting in 1858 that the United States Supreme Court intended to make Illinois a slave state, no important southern politician ever advocated such a cause.[21]

Lincoln had little experience with southerners. Yes, at nineteen and twenty-two he had taken brief trips down the Ohio and Mississippi Rivers to New Orleans. Also, he was born in Kentucky, and his wife came from a slaveowning family in that state, as did his best friend, Joshua Speed. But that part of the border South was all that he knew. After his two youthful journeys to New Orleans in 1828 and 1831, he never traveled in the South beyond Kentucky. Aside from a few Kentuckians, he really did not know any southerners, certainly not any southern politicians. He had in the late 1840s served one term in the United States House of Representatives, where he surely met southerners and was friendly with a few. But that was almost a decade and a half before the crisis of 1860–1861. In the interval he had kept up with none of those men. Fundamentally, he had no friends who could educate him about the South and southern politics.[22]

The record indicates that Lincoln's image of the slave South basically matched common fervent antislavery depictions. In this South rich planters dominated society and politics, pressing in 1860–1861 for secession and cowing nonslaveholding whites. Lincoln appears to have had no understanding of either the widespread ownership of slaves among whites or how deeply embedded slavery had become in southern society. Instead of comprehending that the overwhelming majority of southern whites were committed to their slave society, it seems, he thought of them as conservative Unionists with but a fragile attachment to slavery. In other words, they were much like him, though probably lacking his moral outrage at slavery. Perhaps the mass of southern whites could not or would not act against slavery, but Lincoln could not imagine them either being proslavery or acting against the Union on their own. A South where nonplanters, even nonslaveowners, had an influential voice, feared Republicans, and actively supported secession was both foreign and unknown to Lincoln. When a visitor in early November urged Lincoln to reassure southerners "honestly alarmed" by a Republican triumph, his reply spoke volumes—"There are no such men."[23]

Commenting on the famous epistolary exchange between Lincoln and Alexander H. Stephens of Georgia in November and December 1860, writers often describe them as friends. Such a description is surely an exaggeration, for the two men had seen each other only during sessions of the Thirtieth Congress and had not been in contact since they left Washington in early 1849. In his request on November 30 for a copy of Stephens's recent address before the Georgia legislature, Lincoln mentioned that he had seen newspaper accounts. Responding, Stephens said they were "substantially" accurate.[24]

I wonder how carefully Lincoln had read the speech. Yes, Stephens did deplore the rush to secession because of Lincoln's election. At the same time, however, Stephens left no doubt about his opinion of the Republican party. "If the policy of Mr. Lincoln and his Republican associates shall be carried out," he announced, "no man in Georgia will be more willing or ready than myself to defend our rights, interest, and honor at every hazard and to the last extremity." Defining that policy, Stephens gave primary importance to a congressional prohibition of slavery from the common territory. Of course, for Lincoln that restriction held a place of honor in the Republican catechism. Stephens urged Georgia to delay, not because he found the Republican program acceptable or because he would acquiesce in it, but because he argued that a Congress controlled by Democrats, along with the federal judiciary, would thwart Lincoln. He predicted an enfeebled Lincoln presidency that could do the South no harm.[25]

The four letters between the men do have a certain civility about them, with each man assuring the other of his respect. Stephens drew empathetic attention to Lincoln's massive burden, telling him "no man ever had heavier or greater responsibility resting upon him than you have in the present momentous crisis." Trying to be conciliatory and reassuring, Lincoln, on December 22 in a letter marked "For your eyes only," stated that he "appreciate[d] the present peril." He also told Stephens that the South had nothing to fear from him or a Republican administration. Word even came to Stephens indirectly that Lincoln called him "a great man." Still, Lincoln did recognize that he and Stephens differed on the "right" and "wrong" of slavery.[26]

In his second letter, on December 30, Stephens emphasized, "Personally I am not your enemy—far from it." He then called on Lincoln to do what he could "to save our common country." But Stephens was also pointed. Southerners worried, he wrote, that the Republicans' "leading object seems to be simply, and wantonly, if you please, to put the Institutions of nearly half the States under the ban of public opinion and national condemnation." He connected that "object" to "the influence of fanaticism," which he saw influencing the Republican party. Yet the Georgian concluded that "[a] word 'fitly spoken' by you now, would indeed be 'like apples of gold, in pictures of silver.'" To this entreaty, Lincoln did not reply.[27]

With no firsthand knowledge of the South and with no friends or even serious acquaintances among southern politicians, Lincoln unsurprisingly did not acknowledge distinctions between Fire-Eaters, the zealous evangels of secession, and men like Stephens and even Jefferson Davis, who were fundamentally conservative with no relish for disunion. Lincoln showed no awareness that he understood the political force pressed by the radicals on southern conservatives and regulars.

Although the precise level of popular support for immediate secession in the Deep South remains a tangled issue, no conspiracy took those seven states out of the Union. The Fire-Eaters surely pushed, and they drove for haste; but no secret cabal manipulated events from South Carolina to Texas. Every one of those states held a popular vote for delegates to conventions that would decide on secession.

Concluding, I certainly affirm that secession occurred because of slavery. And I am willing to agree that a myriad of specific factors connected secession to time and place—from fires, to state financial policy, to political muscle, and even to other particulars. Still, I maintain that what took place west of South Carolina depended chiefly on what happened or did not happen in Washington. The critical decision took place there, in the Capitol. The Fire-Eaters secured their goal of disunion only when it became absolutely clear that on the territorial issue the Republicans would not bend at all. When compromise failed, secession succeeded.

10

Where Was Henry Clay?

PRESIDENT-ELECT ABRAHAM LINCOLN AND THE CRISIS OF THE UNION, 1860–1861

This essay also originated in my research for We Have the War Upon Us. *An invitation to contribute to a festschrift for the eminent historian and my excellent friend Michael Holt led to its writing. For the first time in my career, I gave considerable attention to Abraham Lincoln material, both primary, including correspondence, and secondary sources. As have many others, I discovered much that was fascinating. My focus, however, was on the six months between his election as president in November 1860 and the firing on Fort Sumter in April 1861. His reaction as president-elect to congressional efforts to fashion a compromise aimed at settling the crisis of the Union particularly intrigued me. Previous historians had devoted much time to analyzing divisions in Lincoln's Republican party, from radicals to conservatives with most somewhere in the middle. Simultaneously, they noted Lincoln's alignment with the radicals resisting any serious compromise. Although some of these scholars applauded his intransigence, others simply placed him, albeit in a leadership role, in the ranks of the implacably opposed Republicans. It seemed to me, however, that no one had looked carefully at why Lincoln initially opposed and remained steadfast against any serious congressional settlement. I found his stance especially puzzling because he had often praised as his ideal political leader Henry Clay, the Kentuckian who had gained fame as the Great Pacificator, the stalwart and successful supporter of three major sectional compromises from 1820 to 1850. I wanted to investigate why in 1860–61 Lincoln had turned away from his hero's legacy. A final note—on the matter of Lincoln and the South, this essay repeats much of my discus-*

sion in the previous one. It remains in place for two reasons. First, I want to retain the integrity of this essay; second, in my judgment it is extremely important.[1]

Abraham Lincoln occupies a secure place in the pantheon of great United States presidents. Even among that select group, in the view of many, professional historians as well as the general public, he is primus inter pares—the savior of the Union and the Great Emancipator. Recently, numerous Lincoln students seem to be in a contest to extol his greatness. I have no intention of challenging the overwhelming consensus, for I, too, agree that he ranks in the very top tier of our presidents and that he has no equal as a war leader. This widespread agreement focuses, however, on the Civil War. Lincoln's performance in that cauldron forms the foundation of his glowing reputation, a renown that has only brightened in the past two decades.[2]

Rather than Lincoln as a war leader, in this essay my subject is the prewar Lincoln. In fact, I concentrate on a quite narrow time frame, the few months between his election to the presidency on November 6, 1860, and his inauguration as the sixteenth president on March 4, 1861. Even more pointedly, I have a single overriding interest. Why in the great crisis of the Union during the winter of 1860–61 did the self-proclaimed admirer and apostle of the Great Pacificator, Henry Clay, work actively and successfully against any serious compromise designed to defuse, perhaps even settle, the explosive situation? Not only had Clay gained fame as a compromiser, but since the Constitutional Convention, compromise had enjoyed a hallowed place in the American political tradition.

Of course, I am not the first historian to address this question. Several current Lincoln scholars have looked at it, at least in part. Still, none in my judgment has provided a satisfactory explanation. Their analyses fall into two basic camps. The first does not really perceive a serious issue, praising the president-elect for his steadfast loyalty to the Republican platform, his strategy of public silence, and his rejection of any general settlement of the crisis. That outlook is surely a possibility, but it seems to me to come at the study of history backward. A war resulted, a war in which Lincoln prevailed, with the Union intact and slavery abolished.

But no one in the winter of 1860–61, not even Lincoln, could read the future, much less that precise future. The second camp, though not as fixated on a post-1865 perspective, devotes more attention to the efforts at compromise, including the reactions of Republicans and the division within the party. This discussion places Lincoln squarely in the no-compromise column while detailing his determination to derail any plan for adjustment. These writers even note problems in Lincoln's position, such as his delay in taking the secession movement seriously. Yet even here no one has treated systematically why Lincoln remained so inflexible regarding meaningful compromise.[3]

Going back to Lincoln and Henry Clay, I want to underscore two facts that are well known but too little emphasized. First, I want to note Clay's prominence as the Great Pacificator or the Great Compromiser. During his lifetime, and after his death in 1852, tens of thousands of Americans praised the Kentuckian for his central role in settling with compromise the sectional crises over Missouri in 1820–21, over nullification in 1832–33, and over the Mexican Cession in 1850. Second, although Lincoln always praised Clay extravagantly, declaring him "my beau ideal of a statesman," the president-elect spurned compromise in 1860–61.[4]

Perhaps Lincoln's most well-known remarks on Clay came in a eulogy he delivered in Springfield on July 6, 1852, only a week after Clay's death. In it Lincoln praised the Kentucky statesman for "his leading and most conspicuous part" in devising sectional compromise. At the same time, Lincoln underscored that "as a politician or statesman no one was so habitually careful [as Clay] to avoid all sectional ground. Whatever he did he did for the country." Showering adulation on Clay for his willingness and his ability to work with political opponents as well as allies, Lincoln highlighted his main point that Clay "engaged his whole energies" on behalf of the Union. As late as February 1861 Lincoln professed, "During my whole political life, I have loved and revered [Clay] as a teacher and leader."[5]

In the acclamation at Springfield, Lincoln also noted Clay's opposition to slavery. For Lincoln, that antislavery stance was vital, for as a sincere opponent of slavery, he could never embrace as his hero any man identified as proslavery. Several times thereafter Lincoln took care to point to Clay's detestation of slavery and particularly his opposition to the institution's spread. Although Lincoln did not invent an antislavery Clay, he overlooked or downplayed his paladin's willingness to moderate his stance.[6]

Without doubt Clay did detest slavery, even striving unsuccessfully for Kentucky to adopt gradual emancipation. Clay also said he could never support forcing slavery into any area where it had not previously existed. Yet in 1850, referring specifically to the Mexican Cession, he declared that if the citizens there placed slavery in their constitution, he would honor their choice. And Clay did back the Compromise of 1850, which left open the possibility of slavery in the New Mexico and Utah territories. For Clay, no other political or moral issue, slavery included, matched in importance the maintenance of the Union.[7]

Lincoln, too, spoke about compromise and initially did not turn from it. By his own account, he treasured the Missouri Compromise, and he publicly stood for the Compromise of 1850. In fact, in his first major address attacking the Kansas-Nebraska Act for overturning the Missouri Compromise, Lincoln sounded very much like Henry Clay himself. "I too, go for saving the Union," he declared but went on to explain, "Much as I hate slavery, I would consent to the extension of it rather than see the Union dissolved, just as I would consent to any Great evil, to avoid a Greater one." In the late 1850s, however, such declarations disappeared, though as late as 1858 he indicated his acquiescence in the Compromise of 1850.[8]

Positions on major sectional compromise, either in the past or possibly in the future, were certainly not central in the selection of a Republican presidential candidate in 1860. After all, before the nominating convention met in May, nothing had occurred that occasioned calls for compromise or for the party to declare its stance on one. Without question, however, all leading contenders for the nomination accepted what had become almost an article of faith for Republicans—no slavery in any territory.

The convention did not act as most observers thought it would. The leading Republican contender, Senator William Henry Seward of New York, famous for his announcements of a "higher law" than the Constitution and of an "irrepressible conflict" between North and South, between freedom and slavery, was set aside. Seward lost because many

Republican politicians feared he could not win the presidential election. Specifically, they worried that voters in the lower portion of states like Illinois, Indiana, and Pennsylvania—states essential for Republican victory—would reject Seward as being too radical. The convention delegates eventually chose Abraham Lincoln, a man widely seen as less radical than Seward and thus more electable.

Yet a closer look, even by Republicans in 1860, would have cast considerable doubt on any assumption that Lincoln was more conservative than Seward. In his widely distributed "House Divided" speech, Lincoln had explicitly pronounced that the country "cannot endure permanently half *slave* and half *free*." In substance, the notion of the "house divided" and the irrepressibility of conflict mesh perfectly; they were synonymous. One great difference did exist, however. Far more prominent in 1860 than Lincoln, Seward had been the eminent spokesman of antislavery politics for a decade. As far back as 1850 condemning any territorial compromise, he had called on a higher law than the Constitution. For Republicans hungering for victory, Seward had simply been in the public eye for too long. He was passed over.[9]

The Republican decision to jettison Seward and go with Lincoln might well have been the major reason for the party's triumph in the presidential election. Lincoln carried all the critical states on the way to a virtual sweep of the free states, only failing in New Jersey, where he shared the electoral vote. In the nation he won 180 electoral votes, a clear majority, though he received none in any of the slave states. But the popular vote was another matter. He managed only 39.8 percent. In ten slave states he received no votes at all. Since the widespread adoption of popular voting in Andrew Jackson's time, no previous president had gone into office with such a small percentage of the popular vote.

The basic outline of President-Elect Lincoln's position on secession and compromise is well known. Initially, he rejected secession as a serious possibility. One who saw him in Springfield reported that Lincoln considered the secession movement as "a sort of game of bluff." Another visitor wrote, "The threats of secession do not alarm him." To his law partner William H. Herndon, Lincoln confided he "could not in his heart believe the South designed to overthrow of the government." Underscoring his miscalculations, he even defined the military preparation in some

Deep South states as positive, for it would enable "the people the more easily to suppress any uprising there."[10]

At the same time that Lincoln misread the danger of secession, he missed few opportunities to proclaim his steadfast, unyielding opposition to any compromise of the most contentious and vexing question, slavery in the territories. Almost without exception, southerners maintained that the Constitution empowered them to take slave property into any territory, a right affirmed by the United States Supreme Court in the Dred Scott decision of 1857. Even so, many southerners indicated a willingness to accept division of the national domain, with part open to slavery and part closed. In contrast, the Republican platform pronounced no slavery in the territories Republican gospel. Lincoln made clear his devotion; he would "never consent to the *lowering of the Republican standard in the least*." He voiced identical professions to President James Buchanan's unofficial emissary and to Republicans in Congress and out, including Thurlow Weed, the influential New York editor and confidant of Seward. To Weed's suggestion that Republicans entertain compromise, Lincoln responded, "I will be inflexible on the territorial question." As he instructed others, the president-elect had made up his mind to "hold firm, as with a chain of steel."[11]

No matter Lincoln's opinion, secession became neither theory nor threat on December 20, 1860, when South Carolina solemnly left the Union. By the end of the next month, five more Deep South states had seceded, with a sixth, Texas, far down that road. Yet this actual breaking up of the Union did not move Lincoln, nor did the creation in February 1861 of the Confederate States of America. He simply iterated and reiterated that the Union remained whole. On that point he left no doubt: "I hold in contemplation of universal law and the Constitution, the Union of these States is perpetual."[12]

While Lincoln remained unequivocal in opposing compromise even as the Union came apart, his reasons for doing so have not been clearly delineated. To my mind, the evidence leads to three central causes: his ignorance of the South, his vigorous partisanship, and his visceral antislavery commitment. This list has no rank order, for in my judgment the record does not warrant such a ranking. Yet it does appear to me that Lincoln's lack of understanding about the South was formative.

Dismissing the seriousness of secession and looking on it as a conspiracy plotted by a small band of radicals soon to be put down by sensible Union men like himself, Lincoln found no other explanation possible. As he saw it, the drive for secession certainly had nothing to do with anything he or his party had done or said. That conclusion leads inescapably to two observations. First, he clearly rationalized his "house divided" declaration, for in it he bluntly told southerners that the Union of the future had no place for their major economic and social institution. Moreover, the irrepressible-conflict scenario embraced by many Republicans did likewise. Could Lincoln have been tone deaf to how southerners would hear such assertions? He must have been, for he told a conservative Kentuckian that neither he nor any other "prominent Republican had justly made himself obnoxious to the South by anything he had said or done."[13]

Lincoln evidently never stopped to think how he would have reacted to a responsible southern political leader publicly maintaining that the free states had no place in a future Union. Yet he did react forcefully to what he claimed was a plot to nationalize slavery. In his rhetoric that goal was part of a slave power conspiracy. Even though Lincoln struck out on the stump against this specter, even suggesting that the United States Supreme Court intended to make Illinois a slave state, no important southern politician ever advocated such a cause.[14]

Second, it appears indisputable that he assumed such a stance because he knew so little about the South. Yes, at nineteen and twenty-two he had taken brief trips down the Ohio and Mississippi Rivers to New Orleans. Also, he was born in Kentucky, and his wife came from a slave-owning family in that state, as did his best friend, Joshua Speed. But that part of the border South was all that he knew. After his two youthful journeys to New Orleans in 1828 and 1831, he never traveled in the South beyond Kentucky. Aside from a few Kentuckians, he really did not know any southerners, certainly not any southern politicians. He had in the late 1840s served one term in the United States House of Representatives, where he surely met southerners and was friendly with a few. But that was almost a decade and a half before the crisis of 1860–61. In the interim he had kept up with none of those men. Fundamentally, he had no friends who could educate him about the South and southern politics.[15]

The record indicates that Lincoln's image of the slave South basically matched the common abolitionist and fervent antislavery depictions. In this South rich planters dominated society and politics, in 1860–61 agitating for secession and cowing nonslaveholding whites. He appears to have had no understanding either of the widespread ownership of slaves among whites or how deeply slavery had become embedded in southern society. Instead of comprehending that the overwhelming majority of southern whites were committed to their slave society, it appears that Lincoln thought of them as conservative Unionists with little attachment to slavery. In other words, they were like him, though probably without the moral outrage at slavery. Perhaps the mass of southern whites could not or would not act against slavery, but he could imagine them neither proslave nor on their own acting against the Union. A South where nonplanters and even nonslaveholders had an influential political voice, feared Republicans, and actively supported secession was both foreign and unknown to Lincoln. When a visitor in early November urged Lincoln to reassure southerners honestly alarmed by a Republican triumph, his reply spoke volumes: "There are no such men."[16]

In light of the famous epistolary exchange between Lincoln and Alexander H. Stephens of Georgia in November and December 1860, historians have often described the two men as friends. Such a definition is surely an exaggeration, for they had only seen each other during the sessions of the Thirtieth Congress and had not been in contact since Lincoln left Washington in early 1849. In his request on November 30, 1860, for a copy of Stephens's address to the Georgia legislature, Lincoln indicated he had seen newspaper accounts. Responding, Stephens said they were substantially correct.[17]

I wonder how carefully Lincoln read the speech. Yes, Stephens did deplore the rush to secession just because Lincoln had been elected. At the same time, however, Stephens left no doubt about his opinion of the Republican party. "If the policy of Mr. Lincoln and his Republican associates shall be carried out," he announced, "no man in Georgia will be more willing or ready than myself to defend our rights, interest, and honor at every hazard and to the last extremity." Defining that policy, Stephens gave primary importance to a congressional prohibition of slavery from the common territory. Of course, for Lincoln, that restriction was the primary Republican mission. Stephens urged Georgia to delay, not because he found the Republican program acceptable or because he would acquiesce in it, but because he argued that a Congress controlled by Democrats along with the federal judiciary would thwart Lincoln. He predicted an enfeebled Lincoln presidency that could do the South no harm.

The four letters the men exchanged certainly have a civility about them, with each man assuring the other of his respect. Stephens drew empathetic attention to Lincoln's massive burden, telling him that "no man ever had heavier or greater responsibility resting upon him than you have in the present momentous crisis." Trying to be conciliatory and reassuring, Lincoln, on December 22 in a letter marked "For your eyes only," stated that he "appreciate[d] the present peril." He also told Stephens that the South had nothing to fear from him or a Republican administration. Word even came to Stephens indirectly that Lincoln called him "a great man." Still, Lincoln did recognize that he and Stephens differed on the "right" and "wrong" of slavery.

In his second letter, dated December 30, Stephens declared, "Personally, I am not your enemy—far from it." He then called on Lincoln to do what he could "to save our common country." But Stephens was also pointed. Southerners worried, he wrote, that the Republicans' "leading object seems to be simply, and wantonly, if you please, to put the Institutions of nearly half the states under the ban of public opinion and national condemnation." He connected that object to "the influence of fanaticisms," which he saw influencing the Republican party. Yet the Georgian concluded that "a word fitly spoken by you now would be like 'apples of gold in pictures of silver.'" To this entreaty, Lincoln did not reply.

With no firsthand knowledge of the South and no friends or even serious acquaintances among southern politicians, Lincoln unsurprisingly did not acknowledge distinctions between Fire-Eaters, the zealous advocates of secession, and men like Stephens and even Jefferson Davis, who were fundamentally conservative with no relish for disunion. Lincoln gave no awareness that he understood the political force pressed by the radicals on southern conservatives and regulars.

The extent of popular support for immediate secession in the Deep South, still a vexing issue, is not my subject here. Even so, no conspiracy took those states out of the Union. Fire-Eaters surely pushed, and they drove for haste, but no secret cabal manipulated events from South Carolina to Texas. Every one of those states held a popular vote for delegates to conventions that would decide on secession.[18]

While Lincoln's ignorance of the South powerfully influenced his adamant opposition to compromise, his actions also make clear that he approached the crisis not as president-elect of the United States, but as leader of the Republican party. Moreover, he had in November 1860 but a few months as party chief. That brief tenure left him unsure about the security of his leadership and anxious about party unity. During the crisis, many Republicans and non-Republicans alike urged him to make a public statement addressing the issues, in which he would reassure southerners of their rights and his determination to be president of all Americans, southerners as well as northerners. Time and time again Lincoln adamantly refused.[19]

Responding to this cascade of requests, Lincoln embraced a mantra: "I could say nothing which I have not already said, and which is in print, and open to inspection to all." "*Repetition*" as he phrased it, could only do harm to his political position. Three observations seem pertinent. First, to repeat a point made earlier, he seemed to not fathom that some of his most vigorous rhetoric could terrify the South. Second, never did he acknowledge that every one of those statements had been made as a Republican partisan, not as the forthcoming president of a country. Furthermore, none of those declarations had been made when the country faced a monumental crisis.[20]

Lincoln never stepped forward in an effort to conciliate alarmed southerners. Given his unmatched gift for crafting the befitting phrases for a given political moment, one might imagine his theme, if not his words. Such an address could have noted his recognition that he was not one of them and that he represented a party perceived by the multitude of southerners as their enemy. Yet, he would have quickly countered, we are all still Americans, and during this presidency, neither he nor his party would in any way try to harm the South. Not once did Lincoln ever say publicly that he would be president of all Americans. In wedding himself to the Republican platform and claiming he could never deviate from it, he acted like a partisan's partisan, not the leader of a country.

The critical question focuses on the *why* underlying his rigidity. The evidence strongly suggests that he feared alienating his party's most fervent antislavery zealots, or in modern parlance, its left wing. Lincoln constantly expressed concern that any serious compromise would fracture the party—in other words, drive off the left. If that segment bolted because of a sectional compromise, Lincoln worried that the Republican party would disintegrate. That group did not, of course, encompass the Republican party. Undoubtedly, it was a minority, albeit an articulate, vigorous minority. Although precision about numbers is impossible, in a party whose adherents ranged from radicals like Charles Sumner to conservatives like Edward Bates to supreme pragmatists like Thurlow Weed, the hardline left wing could not have been a majority. The closest students of the party during the crisis underscore the divergence of opinion within its ranks and emphasize the strength of a great middle.[21]

A suggestive approach to assess Lincoln's course concentrates on William H. Seward, the preeminent Republican prior to Lincoln's nomination. For that nomination, Seward had been turned aside for being too radical, but in the aftermath of the election, he and his political partner, Thurlow Weed, moved sharply toward the center. During this period, many Republicans still looked to Seward as their chief, believing Lincoln untried and dubious about his ability. The party needed "to see in the lead the only person who can give the country confidence," Massachusetts congressman Charles Francis Adams wrote Seward.[22]

Evidence abounds that Seward was willing to grasp a serious sectional compromise, one that included the territorial issue. In his *Albany Evening Journal* Weed specifically proposed reviving and extending the Missouri Compromise line westward. The two men tried to keep Seward's name apart from that proposal until the political landscape became clearer. Yet the longtime closeness between them and the conversations they had after the election leave little doubt that they agreed. What is indisputable is that a number of Republicans indicated a willingness to take that road. Republican newspapers in cities like New York, Cincinnati, Pittsburgh, and Detroit saw merit in Weed's position. Likewise, businessmen in New York City who had voted for Lincoln lined up behind Weed. Additionally, many Republican politicians signaled their willingness to sign on for compromise.[23]

Although it is impossible to quantify precisely the compromise-inclined Republicans, they surely provided a substantial base for a leader who wanted to guide the party in that direction. Had the party done so, might secession have been thwarted? That is a complex question and not my concern here. But secessionists across the South prayed for Republican intransigence, dreading that a Republican commitment to compromise would torpedo their plans. In my judgment they had a legitimate worry, a worry that Seward recognized. As I read the evidence, Republican backing in November and December for anything resembling Weed's ideas might very well have stymied the Fire-Eaters everywhere but in South Carolina. Then the Nullification Crisis of 1832–33 would have been repeated—South Carolina alone confronting the United States.[24]

My concern here, however, is Seward and why he looked favorably on compromise. In my view he did so for at least three reasons. Early on, certainly by mid-November 1860, he perceived the Union in mortal danger. Above all, he wanted to prevent its dissolution if at all possible. Having been in Washington for the entire decade of the 1850s and knowing many southern politicians, he had a much better grasp than Lincoln of the political force of secession and the political reality facing the more moderate men in the Deep South. Then, he and Weed believed the territorial issue had done its work, elected a Republican to president. To them it was chiefly a political matter. With all the territory controlled by the United States in 1860 already covered by existing law, they thought any chance of adding new land remote and certainly not taking place without Republican concurrence. As Weed put it in a letter to Seward's senatorial colleague from New York: "There is no political temptation in all the territory belonging to us. The fight is over."[25]

Additionally, Seward and Weed saw the Republican victory in no small part as a result of Democratic division. Because they judged that "the normal proclivities of the American people are Democratic" and that "the issues of the late campaign are obsolete," they regarded new issues as necessary to keep the Republicans in power. In 1864 a reunited Democratic party would cause trouble for the Republicans unless the party could expand. Seward wanted to reach out to Unionists in the South, especially in the upper and border slave states. To him, bringing them into the Republican tent was both possible and essential. Without question a number of them, overwhelmingly former Whigs, made clear their willingness to come into a party that focused on the Union, not sectional antagonism. No evidence suggests that Lincoln at the time conceived of a Republican future beyond the borders of the 1860 party.[26]

As for the unity of the newly triumphant Republican party, Seward occupied different ground than Lincoln. Since the inception of the party and even before that as the major spokesman for antislavery northern Whigs, Seward had been the evangelist of the irrepressible conflict. He had the standing to withstand an assault from the Republican left, which would surely have come. Moreover, if a party opting for sectional compromise really distressed the zealots, where could they go? But even if the most radical bolted, the adherence of southern Unionists would offset their loss. Thus, for Seward, the Republican party would become the great Union party, with a solid presence in the slave states, particularly in the upper and border South. Lincoln did turn to the Union party idea, but only during the war. Before hostilities, he absolutely rejected such an initiative.

Although the record is not so clear as one would like, important southern leaders hoped that Seward would prevail in bringing his party to the compromise standard. This interpretation helps explain the timing of the southern reaction to the Senate Committee of Thirteen, created to search for a sectional compromise. Initially, senators from the Deep South, like Jefferson Davis, spurned the committee, but then they reconsidered, agreeing to serve. Davis also made clear his willingness to support any measure the committee adopted similar to the Missouri Compromise admitting southern rights in the territories. Another committee member, the avowed secessionist Robert Toombs of Georgia, stated that if the committee agreed on that kind of arrangement, he would accept it despite his lack of enthusiasm because it would satisfy his state.[27]

In Washington Seward remained publicly quiet, "mum as an oyster" in the colorful image of one Republican congressman. On December 14 Seward left the capital for home; at the same time, Thurlow Weed headed west for a meeting with the president-elect in Springfield. In his newspaper Weed repeated the call for compromise. But he found Lincoln still steadfastly opposed to anything resembling an extension of the Missouri Compromise line. Lincoln underlined to Weed what he had been telling others: no territorial compromise. Party policy on that point was granite. Upon his return to New York State, Weed met with Seward. When the senator returned to Washington, he voted with his fellow Republicans on the committee to refuse any serious territorial compromise. The Committee of Thirteen failed; the Deep South marched out of the Union.[28]

Seward was unwilling to cross the new party leader. And without question Seward's acquiescence in Lincoln's directive signaled that Lincoln was not only president-elect but also unquestionably the Republican chieftain. This is not the place to discuss why Seward bowed to Lincoln, but I want to note that even though Seward acceded to Lincoln's wishes, he kept trying to push the new leader to the right, all the way to Fort Sumter.[29]

In my view a third fundamental underlay Lincoln's rejection of compromise. I am persuaded that he had a much deeper, more visceral hatred of slavery than did Seward. Seward did abhor slavery, never giving it equal billing with freedom. Convinced, however, that the rapid geographic expansion along with the burgeoning economic power of the free states would naturally overpower slavery, he was willing to let the institution and the southern political strength based on it become casualties of America's inevitable progress. Thus, after the territorial issue had accomplished its political task in 1860, Seward was quite willing to shelve it.

Not so Lincoln—to him the territorial issue was never just about politics. To him it spoke about the nation, even if primarily as symbol. That conviction informed his Cooper Union speech of February 1860, which made him a viable presidential possibility to eastern Republicans. In that address Lincoln, concentrating on a discrete group of men, insisted that the Founding Fathers had intended an antislavery future for the new republic. In Lincoln's version of history, that noble goal had somehow been shunted aside. The duty of Republicans was to restore its primacy. On that February evening in New York City, Lincoln's remarks were brilliant as a partisan cry and legal brief, but one-sided as history. For three decades after the ratification of the Constitution, slavery and freedom had marched westward side by side. That simultaneous movement had occurred with powerful support from leading members of the Founding Fathers. New territories open to slavery had been acquired or organized under every president from George Washington to James Monroe.[30]

Those facts did not deter Lincoln. For him, the venerated fathers simply could not have countenanced the extension of the great evil of the country. Thus, for Lincoln, to accept any compromise that even theoretically permitted the possibility of expanding slavery meant turning from a vision he cherished both of past and future. Even if only symbolic, territorial compromise signified a moral blot. Accordingly, for Lincoln, the Union as a good in itself was less powerful than an antislavery Union. To Alexander Stephens he put it starkly: slavery was "wrong." As a result, Lincoln was willing to risk the Union of the fathers to get his antislavery Union. Yet in the winter of 1860–61, he could not imagine the price of his gamble.[31]

To return to my initial query about Lincoln and Henry Clay, in this essay I have advanced my views about why, despite his words, Lincoln in the great crisis of the Union did not look to Henry Clay. In those momentous weeks Seward demonstrated himself, much more than Lincoln, a man of national outlook. In the winter of 1860–61 the New Yorker acted like the disciple of Clay. In this instance Seward had legitimate claim to the mantle of Henry Clay.

NOTES

PREFACE

1. In Lawrence Lee Hewitt and Arthur W. Bergeron, eds., *Confederate Generals in the Western Theater,* vol. 1 (Knoxville, Tenn., 2010).

CHAPTER ONE

1. This essay was originally published in *The Journal of Southern History* 36, no. 2 (May 1970): 189–204.

2. McKitrick, "Party Politics and the Union and Confederate War Efforts," in William N. Chambers and W. Dean Burnham, eds., *The American Party Systems: Stages of Development* (New York, 1967), 119.

3. Many of the works cited below give part of the Lincoln-Davis story.

4. *Richmond Examiner,* September 5, 1864; Edward A. Pollard, *The Second Year of the War* (Richmond, 1863), 302.

5. Pollard, *Second Year of the War,* 302.

6. Pollard, *Life of Jefferson Davis, with a Secret History of the Southern Confederacy* (Philadelphia, 1869), vi.

7. Pollard, *The Lost Cause: A New Southern History of the War of the Confederates* (New York, 1866), 91.

8. Dowdey, *Experiment in Rebellion* (Garden City, N.Y., 1946); and *The Land They Fought For: The Story of the South as the Confederacy, 1832–1865* (Garden City, N.Y., 1955). The quotation comes from *Experiment in Rebellion,* 372.

9. Williams, *Lincoln and His Generals* (New York, 1952), 7.

10. Potter, "Jefferson Davis and the Political Factors in Confederate Defeat," in David Donald, ed., *Why the North Won the Civil War* (Baton Rouge, 1960), 106.

11. Strode, *Jefferson Davis: American Patriot, 1808–1861* (New York, 1955); *Jefferson Davis: Confederate President* (New York, 1959); and *Jefferson Davis: Tragic Hero; The Last Twenty-Five Years, 1864–1889* (New York, 1964).

12. See the superb review by David Donald in the *New York Times Book Review,* September 27, 1964, 6.

13. Jones, *Confederate Strategy from Shiloh to Vicksburg* (Baton Rouge, 1961), 239.

14. Patrick, *Jefferson Davis and His Cabinet* (Baton Rouge, 1944), 44.

15. Vandiver, "Jefferson Davis and Confederate Strategy," in Avery O. Craven and Frank E. Vandiver, eds., *The American Tragedy: The Civil War in Retrospect* (Hampden-Sydney, Va., 1959), 19–32 (quotations on 20 and 32).

16. The only general history of the Army of Tennessee is Stanley F. Horn's *The Army of Tennessee* (Norman, 1953). Two excellent volumes treat the earlier years of the war—Thomas L. Connelly, *Army of the Heartland: The Army of Tennessee, 1861–1862* (Baton Rouge, 1967); and Jones, *Confederate Strategy*—and form the basis for the generalizations on that period.

17. Horn, *Army of Tennessee,* 307–8.

18. Jones, *Confederate Strategy,* passim.

19. The most recent biography of Johnston is Gilbert E. Govan and James W. Livingood, *A Different Valor: The Story of General Joseph E. Johnston, C.S.A.* (Indianapolis and New York, 1956). Jones in *Confederate Strategy* and Alfred H. Burne in *Lee, Grant and Sherman: A Study in Leadership in the 1864–1865 Campaign* (New York, 1939) discuss various aspects of his generalship.

20. Seddon to Johnston, December 18, 1863, *The War of the Rebellion: A Compilation of the Official Records of the Union and Confederate Armies,* 70 vols. in 128 pts. (Washington, D.C., 1880–1901), ser. 1, vol. 31, pt. 3, 842–43 (hereinafter cited as *O.R.*).

21. For the Atlanta Campaign, see Burne, *Lee, Grant, and Sherman,* 70–100; Horn, *Army of Tennessee,* 305–40; and Lloyd Lewis, *Sherman, Fighting Prophet* (New York, 1932), 375–87.

22. For an absorbing account of Lee's fight against Grant, see Clifford Dowdey, *Lee's Last Campaign: The Story of Lee and His Men against Grant—1864* (Boston, 1960).

23. Bragg to Johnston, June 7, 1864, *O.R.,* ser. 1, vol. 38, pt. 4, 762. Thomas R. Hay's "The Davis-Hood Johnston Controversy of 1864," *Mississippi Valley Historical Review* 11 (June 1924): 54–84, has a minutely detailed discussion of the relief of Johnston.

24. Robert G. H. Kean, *Inside the Confederate Government: The Diary of Robert Garlick Hill Kean,* ed. Edward Younger (New York, 1957), 165.

25. Telegrams did arrive at the War Department from the Army of Tennessee between May and July 1864, but they reported minor actions, personnel problems, and similar matters. Never did Johnston talk about the course of his campaign, and he admitted as much. Johnston to Bragg, June 27, 1864, *O.R.,* ser. 1, vol. 38, pt. 4, 795–96.

26. Johnston to Bragg, July 11, 1864, ibid., pt. 5, 876.

27. Davis to Bragg, July 9, 1864, in Dunbar Rowland, ed., *Jefferson Davis, Constitutionalist: His Letters, Papers and Speeches,* 10 vols. (Jackson, Miss., 1923), 6:286.

28. Bragg to Davis, July 13, 1864, *O.R.,* ser. 1, vol. 38, pt. 5, 878; Bragg to Davis, July 15, 1864, ibid., vol. 39, pt. 2, 712–14 (two final quotations on 713).

29. Seddon to Hill, July 13, 1864, ibid., vol. 52, pt. 2, 693–95; Hill to Seddon, July 14, 1864, ibid., 704–7. Hill had a free and open conversation with Johnston. Govan and Livingood, *Different Valor,* 299–300.

30. Davis to Lee, July 12, 1864, Rowland, *Jefferson Davis,* 6:291–92.

31. Lee to Davis, July 12, 1864, Clifford Dowdey and Louis H. Manarin, eds., *The Wartime Papers of R. E. Lee* (Boston and Toronto, 1961), 821–22.

32. Jefferson Davis, *The Rise and Fall of the Confederate Government,* 2 vols. (New York, 1881), 2:560–61; Roy W Curry, "James A. Seddon, a Southern Prototype," *Virginia Magazine of History and Biography* 61 (April 1955): 140.

33. Benjamin to Davis, February 15, 1879, Walter Lynwood Fleming Collection, New York Public Library.

34. Louise B. Hill, *Joseph E. Brown and the Confederacy* (Chapel Hill, 1939), 182–83.

35. Both letters are in *O.R.,* ser. 1, vol. 38, pt. 5, 882–83.

36. Ibid., 885.

37. Lee to Davis, July 12, 1864, Dowdey and Manarin, *Wartime Papers of R. E. Lee,* 821–22.

38. Hay, "Davis-Hood-Johnston Controversy of 1864," 55, 76.

39. Among Hood's critics are W. Birkbeck Wood and James E. Edmonds, *Military History of the Civil War with Special Reference to the Campaign of 1864 and 1865* (New York, 1960), 160–73; and Thomas R. Hay, "The Atlanta Campaign," *Georgia Historical Quarterly* 7 (March and June 1923): 32–43, 100–18.

40. Burne, *Lee, Grant and Sherman,* 110. See also Burne, "General J. B. Hood," *Army Quarterly and Defence Journal* 79 (January 1960): 220–23.

41. J. B. Jones, *A Rebel War Clerk's Diary at the Confederate States Capital,* ed. Howard Swiggett, 2 vols. (New York 1935), 2:277. In addition, consult Mary B. Chestnut, *A Diary from Dixie,* ed. Ben Ames Williams (Boston, 1949), 443.

42. Jones, *Rebel War Clerk's Diary,* 2:288; Horn, *Army of Tennessee,* 371; *Richmond Examiner,* September 5, 1864; Josiah Gorgas, *The Civil War Diary of General Josiah Gorgas,* ed. Frank E. Vandiver (Tuscaloosa, 1947), 140.

43. Horn, *Army of Tennessee,* 372–73; J. B. Hood, *Advance and Retreat: Personal Experiences in the United States and Confederate States Armies* (New Orleans, 1880), 253–55.

44. Hood indicated his thinking on September 22 in a letter to Bragg, *O.R.* ser. 1, vol. 39, pt. 2, 862.

45. Both Bragg and Lieutenant General Richard Taylor, the commander of the Department of Alabama and Mississippi, whom Davis visited when he left Hood's army, objected to an offensive campaign. They argued that Hood's lack of strength and Sherman's overwhelming force made remote the chances of Confederate success. Of course, adopting the defensive in no way guaranteed success either. Richard Taylor, *Destruction and Reconstruction: Personal Experiences of the Late War* (New York, 1879), 205–6; Bragg to Davis, September 29, 1864, quoted in Don C. Seitz, *Braxton Bragg: General of the Confederacy* (Columbia, S.C., 1924), 462.

46. Rowland, *Jefferson Davis,* 6:341–44 (Macon), 345–47 (Montgomery), 356–61 (Augusta), 349–56 (Columbia).

47. Pollard, *Southern History of the War: The Last Year of the War* (New York, 1866), 92.

48. See note 41 above.

49. Alfred Roman, *The Military Operations of General Beauregard in the War Between*

the States 1861 to 1865, 2 vols. (New York, 1883), 2:273–5; Lee to Davis, September 19, 1864, Letterbook, June 7, 1863–October 12, 1864, Robert Edward Lee Papers, Virginia Historical Society, Richmond; T. Harry Williams, *P. G. T. Beauregard: Napoleon in Gray* (Baton Rouge, 1955), 238–40.

50. Undated manuscript on military operations, P. G. T. Beauregard Papers, Manuscript Division, Library of Congress; Roman, *Beauregard,* 2:275–79. The second major segment of Beauregard's new command was Richard Taylor's Department of Alabama and Mississippi.

51. Williams, *Beauregard,* 242 (quotation); Thomas R. Hay, *Hood's Tennessee Campaign* (New York, 1929), 28–29.

52. Jones, *Rebel War Clerk's Diary,* 2:300.

53. Frank E. Vandiver, *Rebel Brass: The Confederate Command System* (Baton Rouge, 1956), 35 (quotation); Craven and Vandiver, *American Tragedy,* 31.

54. Vandiver, *Rebel Brass,* 34–35, 57–59; Jones, *Confederate Strategy,* 89–197 passim.

55. Davis to Hood, September 28, 1864, Rowland, *Jefferson Davis,* 6:344–45.

56. *O.R.,* ser. 1, vol., 39, pt. 3, 782; Davis to Beauregard, November 1, 1864, Rowland, *Jefferson Davis,* 6:368.

57. Johnston's performance as commanding general of the Department of the West illustrates this attitude. Also, consult Williams, *Lincoln and His Generals,* 245.

58. Roman, *Beauregard,* 2:279.

59. Burne, *Lee, Grant, and Sherman,* 125–38; Jacob D. Cox, *Atlanta* (New York, 1882), 225–26.

60. Sherman to his wife, October 11, 1864, M. A. De Wolfe Howe, ed., *Home Letters of General Sherman* (New York, 1909), 310.

61. Sherman to George Thomas, October 20, 1864, quoted in Freeman Cleaves, *Rock of Chickamauga: The Life of General George H. Thomas* (Norman, 1948), 245. Also see Burne, "General J. B. Hood," 225.

62. Hood, *Advance and Retreat,* 264–69; John P. Dyer, *The Gallant Hood* (Indianapolis and New York, 1950), 281–82.

63. Roman, *Beauregard,* 2:287–88; *O.R.,* ser. 1, vol. 45, pt. 1, 647–48; Beauregard to Charles Jones, April 1, 1875, Beauregard Papers.

64. *O.R.,* ser. 1, vol. 39, pt. 3, 841; ibid., pt. 1, 796–98.

65. Actually, he sent Davis a copy of a new dispatch to the War Department. Ibid., pt. 3, 870.

66. For the quotation, see ibid., vol. 45, pt., 1, 1226. See also ibid., 1215; and ibid., vol. 39, pt. 1, 800.

67. Ibid., pt. 3, 913, and Hood, *Advance and Retreat,* 272–74, contain Hood's reasons for his long delay. The closest student of Hood's activities found most of Hood's explanations unconvincing; he suggested that Hood procrastinated but really put forth no new and persuasive reasons for the long stay in Tuscumbia. Hay, *Hood's Tennessee Campaign,* 61–66.

68. Cleave, *Rock of Chickamauga,* 244–50; Wood and Edmonds, *Military History,* 230n; Jacob D. Cox, *The March to the Sea: Franklin and Nashville* (New York, 1884), 7, 14; Hay, *Hood's Tennessee Campaign,* 50–51, 83–102.

69. Davis to Hood, November 7, 1864, Rowland, *Jefferson Davis,* 6:398–99.

70. Davis to Beauregard, November 30, 1864, ibid., 413.

71. Davis, *Rise and Fall,* 2:569–70.

72. Davis to Lucius Northrop, April 9, 1879, Fleming Collection.

73. See notes 62 and 67 above.

CHAPTER TWO

1. This essay was original published in *South Carolina Historical Magazine* vol. 73, no. 4 (October 1972): 209–19.

2. For a summary, see Paul M. Gaston, "The 'New South,'" in Arthur S. Link and Rembert Patrick, eds., *Writing Southern History: Essays in Historiography in Honor of Fletcher M. Green* (Baton Rouge, 1965), 327–31.

3. William J. Cooper Jr., *The Conservative Regime: South Carolina, 1877–1890* (Baltimore, 1968). South Carolina Bourbons called themselves Conservatives and Conservative Democrats; I am merely repeating their usage.

4. Ibid., chap. 6.

5. Augustine Smythe to William A. Courtenay, August 23, 1890, William A. Courtenay Papers, South Caroliniana Library, University of South Carolina, Columbia.

6. There has been no first-rate study of the Haskell movement. For brief comments, see Cooper, *Conservative Regime,* 202 and n.; George B. Tindall, *South Carolina Negroes, 1877–1900* (Columbia, 1952), 51–53; and Francis B. Simkins, *Pitchfork Ben Tillman: South Carolinian* (Baton Rouge, 1944), 164–68.

7. Joseph W. Barnwell (a Haskelite), "Life and Reflections of Joseph W. Barnwell," unpublished autobiography (typescript dated 1929), 468, South Carolina Historical Society, Charleston.

8. For a full account of the convention, the delegates, and the pronouncements, see *Charleston News and Courier,* October 10, 1890.

9. Quoted in Tindall, *Negroes,* 52.

10. Cooper, *Conservative Regime,* 106.

11. The racial proportions refer only to males over twenty-one years of age, the potential voters. *Charleston News and Courier,* July 4, 1882, has a district by district breakdown.

12. Cooper, *Conservative Regime,* 103–7; Tindall, *Negroes,* 61–64, 66–67.

13. Cooper, *Conservative Regime,* 108, 168–73.

14. Table 2.1.

15. *Charleston News and Courier,* November 22, 1886.

16. For the final vote, see table 2.1. The turnout of 73,987 voters in 1890 was greater than in any year since 1882, when the Greenback party mounted a weak and unsuccessful challenge to Democratic supremacy (Cooper, *Conservative Regime,* 70–72), but still the turnout was smaller than one would expect. Even the Tillman managers expressed surprise that the vote had not been larger. *Charleston News and Courier,* November 6, 1890.

17. A "Tillman county" is one that increased its Democratic vote between 1888 and 1890.

18. Table 2.2.

19. The statistical techniques used are the Spearman rank-order formula and the Pearson product-moment formula, the more sophisticated and precise of the two. Both formulae use the coefficient of correlation; this coefficient is a measure of association between two variables, measuring the extent to which they vary in respect to each other. A value of +1.0 indicates a perfect positive association, -1.0 a perfect negative one, zero no association. A value of ±.50 is the criterion for the existence of a significant relationship between two variables. A more detailed discussion is in Hubert M. Blalock, *Social Statistics* (New York, 1960), 285–92, 317–19.

The coefficient of correlation (product-moment correlation) between per-capita agricultural wealth and increased Democratic vote is -.006 in the Tillman counties; in the state as a whole, it is -.20 (rank-order correlation). The coefficient of correlation (product-moment correlation) between per-capita land value and increased Democratic vote is +.47 in the Tillman counties; in the state as a whole it is -.33 (rank-order correlation). Tables 2.3 and 2.4 contain the statistical data for all computations unless otherwise noted.

In my computations in this essay with the Tillman counties, I omitted Orangeburg County, which had an increased Democratic vote of 141 percent—abnormally high for the state. To include Orangeburg, however, does not alter the coefficients of correlation or my findings in any significant way.

20. I termed substantial portion at least 20 percent of the vote in any county. The coefficient of correlation (rank-order correlation) between per-capita agricultural wealth and the Haskell vote is +.03 (omitting Charleston County, whose wealth of $6.53 is far below the average, the coefficient of correlation rank-order correlation is -.01). The coefficient of correlation (rank-order correlation) between per-capita value of land and the Haskell vote is -.11; the coefficient of correlation (rank-order correlation) between total per-capita wealth and the Haskell vote is .00. For figures, see table 2.5.

21. But after gaining power Tillman did nothing to change the South Carolina law. Cooper, *Conservative Regime,* 138. For a description of the crop lien system see Fred A. Shannon, *The Farmers' Last Frontier: Agriculture, 1860–1897,* vol. 5 of Henry David et al., eds., *The Economic History of the United States* (New York, 1945), 89–95.

22. The coefficient of correlation (rank-order correlation) between value of land mortgaged and increased Democratic vote is +.20 in Tillman counties; for the state as a whole, the coefficient of correlation (rank-order correlation) is +.02.

The coefficient of correlation (rank-order correlation) between number of mortgages and increased Democratic vote is +.43 in the Tillman counties.

23. The coefficient of correlation (rank-order correlation) between percentages of farms rented or sharecropped and increased Democratic vote is +.45 in the Tillman counties; for the entire state, it is +.15.

24. The coefficient of correlation (rank-order correlation) between the ascending average-size farm and increased Democratic vote is -.05 in the Tillman counties; for the entire state, it is +.16. In fact the average farm in the Tillman counties, omitting Orangeburg, contained 115.9 acres (omitting Orangeburg and the five counties under 20 percent, it had 131.9 acres). The average for the state was 115 acres. Whether or not rented parts of large farms were counted as independent farms in 1890 is a disputed point. In the agricultural

census of 1890, it is reported that if the average farm in 1890 were smaller than in 1880, it "may be due to reporting certain large plantations in one case as single farms and reporting their various subdivisions in the other case as separate holdings." *Eleventh Census of the United States: 1890, Statistics of Agriculture* (Washington, D.C., 1895), 2. Generally for the plight of agriculture, see Cooper, *Conservative Regime,* 134–35, 217–18; and Shannon, *Farmers' Last Frontier,* chaps. 4 and 5, and p. 415 for cotton prices.

The coefficient of correlation (rank- order correlation) between cotton production and the increased Tillman vote is +.10 in the Tillman counties.

25. The coefficient of correlation (rank-order correlation) between per-capita industrial wealth and increased Democratic vote is -.09 in the Tillman counties; for the entire state, it is -.14. See also Gustauvus G. Williamson Jr., "South Carolina Cotton Mills and the Tillman Movement," *Proceedings of the South Carolina Historical Association* (1949): 44–45.

26. For statistics, see table 2.6.

27. The coefficient of correlation (rank-order correlation) between the increased Democratic vote and the percentage of white voters is +.5 for the state as a whole and +.63 for the Tillman counties. See table 2.7.

Lacking voter registration figures, I used the number of white or Negro males over twenty-one, as listed in the census, for the potential voters. *Compendium of the Eleventh Census: 1890, Part 1, Population* (Washington, D.C., 1892), 798–99.

28. The coefficient of correlation (rank-order correlation) between the percentage of potential Negro voters and the percentage of the Haskell vote is +.5 for the entire state and +.52 for the Haskell counties.

29. Tindall, *Negroes,* 52. Also, see James Welch Patton, "The Republican Party in South Carolina, 1876–1895," in Fletcher Melvin Green, ed., *Essays in Southern History* (Chapel Hill, 1940), 94. The white Republican was E. W. M. Mackey (1882–1884); the Negroes were Robert Smalls (1884–1886) and Thomas E. Miller (1888–1892).

30. The coefficient of correlation (product-moment correlation) between percentage of vote for Haskell, in the Haskell counties, and the percentage of the vote for Benjamin Harrison in 1888 is +.95. See table 2.8.

31. *Charleston News and Courier,* October 7, 1890.

32. *Greenville News,* October 11, 1890, quoted in *Charleston News and Courier,* October 13, 1890.

CHAPTER THREE

1. This essay was originally published in *Agricultural History* 49 (April 1975): 381–91. It appears here courtesy of The Agricultural History Society.

2. Charles W. Ramsdell, "The Natural Limits of Slavery Expansion," *Mississippi Valley Historical Review* 16 (September 1929): 151–71.

3. Eugene D. Genovese, *The Political Economy of Slavery: Studies in the Economy and Society of the Slave South* (New York, 1965). Parts 1, 2, and 4 deal with the topics discussed in this paragraph; for the critique of Ramsdell, see 251–55.

4. Ibid., 243.

5. Robert William Fogel and Stanley L. Engerman, *Time on the Cross,* 2 vols. (Boston and Toronto, 1974).

6. Sam B. Hilliard, *Hog Meat and Hoecake: Food Supply in the Old South, 1840–1860* (Carbondale, 1972).

7. Genovese, *Political Economy of Slavery,* esp. 244–50. Of course all politicians did not advocate expansion, either for economic or any other reasons. Even ardent southern nationalists like James H. Hammond of South Carolina urged that southerners develop the lands they possessed rather than look for new horizons. Hammond to William Gilmore Simms, 20 January 1858, James H. Hammond Papers, Division of Manuscripts, Library of Congress; U.S. Congress, *Congressional Globe,* 35th Cong., 1st Sess., pt. 1, 961.

8. Fogel and Engerman, *Time on the Cross,* 1:103–5 (quotation on 105), 2:87, note 3.10; 2:73, table B.9.

9. Lewis Cecil Gray, *History of Agriculture in the Southern United States to 1860,* 2 vols. (Washington, D.C., 1933; rept. ed., Gloucester, Mass., 1958), 2:641–42.

10. Fogle and Engerman, *Time on the Cross,* 1:97.

11. Genovese, *Political Economy of Slavery,* 246–47.

12. Otis C. Skipper, *J. D. B. De Bow: Magazinist of the old South* (Athens, Ga., 1958), 24, 88.

13. Weymouth T. Jordan, "Noah B. Cloud and the *American Cotton Planter,*" *Agricultural History* 31 (October 1957): 44.

14. These journals were read for the years noted in parenthesis: *De Bow's Review* (1854–1860); *American Cotton Planter* (1853–1858); *Soil of the South* (1850–1860); *Southern Planter* (1850–54, 1858); *Southern Cultivator* (1850–60); *Southern Agriculturalist* (1853).

15. *Southern Cultivator* 9 (January 1851): 9.

16. *De Bow's Review* 26 (January 1859): 92; 26 (May 1859): 582–83; see also 26 (June 1859): 707; 22 (February 1857): 180–93, 197–201; 22 (April 1857): 335–49; and 21 (September 1856): 308–23.

17. *Soil of the South* 2 (January 1853): 393–94; see also 2 (June 1853): 553.

18. *Southern Cultivator* 16 (May 1858): 138–39.

19. *American Cotton Planter* 12 (December 1858): 381; see also 3 (March 1855): 87; and 3 (August 1855): 246.

20. *De Bow's Review* 29 (August, 1860): 216.

21. *Southern Agriculturalist* 1 (October 1853): 296.

22. *American Cotton Planter* 12 (June 1858): 181; 12 (July 1858): 210; *De Bow's Review* 24 (March 1858): 232–36; 29 (September 1860): 375–77; 16 (June 1854): 603.

23. *Southern Agriculturalist* 1 (June 1853): 205.

24. *De Bow's Review* 16 (May 1854): 455.

25. *Southern Cultivator* 13 (January 1855): 9.

26. Even a cursory glance at any volume of any journal substantiates these two generalizations. Very occasionally a contributor expressed concern that some farmers might not heed the cries of reform. See *American Cotton Planter* 3 (February 1855).

27. *Soil of the South* 3 (August 1853): 628.

28. See all journals, passim.

29. For example, *Soil of the South* 3 (April 1853): 499; *Southern Planter* 18 (April 1858): 231; *Southern Cultivator* 13 (March 1855): 76; and 17 (March 1859): 75; *De Bow's Review* 25 (October 1858): 395–404; and 29 (July 1860): 109–10; *American Cotton Planter* 3 (January 1855): 21; and 4 (April 1856): 121–22.

30. Genovese, *Political Economy of Slavery,* 90–91. On this problem Fogel and Engerman point to increasing value of land and improvements as indicating that fertility was maintained. *Time on the Cross,* 1:198.

31. Genovese, *Political Economy of Slavery,* 95.

32. C. Vann Woodward, *Origins of the New South, 1877–1914* (Baton Rouge, 1951), 182; Fred A. Shannon, *The Farmer's Last Frontier: Agriculture, 1860–1897,* Economic History of the United States, vol. 5 (New York, 1945), 114–16.

33. Recent investigators have begun to challenge the traditional view of overproduction; they find production (supply) increasing to meet an increasing demand. See Fogel and Engerman, *Time on the Cross,* 1:96; and Stephen Decanio, "Cotton 'Overproduction' in Late Nineteenth-Century Southern Agriculture," *Journal of Economic History* 33 (September 1973): 608–33.

34. Hereafter "yield" always means specifically "yield per acre."

35. The price quotation for 1860—11.1 cents per pound—is the weighted average for that selling year in the New Orleans market; according to Gray, the New Orleans price more closely approximated the amount received by planters than any other. *Agriculture in the Southern United States to 1860,* 2:696, 1027. The quotation for 1890—8.6 cents per pound—is the average farm price of a pound and is taken from Shannon, *Farmer's Last Frontier,* 415. This difference of 2.5 cents is probably a bit high, for the New Orleans price would exceed the average farm price, even if by a very small amount.

36. In fact Fogel and Engerman claim that the real price in 1890 was higher than in 1860. *Time on the Cross,* 1:96.

37. Rendigs Fels, *American Business Cycles, 1865–1897* (Chapel Hill, 1959), chaps. 7–9.

38. U.S. Bureau of the Census, *Eleventh Census of the United States, 1890. Statistics of Agriculture,* 393–95.

39. Why, then, depression of the land? An old argument placed the blame on the merchants in the countryside and small towns. They yoked cotton growers with the crop-lien system and criminal interest rates that ground down the cotton grower into poverty. However, with merchant and planter often the same individual, the effort to blame the former for hard times loses force. Getting away from the villain idea, Harold Woodman has pointed to the shortage of capital in the South, which precluded the long-term real estate loans that could have offset the ruinous interest rates. A good discussion of this entire question is in Woodman's *King Cotton and His Retainers: Financing and Marketing the Cotton Crop of the South, 1800–1925* (Lexington, 1969), chaps. 26 and 27. In all probability most substantial planters (often planter-merchants) were prospering, but the poverty that marked the mass of agricultural tenants, sharecroppers, and laborers, both black and white, became the accepted characterization of the rural South.

40. Willard Range, *A Century of Georgia Agriculture, 1850–1950* (Athens, Ga., 1954),

102, 122; William Warren Rogers, *The One-Gallused Rebellion: Agrarianism in Alabama, 1865–1896* (Baton Rouge, 1970), 26; William J. Cooper Jr., *The Conservative Regime: South Carolina, 1877–1890* (Baltimore, 1968), 135; R. T. Nesbitt, *Georgia: Her Resources and Possibilities* (Atlanta, 1896), 221. Cf. Alabama, State Department of Agriculture, *A General Description of the State of Alabama* (Montgomery, 1884), 56, 88–91; and U.S. Bureau of the Census, *Tenth Census of the United States, 1890. Cotton Production in the United States,* pt. 1, p. 280.

41. *Tenth Census, 1890. Statistics of Agriculture,* 104–5, 109, 122; *Eleventh Census, 1890. Statistics of Agriculture,* 198–99, 202, 215.

42. For Alabama, see *Eleventh Census, 1890. Statistics of Agriculture,* 51, 198, 393. For Georgia, see ibid., 202–4, 393–94; *Tenth Census, 1890. Cotton Production in the United States,* pt. 2, pp. 269–71; and ibid., *Statistics of Agriculture,* 109–11.

43. Shannon, *Farmer's Last Frontier,* 80–83, 95.

44. Ibid., 96.

45. For a recent study that emphasizes the control white planters retained over the free black as sharecropper, consult Joseph D. Reid Jr., "Sharecropping as the Understandable Market Response: The Post-Bellum South," *Journal of Economic History* 33 (March 1973): 114–20.

46. George P. Rawick, *From Sundown to Sunup: The Making of the Black Community* (Westport, Conn., 1972), xviii.

47. Fogel and Engerman, *Time on the Cross,* 1:191–209.

CHAPTER FOUR

1. Hundley, *Social Relations in Our Southern States* (New York, 1860), vi, 8, 10 (hereinafter cited as *SR*).

2. Ibid., 19–20.

3. W. Brewer, *Alabama: Her History, Resources, War Record and Public Men From 1540 to 1872* (Montgomery, 1872), 313; Thomas McAdory Owen, *History of Alabama and Dictionary of Alabama Biography,* 4 vols. (Chicago, 1921), 3:869.

4. The diary, which used to be on deposit in the Southern Historical Collection, University of North Carolina, was removed in 1952 by the depositor. I am extremely grateful to Mrs. J. Dexter Nilsson, a great-granddaughter of Daniel R. Hundley, for giving me access to a portion of it. Mrs. Nilsson has also placed a copy of that portion in the Department of Archives (now Louisiana and Lower Mississippi Valley Collection), Louisiana State University Library.

5. Tommy W. Rogers, "Daniel R. Hundley's Contribution to Folklore," *Alabama Historical Quarterly* 30 (Fall and Winter 1968): 203–18; and "D. R. Hundley: A Multi-Class Thesis of Social Stratification in the Antebellum South," *Mississippi Quarterly* 22 (Spring 1970): 135–54; Blanche Henry-Clark Weaver, "D. R. Hundley: Subjective Sociologist," *Georgia Review* 10 (Summer 1958): 222–34, which has helpful biographical information.

6. Mrs. J. Dexter Nilsson to William J. Cooper Jr. (hereinafter cited as WJC), Novem-

ber 4, 1976; *Alabama Records, Madison County* 25:95 and 161:35, in Alabama Department of Archives and History; Weaver, "D. R. Hundley," 223.

7. James F. Hopkins, *The University of Kentucky: Origins and Early Years* (Lexington, Ky., 1951), 43–50, 73; Daniel R. Hundley, *Prison Echoes of the Great Rebellion* (New York, 1874), 59; Daniel R. Hundley to James A. Noyes, n.d. [1897], Daniel R. Hundley Biographical Folder, Harvard University Archives, Nathan M. Pusey Library, Harvard University.

8. *SR,* 19; Weaver, "D. R. Hundley," 223; *Harvard College Papers,* Second Series, 20 (1853–54), 99, 109, Pusey Library.

9. Mrs. J. Dexter Lisson to WJC, November 4, 12, 1976; "Hundley Manuscript Diary," May 13, 1861; *SR,* 19–20; Hundley, *Prison Echoes,* 6.

10. Daniel R. Hundley, *Work and Bread; or the Coming Winter & the Poor* (Chicago, 1858), 18; Hundley to Wm. B. Figueres, December 1, 1860, printed in *Huntsville Southern Advocate,* December 12, 1860.

11. "The Evils of Commercial Supremacy," *Hunt's Merchants' Magazine* 36 (March 1, 1857): 316–17; "The Traffic in Coolies," ibid. (May 1857): 570–73.

12. Hundley, *Work and Bread* (quotations on 14 and 22).

13. For a full discussion of *SR,* see below.

14. Hundley to Wm. B. Figueres, December 1, 1860, printed in *Huntsville Southern Advocate,* December 12, 1860.

15. Ibid.; "Hundley Manuscript Diary," April 21–25, 1861. En route back to Alabama, Hundley feared that his property in Chicago would be confiscated; but on May 9 he received word that it had been sold, though at a substantial loss. Ibid., May 1, 4, 9, 1861.

16. Hundley to Citizens of Kentucky, April 27, 1861, printed in *Talladega (Ala.) Democratic Watchtower,* May 15, 1861 (originally published in *Louisville Daily Courier,* April 29, 1861).

17. "Hundley Manuscript Diary," May 14–15, July 8–13, 15, 17–18, 20, 22–23, 25, August 4, 8–9, 1861. The description is from Hundley's Service File, Military Service Records, National Archives.

18. Hundley's Service File; Hundley, *Prison Echoes,* 17–22; Mrs. J. Dexter Nilsson to WJC, November 4, 1976.

19. Hundley, *Prison Echoes,* 4–6, 14. A copy of the oath dated July 11, 1865, is in Hundley's Service File.

20. Hundley, *Prison Echoes,* passim (quotations on 53, 101, 164, 173).

21. Ibid., 6, 14; Hundley's Service File; Mrs. J. Dexter Nilsson to WJC, November 4, 1976; Weaver, "D. R. Hundley," 233.

22. *Huntsville Daily Mercury,* December 28–29, 1899. The only obituary I found outside Hundley's neighborhood was a brief one in *Confederate Veteran* 8 (February 1900): 82.

23. *SR,* 13.

24. *De Bow's Review* 28 (May 1860): 551–66.

25. This might also explain the omission of Hundley from basic works like Jay B. Hubbell, *The South in American Literature, 1607–1900* (Durham, N.C., 1954), and Louis B. Rubin Jr., ed., *A Bibliographical Guide to the Study of Southern Literature* (Baton Rouge, 1969).

26. Phillips, "Economic and Political Essays in the Antebellum South," in Julian A. C.

Chandler et al., eds., *The South in the Building of the Nation,* 12 vols. (Richmond, 1909), 7:188–89.

27. Although Phillips did not make extensive use of *Social Relations,* he did cite it in *American Negro Slavery* (New York, 1918), 200, and in *Life and Labor in the Old South* (Boston, 1929), 107, 343, 353. Dodd, *The Cotton Kingdom: A Chronicle of the Old South* (New Haven, Conn., 1920); and *Statesmen of the Old South: Or From Radicalism to Conservative Revolt* (New York, 1911).

28. Carpenter, *The South as a Conscious Minority, 1789–1861: A Study in Political Thought* (New York, 1930); Gaines, *The Southern Plantation: A Study in the Development and Accuracy of a Tradition* (New York, 1924); Jenkins, *Pro-Slavery Thought in the Old South* (Chapel Hill, 1935).

29. Eaton, *The Mind of the Old South* (Baton Rouge, 1964), 115–16; and *The Waning of the Old South Civilization, 1860s-1880s* (Athens, Ga., 1968), 4–6; Degler, *Place Over Time: The Continuity of Southern Distinctiveness* (Baton Rouge, 1977), 56; Cash, *The Mind of the South* (New York, 1941), 20; Taylor, *Cavalier and Yankee: The Old South and American National Character* (New York and Evanston, 1969), 337; Wyatt-Brown, "The Ideal Typology and Ante-Bellum Southern History: A Testing of a New Approach," *Societas* 5 (Winter 1975): 5n., 8; Kenneth Stampp, *The Peculiar Institution: Slavery in the Ante-Bellum South* (New York, 1956), 180, 256–57.

30. *SR,* 81.

31. For a somewhat different development of this point, see Rogers, "D. R. Hundley: A Multi-Class Thesis."

32. He also placed some members of the middle class in the planter category, but they were not so important as planters as the three primary groups.

33. Eugene D. Genovese, *The Political Economy of Slavery: Studies in the Economy and Society of the Slave South* (New York, 1965).

34. Cash, *Mind of the South,* 3–14; *SR,* 20–76 passim, esp. 21, 23, 27–29, 31–34, 63–64.

35. *SR,* 130–32, 157, 161–62, 166–67, 170–71, 175–76.

36. Ibid., 27–28, 131, 165.

37. Ibid., 251 (italics in original).

38. Jacques Barzun, *Race: A Study in Superstition,* rev. ed. (New York, 1965), chaps. 3–5 (quotations on 52 and 84). See also James Cowles Prichard, *Researches into the Physical History of Man,* ed. George W. Stocking Jr. (Chicago, 1973), lxvi, ci, cii.

39. Taylor, *Cavalier and Yankee,* 337; *SR,* 156–57.

40. Frank L. Owsley, *Plain Folk of the Old South* (Baton Rouge, 1949); *SR,* chaps. 2, 5, 7 passim (quotations on 77 and 192).

41. *SR,* 81–82, 84, 94–95, 193, 198–99, 207, 216–18.

42. Ibid., 54–55, 82–84, 198–99, 201; William J. Cooper Jr., *The South and the Politics of Slavery, 1828–1856* (Baton Rouge, 1978).

43. Not only does Hundley make slavery the subject of his longest chapter, he also treats various aspects of it throughout the book. Quotations from *SR,* 285, 357.

44. Ibid., 132, 140–41, 320.

45. Ibid., 14, 284–92.

46. Ibid., 61, 133, 290, 295–300 (italics in original).

47. Ibid., 302–13; Philip D. Curtin, *The Image of Africa: British Ideas and Action, 1780–1850* (Madison, Wisc., 1964), chaps. 12, 13, and 15 passim.

48. *SR,* 151–52, 316–20.

49. Eric Foner has a full statement of the content and impact of free-labor ideology in his *Free Soil, Free Labor, Free Men: The Ideology of the Republican Party before the Civil War* (New York, 1970). David Brion Davis has a suggestive discussion of its origins in *The Problem of Slavery in the Age of Revolution, 1770–1823* (Ithaca, N.Y., 1975), 489–501 (quotations on 492).

50. *SR,* 324.

CHAPTER FIVE

1. This essay was originally published in Walter J. Fraser Jr. and Winfred B. Moore Jr., eds., *The Southern Enigma: Essays on Race, Class, Folk Culture* (Westport, CT: 1983), 199–215.

2. Two articles discuss portions of the problem: William J. Donnelly, "Conspiracy or Popular Movement: The Historiography of Southern Support for Secession," *North Carolina Historical Review* 42 (January 1965): 70–84; and Ralph A. Wooster, "The Secession of the Lower South: An Examination of Changing Interpretations," *Civil War History* 7 (June 1961): 117–27.

3. William J. Cooper Jr., "The Cotton Crisis in the Antebellum South: Another Look," *Agricultural History* 49 (April 1975): 381–91.

4. Michael F. Holt, *The Political Crisis of the 1850s* (New York, 1978), chap. 8.

5. William J. Cooper Jr., *The South and the Politics of Slavery, 1828–1856* (Baton Rouge, 1978), xi.

6. James D. Richardson, comp., *Messages and Papers of the Confederacy,* 2 vols. (Nashville, 1906), 1:32–36.

7. *Charleston Mercury,* July 25, 1860; *New Orleans Daily Crescent,* November 15, 1860, quoted in Dwight Lowell Dumond, ed., *Southern Editorials on Secession* (Gloucester, Mass., 1964), 240.

8. Michael P. Johnson, *Toward a Patriarchal Republic: The Secession of Georgia* (Baton Rouge, 1977), 30; *Richmond Enquirer,* July 10, 1860.

9. *Daily Nashville Patriot,* September 19, 1860, quoted in Dumond, *Southern Editorials,* 167.

10. Eric Foner, *Free Soil, Free Labor, Free Men: The Ideology of the Republican Party before the Civil War* (New York, 1970); David M. Potter, *The South and the Sectional Conflict* (Baton Rouge, 1968), 34–83; and *The Impending Crisis, 1848–1861* (New York, 1976), 471–75; J. D. Ashmore to Benjamin Perry, May 13, 1860, Benjamin Perry Papers, Alabama Department of Archives and History, Montgomery.

11. Mary Jones to C. C. Jones Jr., November 15, 1860, in *Children of Pride: A True Story of Georgia and the Civil War,* ed., Robert Mason Myers (New Haven, Conn., 1972), 627–38;

Clopton to Clay, December 13, 1860, C. C. Clay Papers, William R. Perkins Library, Duke University, Durham, N.C.

12. J. Mills Thornton III, *Politics and Power in a Slave Society: Alabama, 1800–1860* (Baton Rouge, 1978), 361. On this general point, see also William S. Hitchcock, "The Limits of Southern Unionism: Virginia Conservatives and the Gubernatorial Election of 1859," *Journal of Southern History* 47 (February 1981): 57–72.

13. Although Professor Mering did not use the term "politics of slavery," he definitely described those politics: see "The Constitutional Union Campaign of 1860: An Example of the Paranoid Style," *Mid-America* 60 (April–July 1978): 95–106; and "The Slave-State Constitutional Unionists and the Politics of Consensus," *Journal of Southern History* 43 (August 1977): 395–410. See also Hitchcock, "Limits of Southern Unionism."

14. These and all other slave-related figures refer to 1860 and are taken from the census of that year.

15. *Charleston Mercury,* November 3, 1860.

16. An exception to my lament is J. Mills Thornton's superb study of Alabama, which contains the best analysis of the Fire-Eaters we have, although for only one state. See Thornton, *Politics and Power,* esp. 232–66.

17. William Kauffman Scarborough, ed., *The Diary of Edmund Ruffin,* 2 vols. (Baton Rouge, 1972), 1:473; *Charleston Mercury,* July 10, 1860.

18. Scarborough, *Diary of Edmund Ruffin,* 1:442–43.

19. Thornton, *Politics and Power,* 266.

20. *Bee,* December 5, 1860; Daniel R. Hundley, *Social Relations in Our Southern States,* ed. William J. Cooper Jr. (Baton Rouge, 1979), xxi; Don E. Fehrenbacher, *The South and Three Sectional Crises* (Baton Rouge, 1980), chaps. 2 and 3 passim, esp. p. 31.

21. Thornton, *Politics and Power,* 452.

22. Brown to Howell Cobb, December 15, 1860, Howell Cobb Papers, Ilah Dunlap Little Memorial Library, University of Georgia, Athens; Vance to William Dickinson, December 11, 1860, in *The Papers of Zebulon Baird Vance: Volume One, 1843–1862,* ed. Frontis W. Johnson (Raleigh, 1963), 71.

23. Davis to R. B. Rhett Jr., November 10, 1860; and to J. J. Pettus, December 26, 31, 1860, January 4, 1861, in Dunbar Rowland, ed., *Jefferson Davis, Constitutionalist: His Letters, Papers, and Speeches,* 10 vols. (Jackson, Miss., 1923), 4:541–43, 559–61, 564–65; David M. Potter, *Lincoln and His Party in the Secession Crisis* (New Haven, Conn., 1962), 171, 205.

24. Slidell to Edward G. W. Butler, November 1, 1860, Edward G. W. Butler Papers, Perkins Library, Duke University, Durham N.C.; Slidell to Buchanan, November 13, 1860, James Buchanan Papers, Historical Society of Pennsylvania, Philadelphia.

25. *Augusta Daily Chronicle and Sentinel,* December 22, 1860, quoted in Dumond, *Southern Editorials,* 361–63.

26. Daniel W. Crofts, "The Union Party of 1861 and the Secession Crisis," *Perspectives in American History* 2 (1977–78): 327–76 (quotation on 328).

27. *Charlottesville Review,* January 4, 1861, quoted in Dumond, *Southern Editorials,* 389.

28. Ibid. See also *Charlottesville Review,* January 25, 1861, ibid., 415.

29. For example, see William J. Evitts, *A Matter of Allegiances: Maryland, 1850–1861* (Baltimore, 1974).

CHAPTER SIX

1. *Congressional Globe,* 30th Cong., 2nd Sess., Appendix, 175 (hereinafter cited as *CG;* all citations are to this Congress and session).

2. George M. Dallas Diary, December 12, 1848, in Roy F. Nichols, "The Mystery of the Dallas Papers," *Pennsylvania Magazine of History and Biography* 73 (1949): 485–86.

3. *CG,* 33, 440, 456, Appendix, 105, 175, 213; William J. Cooper Jr., *The South and the Politics of Slavery, 1828–1856* (Baton Rouge, 1978), 270.

4. *CG,* 181, 309, 347, Appendix, 101; *Albany Evening Journal,* February 23, 1849.

5. On the South and the territories, see Cooper, *The South and the Politics of Slavery,* 238–44.

6. The most complete treatment of the northern perception of the territories is in Eric Foner, *Free Soil, Free Labor, Free Men: The Ideology of the Republican Party before the Civil War* (New York, 1970).

7. David M. Potter, *The Impending Crisis, 1848–1861* (New York, 1976), 69–76.

8. Ibid., 78–82; Cooper, *The South and the Politics of Slavery,* 244–53; Michael F. Holt, "Winding Roads to Recovery: The Whig Party from 1844 to 1848," in Stephen E. Maislish and John J. Kushma, eds., *Essays on American Antebellum Politics, 1840–1860* (College Station, Tex., 1982), 122–65.

9. *Washington Daily Union,* December 9, 1848.

10. H. D. Gilpin to Martin Van Buren, December 21, 1848, Martin Van Buren Papers, Library of Congress. Every newspaper that I looked at for this essay carried numerous California stories.

11. William B. Preston to William C. Rives, December 6, 1848; and Jonathan Pendleton to Rives, December 28, 1848, William C. Rives Papers, Library of Congress; Charles Francis Adams to John G. Palfrey, December 12, 1848, Adams Family Papers, Massachusetts Historical Society, Boston; *Albany Evening Journal,* December 15, 1848.

12. John M. Clayton to John J. Crittenden, December 13, 1848, John J. Crittenden Papers; and Crittenden to Clayton, January 7, 1849, John M. Clayton Papers, Library of Congress; Alexander Stephens to Crittenden, December 6, 1848, Crittenden Papers.

13. George M. Dallas to his wife, December 7, 1848, in Nichols, "Mystery of the Dallas Papers," 477.

14. James D. Richardson, comp., *A Compilation of the Messages and Papers of the Presidents, 1789–1897,* 10 vols. (Washington, D.C., 1896–99), 4:633–43 (quotations on 639–40).

15. Ibid., 641–42.

16. Milo Milton Quaife, ed., *The Diary of James K. Polk during His Presidency, 1845–1849,* 4 vols. (Chicago, 1910), 4:251.

17. *CG,* 1, 21. For a full account of Douglas's activities, see Robert W. Johannsen, *Stephen A. Douglas* (New York, 1973), 241–48.

18. *CG,* 37, 46–49; Dallas Diary, December 18, 1848, in Nichols, "Mystery of the Dallas Papers," 487.

19. *CG,* 49; Louis T. Wigfall to John C. Calhoun, January 4, 1849, in Chauncey S. Boucher and Robert P. Brooks, eds., *Correspondence Addressed to John C. Calhoun, 1837–1849* (Washington, D.C., 1930), 494; *Charleston Mercury* quoted in *Niles' National Register* 75 (February 28, 1849): 139.

20. *CG,* 83–84. For Calhoun's movement, see Cooper, *The South and the Politics of Slavery,* 269–70, 287–88; and Charles M. Wilste, *John C. Calhoun: Sectionalist, 1840–1850* (Indianapolis, 1951), 378–88.

21. These totals exclude the border states.

22. Robert Toombs to John J. Crittenden, January 3, 1849, in Ulrich B. Phillips, ed., *The Correspondence of Robert Toombs, Alexander H. Stephens, and Howell Cobb* (Washington, D.C., 1913), 139 (hereinafter cited as *Correspondence of Toombs, Stephens, and Cobb*). Also see Alexander Stephens to [unknown], December 27, 1848, Alexander Stephens Papers, Library of Congress.

23. Toombs to Crittenden, January 3, 1849, in Phillips, *Correspondence of Toombs, Stephens, and Cobb,* 139; John C. Calhoun to James Edward Calhoun, January 17, 1849, John C. Calhoun Papers, William R. Perkins Library, Duke University, Durham, N.C.

24. John C. Calhoun to Henry W. Conner, February 2, 1849, Henry W. Conner Papers, South Carolina Historical Society, Charleston.

25. Robert Toombs to John J. Crittenden, January 22, 1849, in Phillips, *Correspondence of Toombs, Stephens, and Cobb,* 141; Alexander Stephens to John J. Crittenden, January 17, 1849, Alexander Stephens Papers, Perkins Library, Duke University, Durham, N.C.

26. David Outlaw to Emily Outlaw, December 14, 1848, David Outlaw Papers, Southern Historical Collection, University of North Carolina, Chapel Hill; *CG,* 83–84, 105, 216; *New York Tribune,* January 7, 1849; Nathan K. Hall to Millard Fillmore, December 30, 1848, Millard Fillmore Papers, State University of New York, Oswego.

27. Toombs to Crittenden, January 3, 1849, in Phillips, *Correspondence of Toombs, Stephens, and Cobb,* 140.

28. Thomas B. Stevenson to Caleb B. Smith, December 12, 1848, Caleb B. Smith Papers, Library of Congress; N. K. Hall to Millard Fillmore, January 8, 1849, Fillmore Papers; John G. Palfrey to Charles Francis Adams, December 7, 1848, Adams Family Papers.

29. Palfrey to Adams, December 7, 1848, Adams Family Papers; Daniel Lee to Millard Fillmore, January 25, 1849, Fillmore Papers; *CG,* Appendix, 223; *Louisville Daily Journal,* January 18, 1849.

30. *Richmond Whig,* December 22, 1848; *Louisville Daily Journal,* December 21, 1848; Clayton to Crittenden, December 13, 1848, Crittenden Papers; Crittenden to Clayton, January 7, 1849, Clayton Papers.

31. These totals include two Democratic senators from Iowa who took their seats in late December 1848 and one Democratic congressman from South Carolina who did not arrive in the House until early February 1849.

32. Quaife, *Polk Diary,* 4:231, 233, 235, 236–37, 238, 254–55, 257–58, 279, 286–87, 293, 299–300, 302–3, 312–13, 316; Johannsen, *Stephen A. Douglas,* 244–45.

33. *Washington Daily Union,* December 9, 10, 1848, January 16 (quotation), 21, 28, February 4, 8 (quotation), 15, 1849.

34. *CG,* 477; Toombs to Crittenden, January 22, 1849, in Phillips, *Correspondence of Toombs, Stephens, and Cobb,* 141. Toombs indicated that Preston would "move," but he gave no indication of why Preston was chosen.

35. For Preston's speech, see *CG,* 477–80.

36. Robert Toombs to John J. Crittenden, February 9, 1849, in Phillips, *Correspondence of Toombs, Stephens, and Cobb,* 147; *Niles' National Register* 75 (February 28, 1849): 133–37.

37. *Richmond Whig,* February 13, 16, 1849; William C. Rives to William B. Preston, February 13, 1849; and John B. Floyd to Preston, February 19, 1849, William B. Preston Papers, Virginia Historical Society, Richmond; *CG,* Appendix, 213.

38. *CG,* Appendix, 106–7 (quotation), 120–21 (quotation), 157, 220–21, 241, 247.

39. Hopkins Holsey to Howell Cobb, February 13, 24, 1849, in Phillips, *Correspondence of Toombs, Stephens, and Cobb,* 148–55 (quotation on 154); *CG,* Appendix, 101, 162, 220.

40. *CG,* Appendix, 248; *New York Tribune,* January–February 1849 passim; *Albany Evening Journal,* February 23, March 2, 1849; John G. Palfrey to Charles Francis Adams, December 7, 1848, and February 18, 1849, Adams Family Papers.

41. *CG,* 340–41, 435, 552, 553, 562–66, 573; *Washington National Intelligencer,* February 21, 1849 (quotation).

42. *CG,* 607–8.

43. Ibid., 609. Nor did any of the newspapers I consulted have a roll call.

44. Ibid., 561–62, 573–74, 664–65, 666, 668, 682–91; *New York Tribune,* February 28, March 1, 1849; John G. Palfrey to Charles Francis Adams, March 2, 1849, Adams Family Papers; Francis P. Blair to Martin Van Buren, March 5, 1849, Van Buren Papers.

45. Robert Toombs to William B. Preston, May 18 1849, Preston Papers.

46. Cooper, *The South and the Politics of Slavery,* 275–76, 283–87.

CHAPTER SEVEN

1. Louis M. Starr, *Bohemian Brigade: Civil War Newsmen in Action* (New York, 1954), 3–11.

2. Edwin Forbes, *Thirty Years After: An Artist's Memoir of the Civil War* (1890; Baton Rouge, 1993), 257. Subsequent citations are given parenthetically in the text.

3. Jacob Edward Kent Aherns, "Edwin Forbes" (M.A. thesis, University of Maryland, 1966), 15. This thesis has the most biographical detail on Forbes readily available, but it is still extremely sketchy.

4. Ibid.; F. Weitenkampf, *American Graphic Art,* rev. ed. (New York, 1924), 1.

5. Aherns, "Edwin Forbes," 51–53.

6. Mrs. Ida B. Forbes, *Gen'l Wm. T. Sherman: His Life and Battles; or From Boy-Hood to His "March to the Sea"* (New York, 1886); Mrs. Helen W. Pierson, *Life and Battles of Napoleon Bonaparte* (New York, 1886); George F. Williams, *Bullet and Shell: A Soldier's Romance* (New York, 1882); and *Bullet and Shell: War as the Soldier Saw It* (New York, 1883).

7. *New York Times,* May 7, 1895, 3; Aherns, "Edwin Forbes," 49.

8. Starr, *Bohemian Brigade,* 6.

9. Ibid.; W. Fletcher Thompson Jr., *The Image of War: The Pictorial Reporting of the American Civil War* (New York, 1960); J. Cutler Andrews, *The North Reports the Civil War* (Pittsburgh, 1955); and *The South Reports the Civil War* (Princeton, 1970).

10. Budd Leslie Gambee Jr., *Frank Leslie and His Illustrated Newspaper, 1855–1860* (Ann Arbor, 1964), 80.

11. Stuart William Becker, "Frank Leslie's Illustrated Newspaper from 1860 to the Battle of Gettysburg" (M.A. thesis, University of Missouri, 1960), 25.

12. Mark E. Neely Jr., Harold Holzer, and Gabor S. Boritt, *The Confederate Image: Prints of the Lost Cause* (Chapel Hill, 1987), 23–30; Frederic Ray, "With Pen and Palette: Artists of the Civil War," *Civil War Times Illustrated* 21 (April 1982): 27.

13. Thompson, *Image of War,* 81.

14. Ibid., 83; Aherns, "Edwin Forbes," 17.

15. Thompson, *Image of War,* 21.

CHAPTER NINE

1. This essay was originally published in *The Journal of Southern History* 77, no. 1 (February 2011): 3–16.

2. John Amasa May and Joan Reynolds Faunt, *South Carolina Secedes* (Columbia, 1960), 7.

3. William W. Freehling, *The Road to Disunion,* vol. 2, *Secessionists Triumphant, 1854–1861* (New York, 2007); Dwight Lowell Dumond, *The Secession Movement, 1860–1861* (New York, 1931). I am not going to list books, but a glance at those by some major historians who have written about the late 1850s makes my point about historians' unanimity on the importance of slavery to secession. For instance, see the work of Michael F. Holt, Robert W. Johannsen, Allan Nevins, Roy F. Nichols, and David M. Potter.

4. I first noted the necessity to account for three different reactions in Cooper, "The Politics of Slavery Affirmed: The South and the Secession Crisis," in Walter J. Fraser Jr. and Winfred B. Moore Jr., eds., *The Southern Enigma: Essays on Race, Class, Folk Culture* (Westport, 1983), 199–215; and Cooper, *Liberty and Slavery: Southern Politics to 1860* (New York, 1983), 273–81—a point Freehling graciously acknowledges in *Road to Disunion,* 2:574n1. Also see Michael F. Holt, *The Political Crisis of the 1850s* (New York, 1978), chap. 8, which discusses contrasting courses in the lower and upper South.

5. The first volume is William F. Freehling, *The Road to Disunion,* vol. 1, *Secessionists at Bay: 1776–1854* (New York, 1990).

6. Steven A. Channing, *Crisis of Fear: Secession in South Carolina* (New York, 1970); Lacy K. Ford Jr., *Origins of Southern Radicalism: The South Carolina Upcountry, 1800–1860* (New York, 1988); Stephanie McCurry, *Masters of Small Worlds: Yeoman Households, Gender Relations, and the Political Culture of the Antebellum South Carolina Low Country* (New York, 1995); Manisha Sinha, *The Counterrevolution of Slavery: Politics and Ideology in Antebellum South Carolina* (Chapel Hill, 2000).

7. Christopher J. Olsen, *Political Culture and Secession in Mississippi: Masculinity, Honor, and the Antiparty Tradition, 1830–1860* (New York, 2000); J. Mills Thornton III, *Politics and Power in a Slave Society: Alabama, 1800–1860* (Baton Rouge, 1978); William L. Barney, *The Secessionist Impulse: Alabama and Mississippi in 1860* (Princeton, 1974); Michael P. Johnson, *Toward a Patriarchal Republic: The Secession of Georgia* (Baton Rouge, 1997); Anthony Gene Carey, *Parties, Slavery, and the Union in Antebellum Georgia* (Athens,

Ga., 1997); John M. Sacher, *A Perfect War of Politics: Parties, Politicians, and Democracy in Louisiana, 1824–1861* (Baton Rouge, 2003); Donald E. Reynolds, *Texas Terror: The Slave Insurrection Panic of 1860 and the Secession of the Lower South* (Baton Rouge, 2007).

8. Freehling, *Road to Disunion,* vol. 2, chaps. 22–27.

9. Ibid., chap. 28.

10. *Congressional Globe,* 36th Cong., 2nd Sess., December 3, 1860, 1–2; William J. Cooper Jr., *Jefferson Davis, American* (New York, 2000), chap. 10; Jefferson Davis to Frank H. Alfriend, August 17, 1867, in Cooper, ed., *Jefferson Davis: The Essential Writings* (New York, 2003), 393–97.

11. For the report of the Committee of Thirteen, see *Senate Reports,* 36th Cong., 2nd Sess., no. 288 (serial 1090) (quotation on 4). Robert W. Johannsen, *Stephen A. Douglas* (New York, 1973), chap. 30; and Albert D. Kirwan, *John J. Crittenden: The Struggle for the Union* (Lexington, Ky., 1962), chap. 18, contain helpful discussions of the committee's activity.

12. Every student of the Republican Party in the 1850s and during the crisis emphasizes that point. Note, for example, David M. Potter, *Lincoln and His Party in the Secession Crisis* (1942; new ed., Baton Rouge, 1995). Jefferson Davis provides a good example of southern thinking; consult Cooper, *Jefferson Davis,* 304–6.

13. Cooper, *Jefferson Davis,* 318–20; Davis to Frank H. Alfriend, August 17, 1867, in Cooper, *Jefferson Davis: The Essential Writings,* 393–97; Ulrich Bonnell Phillips, *The Life of Robert Toombs* (New York, 1913), 206–8.

14. Robert Toombs to E. B. Pullin and Others, December 13, 1860; Toombs to the People of Georgia, December 23, 1860; and Alexander H. Stephens to J. Henly Smith, December 31, 1860 (quotations), all in Ulrich B. Phillips, ed., *The Correspondence of Robert Toombs, Alexander H. Stephens, and Howell Cobb* (Washington, D.C., 1913), 519–22, 525, 526; "The Future," *Charleston Mercury,* January 22, 1861, 1; William Henry Seward to Hamilton Fish, December 11, 1860, Hamilton Fish Papers, Manuscript Division, Library of Congress, Washington, D.C. (hereinafter cited as LC).

15. *Senate Reports,* 36th Cong., 2nd Sess., no. 288, 17–18.

16. Potter, *Lincoln and His Party;* Russell McClintock, *Lincoln and the Decision for War: The Northern Response to Secession* (Chapel Hill, 2008). Cf. Michael Burlingame, *Abraham Lincoln: A Life* 2 vols. (Baltimore, 2008); and Harold Holzer, *Lincoln President-Elect: Abraham Lincoln and the Great Secession Winter, 1860–1861* (New York, 2008). For pertinent comments on Lincoln's scholarly admirers and Lincoln as president-elect, see Daniel W. Crofts, "A Fresh Look at *The Diary of a Public Man,*" *Civil War History* 55 (December 2009): 442–68, esp., 465–66.

17. For suggestive introductions to Seward's activities, see Daniel W. Crofts, *Reluctant Confederates: Upper South Unionists in the Secession Crisis* (Chapel Hill, 1989), chaps. 8–9; and Michael Robinson, "William Henry Seward, Compromise, and the Secession Crisis, November–December 1860" (unpublished seminar paper, Louisiana State University, 2007).

18. The Abraham Lincoln Papers (LC) contain many examples of letters giving him advice. His letters to Lyman Trumbull, December 10 and 17, 1860, and to Thurlow Weed,

December 17, 1860, underscore his implacable opposition to compromise on the territories. See Roy B. Basler et al., eds., *The Collected Works of Abraham Lincoln,* 8 vols. plus index (New Brunswick, N.J., 1953–55), 4:149–50, 153, 154 (hereinafter cited as *CWL*).

19. Burlingame, *Abraham Lincoln,* vol. 1, chap. 17; Holzer, *Lincoln President-Elect.*

20. "Passage Written for Lyman Trumbull's Speech at Springfield Illinois," November 20, 1860, in *CWL,* 4:142; Lincoln to Peter H. Silvester, December 22, 1860, ibid., 160; "'A House Divided': Speech at Springfield Illinois," June 16, 1858, ibid., 2:461–69; Donn Piatt, *Memories of the Men Who Saved the Union* (New York, 1887), 30; Don E. Fehrenbacher and Virginia Fehrenbacher, comps. and eds., *Recollected Words of Abraham Lincoln* (Stanford, Calif., 1996), 341 (quotation).

21. "'A House Divided': Speech at Springfield Illinois," June 16, 1858, in *CWL,* 2:461–69.

22. Any substantive Lincoln biography illustrates this fact—for example, see David Herbert Donald, *Lincoln* (New York, 1995); Ronald C. White Jr., *A. Lincoln: A Biography* (New York, 2009); and Burlingame, *Abraham Lincoln.*

23. Fehrenbacher and Fehrenbacher, comps. and eds., *Recollected Words of Abraham Lincoln,* 341.

24. Lincoln to Stephens, November 30, 1860, in *CWL,* 4:146; Lincoln to Stephens, December 22, 1860, ibid., 160; Stephens to Lincoln, December 14, 1860, Lincoln Papers (quotation); Stephens to Lincoln, December 30, 1860, in Stephens, *A Constitutional View of the Late War Between the States . . . ,* 2 vols. (Philadelphia 1868–70), 2:267–70. Stephens's speech is printed in William W. Freehling and Craig M. Simpson, eds., *Secession Debated: Georgia's Showdown in 1860* (New York, 1992), 51–79.

25. Freehling and Simpson, *Secession Debated,* 51–79 (quotations on 69).

26. Stephens to Lincoln, December 14, 1860, Lincoln Papers (first quotation); Lincoln to Stephens, December 22, 1860, in *CWL,* 4:160 (second, third, fifth, and sixth quotations). For Lincoln's calling Stephens "a great man," see Linton Stephens to Alexander Stephens, February 8, 1861, Alexander H. Stephens Collection, Rare Books and Manuscripts, Special Collections, Manhattanville College Library, Purchase, N.Y.

27. Stephens to Lincoln, December 30, 1860, in Stephens, *Constitutional View of the Late War,* 2:267–70.

CHAPTER TEN

1. This essay was originally published in Gary W. Gallagher and Rachel A. Shelden, eds., *A Political Nation: New Directions in Mid-Nineteenth-Century American Political History,* (Charlottesville, 2012), 126–140. Reprinted here courtesy of the University of Virginia Press.

2. Notable recent Lincoln books include Michael Burlingame, *Abraham Lincoln: A Life,* 2 vols. (Baltimore, 2008); George M. Fredrickson, *Big Enough to Be Inconsistent: Abraham Lincoln Confronts Race and Slavery* (Cambridge, Mass., 2008); William C. Harris, *Lincoln's Rise to the Presidency* (Lawrence, Kan., 2007); Harold Holzer, *Lincoln President-Elect: Abraham Lincoln and the Great Secession, Winter 1860–1861* (New York, 2008); James M.

McPherson, *Tried by War: Abraham Lincoln as Commander in Chief* (New York, 2008); William Lee Miller, *President Lincoln: The Duty of a Statesman* (New York, 2008); Craig L. Symonds, *Lincoln and His Admirals* (New York, 2008); and Ronald C. White Jr., *A. Lincoln: A Biography* (New York, 2009).

3. The classic account, which still retains great value, is David M. Potter, *Lincoln and His Party in the Secession Crisis* (1942; Baton Rouge, 1995). It is in the second camp along with Patrick Michael Sowle, "The Conciliatory Republicans during the Winter of Secession" (Ph.D. diss., Duke University, 1963); and Russell McClintock, *Lincoln and the Decision for War: The Northern Response to Secession* (Chapel Hill, 2008). For the first, see Burlingame, *Abraham Lincoln*, vol. 1, chap. 17; and Holzer, *Lincoln President-Elect.* A balanced treatment is Harris, *Lincoln's Rise.*

4. Roy P. Basler et al., eds., *The Collected Works of Abraham Lincoln*, 8 vols. (New Brunswick, N.J., 1953–55), 3:29 (hereinafter cited as *CWL*). The best biography of Clay is Robert V. Remini, *Henry Clay: Statesman for the Union* (New York, 1991).

5. *CWL*, 2:121–32 (quotations on 125, 126, 129); Lincoln to Daniel Ullman, February 1, 1861, ibid., 4:184.

6. Ibid., 2:130–31, 3:29, 89, 300–305.

7. Robert Seager et al., eds., *The Papers of Henry Clay*, 10 vols. and supp. (Lexington, Ky.,1959–92), 10:658, 664. For Clay and the compromise, consult Remini, *Clay*, chap. 40.

8. *CWL*, 2:232–33, 241–42, 270 (quotation), 272, 3:119–20.

9. Ibid., 2:461. Still best on the 1850s is David M. Potter, *The Impending Crisis, 1848–1861*, completed by Don E. Fehrenbacher (New York, 1976), which has considerable material on Seward.

10. *CWL*, 4:142, on military preparation; Donn Piatt, *Memories of the Men Who Saved the Union* (New York and Chicago, 1887), 30 (first quotation); Lincoln to Peter H. Silvester, December 22, 1860, *CWL*, 4:160 (second quotation); Don E. Fehrenbacher and Virginia Fehrenbacher, comps. and eds., *Recollected Words of Abraham Lincoln* (Stanford, Calif., 1996), 253 (third quotation) (hereinafter cited as *Words*).

11. Hawkins Layton to John Allison, December 12, 1860, Abraham Lincoln Papers, Library of Congress (hereafter LC) (first quotation); Lincoln to Lyman Trumbull, December 17, 1860, to Elihu Washburne, December 13, 1860 (third quotation), to Thurlow Weed, December 17, 1860 (second quotation), *CWL*, 4:149–50, 151, 154; *Words*, 253; Duff Green to James Buchanan, December 28, 1860, James Buchanan Papers, Historical Society of Pennsylvania, Philadelphia; Harold G. Villard and Oswald Garrison Villard, eds., *Lincoln on the Eve of '61: A Journalist's Story by Henry Villard* (New York, 1941), 23; Carl Schurz to his wife, February 9, 1861, in Joseph Schafer, trans. and ed., *Intimate Letters of Carl Schurz* (Madison, Wis., 1928), 247.

12. *CWL*, 4:264.

13. *Words*, 341.

14. See his "House Divided" speech, *CWL*, 2:461–69.

15. Biographies of Lincoln, such as those by Blasingame and White cited in note 1, cover this material. No Lincoln scholar has uncovered any serious contact; neither have I.

16. *Words*, 341.

17. Lincoln to Stephens, November 30, December 22, 1860, *CWL,* 4:146, 160; Stephens to Lincoln, December 14, 1860, Lincoln Papers, LC; Stephens to Lincoln, December 30, 1860, in Stephens, *A Constitutional View of the Late War Between the States . . . ,* 2 vols. (Philadelphia, 1868), 2:267–70. Stephens's speech is printed in William W. Freehling and Craig M. Simpson, eds., *Secession Debated: Georgia's Showdown in 1860* (New York, 1992), 51–79 (quotation on 69). For Lincoln calling Stephens a great man, see Linton Stephens to Alexander Stephens, February 8, 1861, Alexander H. Stephens Collection, Rare Books and Manuscripts, Special Collections, Manhattanville College Library, Purchase, N.Y.

18. The most recent study as well as the best is William W. Freehling, *The Road to Disunion,* vol. 2, *Secessionists Triumphant, 1854–1861* (New York, 2007).

19. For example, see N. Paschall to Lincoln, November 18, 1860; John Gilmer to Lincoln, December 11, 1860; and Montgomery Blair to Lincoln, December 14, 1860, all in Lincoln Papers, LC; and Thomas J. McCormack, ed., *Memoirs of Gustave Koerner, 1809–1896,* 2 vols. (Cedar Rapids, Iowa, 1909), 2:104–5, 109.

20. Lincoln to Truman Smith, November 10, 1860 (first quotation); and to N. Paschall, November 16, 1860 (second quotation), *CWL,* 4:138, 140.

21. Especially consult McClintock, *Lincoln and the Decision for War;* Potter, *Lincoln and His Party;* and Sowle, "Conciliatory Republicans."

22. Adams to Seward, November 11, 1860, William Henry Seward Papers, Rush Rhees Library, University of Rochester (hereafter UR). For suggestive introductions to Seward's activities, see Daniel W. Crofts, *Reluctant Confederates: Upper South Unionists in the Secession Crisis* (Chapel Hill, 1989), chaps. 8–9; and Michael Robinson, "William Henry Seward, Compromise, and the Sectional Crisis, November–December 1860" (unpublished seminar paper, Louisiana State University, 2007).

23. *Albany Evening Journal,* November 24, December 17, 24, 1860; Sowle, "Conciliatory Republicans," 50, 84–86; Phillip S. Foner, *Business and Slavery: New York Merchants & the Irrepressible Conflict* (Chapel Hill, 1941), 235; J. Watson Webb to Lincoln, December 1, 1860, Lincoln Papers, LC; James Dixon to Gideon Welles, January 2, 1861, Gideon Welles Papers, LC; W. S. Gelman to Lyman Trumbull, December 11, 1860, Lyman Trumbull Papers, LC; George D. Morgan to Thurlow Weed, December 8, 1860, Thurlow Weed Papers, UR.

24. For examples, see *Charleston Mercury,* January 22, 1861; J. L. Pugh to William Miles, January 24, 1861, William P. Miles Papers, Southern Historical Collection, University of North Carolina, Chapel Hill; Robert Toombs to E. B. Pullin and others, December 13, 1860; and to People of Georgia, December 23, 1860, in Ulrich Bonnell Phillips, ed., *The Correspondence of Robert Toombs, Alexander H. Stephens, and Howell Cobb* (Washington, 1913), 519–22, 525. Seward noted the Fire-Eater hope in a letter to Hamilton Fish, December 11, 1860, Hamilton Fish Papers, LC.

25. Weed to Preston King, December 10, 1860, in Thurlow Weed Barnes and Harriet A. Weed, eds., *The Life of Thurlow Weed . . . ,* 2 vols. (Boston, 1883–84), 2:309 (quotation); J. H. McKee to Lincoln, December 12, 1860; and Henry Winter Davis to Lincoln, February 1861, Lincoln Papers, LC; John P. Kennedy to George S. Bryan, December 27, 1860, Letterbook, John Pendleton Kennedy Papers, Enoch Pratt Free Library, Baltimore; H. R. Riddle to Thurlow Weed, December 24, 1860, Weed Papers, UR; J. M. Taylor to Seward, January 21,

1861; J. R. Bailey to Seward, February 11, 1861; and H. Fountleroy to Seward, February 12, 1861, Seward Papers, UR; Thomas Fitnam to Seward, February 19, 1861; and M. J. Crawford to Robert Toombs, March 8, 1861, in Frederic Bancroft, *The Life of William H. Seward,* 2 vols. (New York, 1900), 2:537, 109–10n.

26. Weed to Preston King, December 10, 1860, in Barnes and Weed, *Thurlow Weed,* 2:309.

27. Davis to Frank H. Alfriend, August 17, 1867, in William J. Cooper Jr., ed., *Jefferson Davis: The Essential Writings* (New York, 2003), 393–97; Samuel S. Cox, *Union-Disunion-Reunion: Three Decades of Federal Legislation, 1855–1885* (1885; Freeport, N.Y., 1970), 77; Ulrich Bonnell Phillips, *The Life of Robert Toombs* (New York, 1913), 206–8.

28. George C. Fogg to Lincoln, December 19, 1860, Lincoln Papers, LC; *Albany Evening Journal,* December 17, 1860.

29. There is no other persuasive explanation for Seward's striving to get Lincoln to conciliate the upper and border South, moderate his inaugural address, and evacuate Fort Sumter.

30. Harold Holzer, in his *Lincoln at Cooper Union: The Speech that Made Abraham Lincoln President* (New York, 2004), agrees with Lincoln's interpretation.

31. Lincoln to Stephens, December 22, 1860, *CWL,* 4:160.

ACKNOWLEDGMENTS

From our initial conversation about the possibility of this volume, Rand Dotson, editor in chief at LSU Press, has been enthusiastically supportive. Without his keen interest and unflagging attention, *Approaching Civil War and Southern History* would not be coming out at this time.

Once more I want to express my thanks to Victor Stater, chair of the LSU History Department, and to Darlene Albritton, the office manager, for their continuing willingness to answer calls even from an emeritus professor. In the office Ali Wolfe also willingly helped. Moreover, the department as well as the University still generously support my research, as they have for a half century.

For helping with the preparation of this manuscript, I am indebted to Jeff Hobson, a LSU graduate student, who has again served as my research assistant. Jeff's dedication, initiative, and intelligence make him the ideal research assistant. For this book, his assistance has been absolutely essential.

I also gratefully recognize the several organizations and publishers that have granted permission to reprint essays that originally appeared in their journals and books. They are the Agricultural History Society, Greenwood Press, LSU Press, South Carolina Historical Society, Southern Historical Association, and University of Virginia Press. Herein on page 181 Original Citations for Essays provides full and specific citations.

Finally, I want to acknowledge my special debt to Patricia, who has been stalwart beside me throughout my career in History.

ORIGINAL CITATIONS FOR INCLUDED ESSAYS

(*in chronological order*)

"A Reassessment of Jefferson Davis as War Leader: The Case from Atlanta to Nashville." *Journal of Southern History* 36 (May 1970): 189–204.

"Economics or Race: An Analysis of the Gubernatorial Election of 1890 in South Carolina." *South Carolina Historical Magazine* 73 (October 1972): 209–19.

"The Cotton Crisis in the Antebellum South: Another Look." *Agricultural History* 49 (April 1975): 381–91.

"Daniel R. Hundley, Interpreter of the Antebellum South." In Daniel R. Hundley, *Social Relations in Our Southern States,* edited by William J. Cooper, xiii–xlv. Baton Rouge, 1979.

"The Politics of Slavery Affirmed: The South and the Secession Crisis." In *The Southern Enigma: Essays on Race, Class, and Folk Culture,* edited by Walter J. Fraser and Winfred B. Moore, 199–215. Westport, Conn., 1983.

"'The Only Door': The Territorial Issue, the Preston Bill, and the Southern Whigs." In *A Master's Due: Essays in Honor of David Herbert Donald,* edited by William J. Cooper et al., 59–86. Baton Rouge, 1985.

"Edwin Forbes and the Civil War." In Edwin Forbes, *Thirty Years After: An Artist's Memoir of the Civil War,* vii–xvi. 1890. Baton Rouge, 1993.

"Jefferson Davis Confronts a Changed World." In *The Papers of Jefferson Davis,* 14 vols., edited by Lynda L. Crist et al., 12:vii–xv. Baton Rouge, 1971–2015.

"The Critical Signpost on the Journey toward Secession." *Journal of Southern History* 76 (February 2011): 3–16.

"Where Was Henry Clay? President-Elect Abraham Lincoln and the Crisis of the Union, 1860–1861." In *A Political Nation: New Directions in Mid-Nineteenth Century American Political History,* edited by Gary W. Gallagher and Rachel A. Shelden, 126–40. Charlottesville, Va., 2012.

INDEX